Empire, the National, and the Postcolonial, 1890–1920

Resistance in Interaction

ELLEKE BOEHMER

OXFORD
UNIVERSITY PRESS

OXFORD
UNIVERSITY PRESS

Great Clarendon Street, Oxford OX2 6DP

Oxford University Press is a department of the University of Oxford.
It furthers the University's objective of excellence in research, scholarship,
and education by publishing worldwide in

Oxford New York

Auckland Cape Town Dar es Salaam Hong Kong Karachi
Kuala Lumpur Madrid Melbourne Mexico City Nairobi
New Delhi Shanghai Taipei Toronto

With offices in
Argentina Austria Brazil Chile Czech Republic France Greece
Guatemala Hungary Italy Japan South Korea Poland Portugal
Singapore Switzerland Thailand Turkey Ukraine Vietnam

Oxford is a trade mark of Oxford University Press
in the UK and in certain other countries

Published in the United States
by Oxford University Press Inc., New York

British Library Cataloguing in Publication Data

Data available

Library of Congress Cataloging in Publication Data

Data available

ISBN 0-19-818446-8
ISBN 0-19-818445-x (pbk.)

1 3 5 7 9 10 8 6 4 2

Typeset in Sabon
by Alliance Phototypesetters, Pondicherry, India
Printed in Great Britain
on acid-free paper by
Biddles Ltd,
King's Lynn, Norfolk

Acknowledgements

I am grateful to the British Academy Small Grants scheme for support to do research at the National Library, Dublin; to the School of English, University of Leeds, for research leave in 1999 to complete an essential period of work on this book; and to the Department of English and Media, the Nottingham Trent University, for support in consulting the Leonard Woolf Papers at the University of Sussex Library. Warm thanks are also due to the tirelessly helpful staff of the Bodleian and Brotherton Libraries, the National Library, Dublin, and the University of Sussex Library Special Collections.

My gratitude is to Matthew Frost and Manchester University Press for permission to produce a part of an earlier essay, entitled ' "Immeasurable Strangeness" in Imperial Times', which appeared as chapter 4 in *Modernism and Empire*, edited by Howard Booth and Nigel Rigby (Manchester UP, 2000). Extended and substantially reworked this now forms a part of the final chapter of this book.

Seminar and conference groups paid generous and helpfully critical attention to earlier versions of some of the chapters which follow: my thanks are to audiences at the AUETSA 25th Anniversary Conference, University of the Western Cape, 1996; the South African War Conference, UNISA, South Africa, 1998; the School of English Seminar, University of Kent, Canterbury, 1998; the 'Defining Colonies' Third Galway Conference on Colonialism, 1999; the Imperial History Seminar, University of Oxford, 2000, especially Judith Brown; the Centre for Irish and Scottish Studies, University of Aberdeen, in particular Glenn Hooper; Susheila Nasta and the NILE MA seminar, Institute of English Studies, University of London, 2000; the Postcolonial Seminar, University of Warwick, 2001, in particular Neil Lazarus, Benita Parry, and Jane Poyner; and the Colonial Desire Colloquium at the University of Kent's Centre for Colonial and Postcolonial Research, 2001.

For their constructive interest, sharp-eyed advice, and intellectual and moral support, variously given, my sincere thanks are to David Attwell, Bridget Bennett, Judith Brown, Shirley Chew, Alison

Donnell, Rod Edmond, Denis Flannery, Kate Flint, Liz Gunner, Jeff Guy, Stephen Howe, Lyn Innes, Hermione Lee, Joseph Lennon, Donal Lowry, John McLeod, Gail Marshall, Bart Moore-Gilbert, Benita Parry, Sarah Salih, Jon Stallworthy, Alex Tickell, Gauri Viswanathan, Patrick Williams, Robert Young. For enthusing conversation about historical interconnection, I thank Barbara Harlow.

Immense thanks are due to Danielle Battigelli and James Rogers, Astrid and Jeremy James, Marianne Thrower and Anneke Lucassen and Tim Elliott, who have been wonderfully generous with their friendship and offers of childcare over the years, so creating precious hours for further squirrelling at this book. To Thomas, too, though my 'pitter-pattering' on the computer has produced no more than this book with no pictures, thanks for your astonishing patience, humour, and forbearance.

Without Steven Matthews barely a word would have seen the light of day. My debt to him is greater than gratitude; I acknowledge it with respect, and much love.

E. B.

Contents

Abbreviations

Full bibliographical details for works listed below may be found in the Bibliography.

AH	Nivedita, *Aggressive Hinduism*
APO	African People's Organization
ASAPS	Anti-Slavery and Aborigines' Protection Society
BCL	Aurobindo, *Birth Centenary Library*
CS	Civil Service
CW	Nivedita, *Collected Works*
Doctrine	Aurobindo, *The Doctrine of Passive Resistance*
EI	W. B. Yeats, *Essays and Introductions*
Kali	Nivedita, *Kali, the Mother*
Karmayogin	Aurobindo, *The Ideal of the Karmayogin*
LWP	Leonard Woolf Papers
Master	Nivedita, *The Master as I Saw Him*
NLSA	Solomon Plaatje, *Native Life in South Africa*
'PS'	Leonard Woolf, 'Pearls and Swine'
SANNC	South African Native National Congress
SW	Solomon Plaatje, *Selected Writings*
TLS	*Times Literary Supplement*
UI	*United Irishman*
UP	University Press
Village	Leonard Woolf, *The Village in the Jungle*
Web	Nivedita, *The Web of Indian Life*

1 Anti-imperial Interaction across the Colonial Borderline: Introduction

We must also notice in this ripening process the role played by the history of the resistance at the time of the conquest. . . .

A colonized people is not alone. In spite of all that colonialism can do, its frontiers remain open to new ideas and echoes from the world outside. It discovers that violence is in the atmosphere, that it here and there bursts out, and here and there sweeps away the colonial regime.

(Frantz Fanon, 'Concerning Violence', 1961)[1]

Hark! to the curses ringing
 From all smitten lands;
In sob and wail, they tell the tale
 Of England's blood-red hands.

And wheresoe'er her standard flings
 Forth its folds of shame,
A people's cries to heaven arise
 For vengeance on her name!

(Lady Gregory, 'A New Song
for the Boers', c.1900)[2]

CROSS-NATIONAL INTERTEXTUALITY

With few exceptions postcolonial theories of colonial power and anti-colonial resistance have privileged the relationship of European self and other; of colonizer and colonized. The aim of *Empire, the National, and the Postcolonial* is to swivel this conventional axis of interaction laterally by examining how, around the turn of the nineteenth into the twentieth century, certain early anti-imperial and

[1] Frantz Fanon, *The Wretched of the Earth*, trans. Constance Farrington (1961; Harmondsworth: Penguin, 1986), ch. 1 'Concerning Violence', 54–5.

[2] Lady Gregory, 'A New Song for the Boers', *Poets and Dreamers: Studies and Translations from the Irish* (1903; Gerrards Cross: Colin Smythe, 1974), 76.

nationalist movements, and nationalist and anti-colonial leaders and writers, found inspirational solidarity and instructive models in *one another*'s work and experience.[3] The 'contact zone' of cultural and political exchange conventionally located between the European colonial centre and its periphery will instead be positioned *between* peripheries.[4]

Whereas, following the Subaltern school of Indian historiography, or the Lacanian theory of Homi Bhabha and others, critics have in recent years given more attention to the 'continuities and intimacies' as well as the antagonisms of the colonial relationship, to rereadings of the colonial tradition from the position of otherness, the intention here will rather be to consider the ways in which such continuities were manifested between colonial (and proto-national) spaces, especially between native elites, during the decades of formal or high empire, 1890–1920.[5] The book will investigate how definitive concepts of self-realization often seen as originating within European political traditions (self-help; boycott; imperial 'loyalty'), were critically appropriated and remade not only by native nationalists as such, but through borrowing, exchange, and even collaboration between anti-colonial regions.[6] The central question will be how resistance emerged not so much from the place of otherness as *amongst others*.

As the key theorist of anti-colonial resistance Frantz Fanon claimed some forty years ago, native resistance movements are by no means sealed off from one another. In the oppressive conditions they share with other colonized peoples, they find not only 'informatory' but 'operative', stirring images of preparedness and zeal springing out of situations of resistance analogous to their own. These come to life 'with peculiar intensity' at that time when a movement finds itself ready to go forward to change the course of colonization and 'make

---

[3] See Gillian Beer, *Open Fields* (Oxford: Clarendon, 1996), 5, which considers how ideas are transferred and adapted through '[l]ateral encounter, between groups and individuals alive in the same time but in different initial conditions'.

[4] On contact zones as points of intercultural meeting, usually under colonization, the now standard reference is Mary Louise Pratt, *Imperial Eyes: Travel Writing and Transculturation* (London: Routledge, 1992).

[5] See Gyan Prakash, 'Introduction', to his edited *After Colonialism: Imperial Histories and Postcolonial Displacements* (Princeton: Princeton UP, 1995), 5–6. See also Leela Gandhi's ch. 1, 'After Colonialism', *Postcolonial Theory: A Critical Introduction* (Edinburgh: Edinburgh UP, 1998), 1–22.

[6] On the 'colonized' remaking of imperial power relations *within* the metropolis, see Antoinette Burton, *At the Heart of the Empire: Indians and the Colonial Encounter* (Berkeley and Los Angeles: University of California Press, 1998).

history'.[7] In a development that continued across the twentieth century, movements may thus be both nationally focused in terms of political organization, and yet cross- or transnational in their range of reference and reception of influence. As Ania Loomba insightfully acknowledges: 'anti-colonial resistances . . . inspired one another, but also debated with one another about . . . how best [colonial authority] should be challenged'.[8]

Therefore, departing from the culturalist definitions of the nation made by Anthony Smith on the one hand, and the modular, chiefly Europe-derived socio-political categories of the early Benedict Anderson and Eric Hobsbawm on the other, this study will propose that the stimuli to an anti-imperial and/or national consciousness may in certain situations lie not so much outside the unitary domain of the nation, but specifically within other similarly anti-imperial contexts.[9] Especially under the difficult, beleaguered conditions of emergent colonial resistance, oppositional nationalist, proto-nationalist, and anti-colonial movements learn from one another as well as drawing from their own internal political and cultural resources or the political culture of their oppressors. Looked at from this perspective, anti-colonial nationalism emerges as an allusive, cross-cultural, intertextual, or interdiscursive phenomenon, strung across borders of different descriptions as well as staked out within geopolitical boundaries. It is haunted by (in Anderson's own more recent phrase) 'spectres of comparison' with apparently like-minded movements located in sometimes very different political spaces.[10]

---

[7] Fanon, *The Wretched of the Earth*, 54–5, and see the epigraph above.

[8] Ania Loomba, *Colonialism/Postcolonialism* (London: Routledge, 1998), 185, and see also 174, 196, and 214. James M. Blaut, *The National Question: Decolonizing the Theory of Nationalism* (London: Zed, 1987), remarks that liberation movements may simultaneously hold particularist views, yet help other struggles 'as best they can'.

[9] Anthony D. Smith, *Theories of Nationalism* (London: Duckworth, 1971), and his *National Identity* (London: Penguin, 1991); Benedict Anderson, *Imagined Communities: Reflections on the Origin and Spread of Nationalism*, rev. edn. (London: Verso, 1991); Eric Hobsbawm, *Nations and Nationalism since 1780* (Cambridge: Cambridge UP, 1990). In the latter category, see also Ernest Gellner, *Nations and Nationalism* (Oxford: Blackwell, 1983).

[10] Benedict Anderson's *The Spectre of Comparisons: Nationalism, Southeast Asia and the World* (London: Verso, 1998) examines the world standardization of a language of nationalist politics. Where its emphasis however is on the interaction between the idiosyncratic local (of Southeast Asia) and the homogeneous empty time of the modern industrial nation, the focus of *Empire, the National, and the Postcolonial* is rather on certain political parallels and form-giving cultural moments of cross-national exchange, and on how these impinged on emergent polemical and literary nationalisms. Whereas this book's

Taking off from the (differing) transnational methodologies of Antoinette Burton, Parama Roy, and Gauri Viswanathan, this book will explore some of the political and cultural conditions, as well as the writerly and textual ramifications, of such cross-national lessons and debates.[11] Close readings of key texts which reflect or effect cross-national movement will be used to draw out the signs and significance of these formative, in some cases transformative, interactions. In particular I will consider symptomatic instances of cross-national borrowing and conversation, and certain key cusp or transitional figures (situated between modernity and tradition, Europe and the other) who carried out such borrowing. These will be further located along the interconnected triangle of Ireland and England, India, and South Africa, and during the protracted critical period for British imperialism of 1890–1920.

The disaster of the early Anglo-Boer War (1899–1900), which dragged on for far longer than anticipated, inaugurated over a decade of imperial crises for Britain including the efflorescence or resurgence of nationalist and anti-imperial movements in South Africa, Ireland, Bengal, and Egypt. The period culminated in the conflagration of 1914–18, a war of imperial rivalry between European powers. During the same 1890–1920 period the metropolis witnessed a rising social and political radicalism, galvanized at crucial points by the campaigns for Irish Home Rule, by women's struggle for self-representation, and by the international spread of socialist and Marxist ideas, formalized within the (Europe-centred) Second International (1889–1914). The time therefore marked the beginning of the development of a more global dimension to radical political networking and organization. It was also the period when modernity with its message of individuation, rationalized social order, and capitalist progress was systematically disseminated to the non-West via speeded-up imperial channels of communication. The globalized formations of empire therefore paradoxically facilitated the rise of

interest is in the exchange between margins, Anderson explores the global 'serialization' of political ideas (the metropolis remaining the dominant venue of 'empty time'). I am highly indebted to Anderson's ideas concerning the circulation and dissemination of nationalist vocabularies.

[11] Burton, *At the Heart of the Empire*; Parama Roy, *Indian Traffic: Identities in Question in Colonial and Postcolonial India* (Berkeley and Los Angeles: University of California Press, 1998); Gauri Viswanathan, *Outside the Fold: Conversion, Modernity and Belief* (Princeton: Princeton UP, 1998). See also Inderpal Grewal, *Home and Harem: Nation, Gender, Empire and the Cultures of Travel* (London: Leicester UP, 1996).

cross- or transnational resistances, as continued to be the case later in the century also.

The paradigm shift which *Empire, the National, and the Postcolonial* proposes emerges in a clearer light if we consider the extent to which the interactive conceptualization of the anti-colonial nation, or of cultural resistance, undercuts the notions both of top-down and of bottom-up discursive impacts that still organize definitions of the colonial relationship. In the reoriented global picture which unfolds, we find, for example, advanced Irish nationalists discovering in the Boer War an arena for their own struggle; or the South African nationalist Sol Plaatje adapting his ideas of anti-imperial refusal relative to suffragette activism in 1910s London, just as M. K. Gandhi did. We also find the Irish-born Hindu revivalist Margaret Noble/ Sister Nivedita assessing the limitations of 1905 passive resistance *in dialogue with* the Bengali extremist leader Aurobindo Ghose. The flow of power relations in this new picture, the movement and exchange of anti-colonialist, nationalist, class, gender, and other discourses, appears as more constellated and diversified, far more multiply-mediated than in standard dualistic configurations of the colonial relationship.[12]

True, anti-imperial, cross-border exchanges were, in their initial stages at least, secretive and coded, even contingent, accidental, and ad hoc; yet in relation to any one of the cross-national scenarios just cited, colonial authority would have felt itself threatened and unsettled. Consider only the Viceroy Lord Dufferin's repeated worry in the mid- to late 1880s about a nationalist domino effect as he saw it running from Ireland to India in the aftermath of Land League agitation.[13] In constructing a lateral or reoriented world picture of political and discursive relations, therefore, it is not only that we become committed to implicating both centre and margin in the making of colonial and national ideologies, as Rosemary M. George has suggested, or to the interconnection of the histories of '"metropolis"'

---

[12] On power, space, and/or identities conceived as diversified or rhizomic, see Gilles Deleuze and Félix Guattari, *On the Line*, trans. John Johnson (New York: Semiotext(e), 1983), 13; Teresa de Lauretis, *Technologies of Gender* (London: Macmillan, 1987).

[13] See Howard Brasted, 'Irish Home Rule Politics and India 1873–1886', unpublished Ph.D. thesis (Edinburgh: University of Edinburgh, 1974), 42–5; T. G. Frazer, 'Ireland and India', in Keith Jeffery (ed.), *'An Irish Empire': Aspects of Ireland and the British Empire* (Manchester: Manchester UP, 1996), 86–7; Michael Holmes and Denis Holmes (eds.), *Ireland and India: Connections, Comparisons, Contrasts* (Dublin: Folens, 1997); Anne Taylor, *Annie Besant: A Biography* (Oxford: Oxford UP, 1992), 270–1.

and '"peripheries"' outlined by Catherine Hall.[14] Rather the entire imperial framework becomes from this perspective at once decentred and multiply-centred, a network, one might say, of interrelating margins. Within this reshaped framework, attention is focused not only on the emergence of alternative agencies and knowledges within colonialism,[15] though this is crucial, but on how those different agencies may have impinged on one another, and how these contacts were then processed into emerging concepts of the new post-imperial nation.[16]

As will be evident throughout, my readjusted focus also has bearings both on conventional chronological definitions of the 'postcolonial' as mainly post-independence (post-1950), as well as on Eurocentric theories of anti-colonial struggles as largely reactive, repetitive, or 'derivative' of European 'modular' forms, in the phraseology of Partha Chatterjee's now classic rebuttal of this phenomenon in the South Asian context.[17] The study of often two-way influences and moments of interchange will demonstrate how Indian, southern African, and Irish (as also Caribbean, West African, and Egyptian) nationalisms and resistance movements were in fact multiply-constituted, opportunistic, and fluid, and in more complex ways than current definitions of syncretism or imperfect mimicry, usually applied to post-1950 identity constructions, generally allow.[18] Put differently, native and early nationalist attempts at

---

[14] Rosemary M. George, *The Politics of Home: Postcolonial Relocations and Twentieth-Century Fiction* (Cambridge: Cambridge UP, 1996), 1–9; Catherine Hall, 'Histories, Empire, and the Post-Colonial Moment', in Iain Chambers and Lidia Curti (eds.), *The Post-colonial Question* (London: Routledge, 1996), 70.

[15] Ania Loomba, 'Overworlding the "Third World"', in Robert Young (ed.), *Neo-colonialism, Oxford Literary Review*, 3 (1991), 178.

[16] This idea of processing back, with its inevitable accompaniment of hybridization, helps account for the fact that the racial chauvinism of some nationalist movements, such as the anti-Semitism of early Sinn Féin and its affiliates, did not necessarily filter into the nationalisms which they otherwise influenced. See the Resolution of the Irish Socialist Republican party in 'Ireland and the Transvaal', *United Irishman* (2 Sept. 1899), 6, which commends Boer naturalization laws for keeping both 'bloated' Jews and English adventurers at bay.

[17] See Partha Chatterjee's interrelated studies of the mediation by native elites of the inherited forms of the colonial state through the addition of their own often religious and cultural 'marks of difference': *Nationalist Thought and the Colonial World: A Derivative Discourse?* (London: Zed, 1986), and *The Nation and its Fragments: Colonial and Post-colonial Histories* (Princeton: Princeton UP, 1994). See also Loomba, *Colonialism/ Post-colonialism*, 174, 188–9.

[18] For the now standard definitions of these and related terms, see Bill Ashcroft, Gareth Griffiths, and Helen Tiffin, *The Empire Writes Back* (London: Routledge, 1989), and their

cross-allusion and adaptive copying from political and cultural contexts perceived as corresponding to their own, in fact prefigure by many decades, and through complex, at times conflicted channels, the crossed registers and diasporic intertextuality with which contemporary migrant and postcolonial criticism is concerned. Nationalism in this respect emerges not as a purely oppositional, or purely inwardly directed discourse but as multi-layered and polyphonic, a site of enunciation to which different agents may lay claim. In consequence, the book would necessarily question certain postcolonialist assumptions that in a multinationally organized world the nation as a historical and political entity has been practically transcended as well as exhaustively treated as a subject of investigation. Here I would agree with Edward Said when he notes that we must continue to acknowledge the success of nationalism in mobilizing peoples against oppression (within *and* across borders), while at the same time conceding its ideological and socio-political flaws, its mostly oppressive rather than liberatory postcolonial legacy.[19]

In the terms of Tapan Raychaudhuri in *Europe Reconsidered*, the imprint of European empire on the native, far from being an imperfect copy or misconceived replication, should be seen as but one element amongst others in the development of colonial/postcolonial ideas of, for instance, modern selfhood and national interrelationship.[20] Anti-colonial nationalisms, that is to say, took over the premisses of modernity (individualism, state-organized politics, and social improvement), yet adapted or married these to both native and other imported forms of knowledge for anti-colonial purposes. *Empire, the National, and the Postcolonial* therefore also expands the parameters (and perimeters) of Paul Gilroy's influential thesis concerning the intercultural or 'outer-national' formation of identity and modernity within the 'Black Atlantic' diaspora.[21] It considers

Key Concepts in Post-colonial Studies (London: Routledge, 1998); Homi K. Bhabha, *The Location of Culture* (London: Routledge, 1995), 85–92.

[19] Edward Said, 'Yeats and Decolonization', Field Day Pamphlet 15 (Derry: Field Day Theatre Co., 1988), 8–9.

[20] Tapan Raychaudhuri, *Europe Reconsidered: Perceptions of the West in Nineteenth Century Bengal* (New Delhi: Oxford UP, 1988).

[21] Paul Gilroy, *The Black Atlantic: Modernity and Double Consciousness* (London: Verso, 1993). Neil Lazarus, *Nationalism and Cultural Practice in the Postcolonial World* (Cambridge: Cambridge UP, 1999), 51–67, mounts a vigorous critique of Gilroy's neglect of the capitalist formations of modernity. It is doubtful however that Gilroy's liberatory and boundary-shifting thesis is *fundamentally* flawed due to its neglect of the Marxist category of class.

the borrowing, transmutation, and general transcontinental *sifting* of strategies and idioms of resistance between widely spaced nationalist elites (for example, home rule; the hunger strike as moral weapon; images of the small but strong nation(s) v. the vast empire, or of the vengeful National Mother). In this way the book broadens Gilroy's Atlantic basin of exchange to include other intercultural and interdiscursive pathways. By examining for instance the corroborative citation of another's nationalist struggle by a resistance movement perhaps located in a very different country, the book embraces a more diverse and expansive web of interactive, cross-national, *and yet still* nationalist, resistance formations than Gilroy's mapping permits.

The dual emphasis in these paragraphs on the development of national selfhood *in the context of* interrelationship ('resistance *in* interaction'), will remain important across the study. Adapting Benedict Anderson's notion in both *Imagined Communities* and *The Spectre of Comparisons* that modern media networks created horizontal contexts within which new national communities could be imagined, the concept of *cross-border interdiscursivity*—of a transformative transmission of different political vocabularies and cultural discourses between anti-colonial spaces—creatively qualifies one of the central constitutive concepts of any nationalism, that it is based on an essence or core of self.[22] By contrast, as in the five case studies which are brought together here, a nation's self is seen as in part intersubjectively constructed through forms of cross-border exchange between bourgeois native elites, and through the medium of different signifying systems (including oral traditions, newspapers and other print media, as well as gestural and performative strategies of resistance such as, for instance, Sister Nivedita's controversial Kali-worship discussed in Chapter 2). As we are dealing with the transmission of influence through channels including political hearsay, common-knowledge history, and public expressions of solidarity, the term *interdiscursivity* will here be preferred over intertextuality.

---

[22] For Ato Quayson's definition of interdiscursivity as embracing a variety of semiotic (or 'outer-textual' as well as textual) systems, see his *Strategic Transformations in Nigerian Writing* (Oxford: James Currey, 1997), 17–18. On cross-border exchange, see also Lewis Nkosi, 'Constructing the "Cross-Border" Reader', in Elleke Boehmer, Laura Chrisman, and Kenneth Parker (eds.), *Altered State? Writing and South Africa* (Sydney: Dangaroo, 1994), 37–50.

Also as regards terminology, although the discussion will privilege moments of transmission and intercultural translation, I will prefer the terms *cross*-national and *cross*-nationalist over transnational and its variants, because of the emphasis throughout on formations of national selfhood *alongside* intersubjectivity, and on exchanges (*crossings*) between different political and cultural contexts. The crossing between (proto-)national entities which is connoted by the former terms, holds in tension the idea of separate locations maintaining a political integrity, *and yet* of these in some form of relationship with one another.[23] As in our contemporary globalized context, transnationalism by contrast often tends to designate the formation of neo-imperial capitalist structures overarching or inter-penetrating the self-legitimating nation. The operation of multi-national companies and worldwide information systems as well as new economic migrations of people now have the ability to corrode though not necessarily to undercut the autonomy of the nation-state.[24] To further distinguish cross-border or cross-national movements in a technical sense from the political, or specifically national*ist*, formations shaped by such movements, the terms cross-national and cross-nationalist will be used non-interchangeably, respectively to signify this difference.

The concept of a crossing between (proto-)national entities also requires nuancing. Cross-national interrelations, it is important to note, in fact arrange along a scale which takes in, on one end, the observable movement and transplantation of ideas, theories, and individuals between different anti-colonial spaces (as reflected in Edward Said's account of travelling theory).[25] It also embraces potentially subversive expressions of solidarity or joint inspiration (without an

[23] See Sudipta Kaviraj, *The Imaginary Institution of India* (New Delhi: Teen Murti Publications, 1991), for his distinction between 'fuzzy' or non-territorial, pre-national communities, and enumerated nations centred on the notion of a defining collective will.

[24] See Steven Vertovec, 'Conceiving and Researching Transnationalism', *Ethnic and Racial Studies*, 22.2 (1999), 447–62; and Michael Peter Smith and Luis Eduardo Guarnizo (eds.), *Transnationalism from Below* (Somerset, NJ: Transaction, 1998), for their argument that transnationalism, while transforming intercommunity relations, does not necessarily signify post-nationalism. I am grateful to John McLeod for his advice in this area. See also Jean Baudrillard, ch. 2 'Figures of the Transpolitical', in *Fatal Strategies*, trans. Philip Beitchman and W. G. J. Niesluchkowski (London: Pluto, 1999), 25–70.

[25] Edward Said, *The World, the Text, and the Critic* (London: Faber, 1984), ch. 10 'Travelling Theory', especially pp. 226–8. See also Grewal, *Home and Harem*, 17–18, for her outline of the comparative methodology of 'transnational cultural flows'.

actual interchange of influences or ideas), as captured in Daniel O'-Connell's often repeated 1840s slogan, 'England's Difficulty is Ireland's Opportunity', which was revived by Irish nationalists in 1899 to broadcast their support for the Boers. At its other end, the scale includes more appropriative, localized moments of cultural and political allusion and citation, as when Bengal evolved its concept of swadeshi in the awareness of Sinn Féin's emphasis on self-help and self-reliance, yet not in direct emulation of it, drawing also on internal cultural traditions of *atmasakti* or 'own force'. In other words, a long-established anti-imperial nationalism, such as was found in Ireland at this time, did not necessarily stand as an inflexible blueprint but rather as a frame of reference in relation to which emergent nationalist and/or anti-colonial movements elsewhere might encode their own attitudes to British rule.[26]

Where the intention is to draw together apparently related political, cultural, and textual phenomena from across the globe, further qualification is again in order. Moments of cross-national contact between native intellectuals were not only secretive, and often sporadic and impressionistic, but also highly context-specific. On this basis *Empire, the National, and the Postcolonial* would want to avoid constructing any overarching theory of anti-colonial or nationalist commonality connecting vastly different cultural and geopolitical spaces. In fact, apparent cooperation or hand-holding, such as was offered to the Boers by Irish nationalists during 1899–1900, usually operated as a medium for local self-identification. Resisting (proto-)nations, even if cross-imperially connected, were primarily concerned with their *own particular* projects of self-definition and/or anti-colonial subversion.

[26] See C. L. Innes, *The Devil's Own Mirror: The Irishman and the African in Modern Literature* (New York: Three Continents Press, 1990), 6, 21, as to how the Harlem Renaissance and the Irish literary revival codified their cultural nationalism in related ways. As another expression of Irish solidarity, Keith Jeffery in the Introduction to his edited *'An Irish Empire'*, 8, remarks that in 1882 Frank Hugh O'Donnell, MP for Dungarven, told the House of Commons that his Irish Party were the 'natural representatives and spokesmen of the unrepresented nationalities of the Empire'. The anomalous colonial position of Ireland—its class structure locked into imperial hierarchies, its resistance movements an example to nationalists across the empire—has been widely and heatedly debated. See, for example: Luke Gibbons, *Transformations in Irish Culture* (Cork: Cork UP and Field Day, 1996), especially 171–80; Liam Kennedy, *Colonialism, Religion and Nationalism in Ireland* (Belfast: Queen's University Institute of Irish Studies, 1996); Declan Kiberd, *Inventing Ireland* (London: Cape, 1995). Stephen Howe, *Ireland and Empire: Colonial Legacies in Irish History and Culture* (Oxford: Oxford UP, 2000), offers a comprehensive analytical discussion of the application of colonial models to the Irish situation.

We would therefore want to steer clear of conflating nationalist self-expression with international collaboration against empire, or indeed of regarding the national as synonymous with the anti-colonial. Though as part of the development of resistance to empire, nationalism often served as a vehicle for anti-colonialism, anti-colonialisms were (and are) not invariably nationalist, and nationalisms in turn were not necessarily anti-colonialist. In fact resistant nationalisms take widely differing forms: revolutionary but fundamentalist; 'advanced' yet anti-Semitic; anti-imperial and pan-nationalist but not necessarily anti-British; or, nostalgically reactionary, yet modernizing at economic and political levels. More specifically, (proto-)nationalists in the 1890–1920 period tended in the main to be moderate and constitutionalist: this approach significantly modified any anti-imperialist tendencies they may have entertained, and limited the subversive impact of their cross-nationalist interactions.

However, what probably separates this study from a mere retrospective attribution of analogies, is what appears to be a distinct and enabling perception of correspondence *at the time*. As Frantz Fanon already suggested, early anti-colonial intellectuals, who often occupied isolated and even threatened positions in their various colonial homelands, or who worked from the even more isolated condition of exile, drew on situations analogous to their own for political inspiration and support. They were aware that other elites, colonially educated, professionally or bureaucratically employed, inhabited situations similar to their own, and that both actual and gestural hand-holding could therefore be seen to be of mutual benefit. As newspaper commentaries and editorials of the period show, whether in the *United Irishman*, as we will see, or in the *Bengalee*, or in Sol Plaatje's *Bechuana Gazette*, nationalists and anti-colonialists kept a keen eye on resistance unfolding in other regions of the empire. From this developed a growing awareness of the tactical, rhetorical, imaginative, or emotional support which might be obtained from building on juxtapositions and contacts between oppressed conditions. This awareness was widespread and substantial enough, I would want to propose, to allow us to speak of an anti-colonial interdiscursivity as manifest in literary nationalist as well as more overtly political writing as early as the late nineteenth century.

It dislodged the yoke of ideological dependency, it inspired the cowed colonized mind, so Aurobindo Ghose certainly urged in 1907, to seek 'instructive spectacle' from the struggles and successes of other colonized nations.[27] As the opening to Aimé Césaire's later *Discours sur le colonialisme* (1955) also implies, the spectacle of worldwide injustice and anti-colonial action gives resistance movements a sense of collective power, of the power of the collectivity.[28] Laying emphasis on actual cooperation rather than instructive example, Arthur Griffith the Irish nationalist editor and leader was perhaps even more optimistic, claiming in 1905 that if a Sinn Féin-propelled anti-recruitment drive had been in place at the time of the Boer War, Ireland would by now have its independent parliament sitting in College Green, and 'the Transvaal flag would . . . be flying over a united South Africa'.[29] Griffith, who had closely scrutinized nineteenth-century Hungarian nationalism and *its* use of parliamentary boycott, moreover established the Sinn Féin movement, and propagated ideas of self-help and home industry, at the time that swadeshi and boycott were being inaugurated as tactics of anti-imperial resistance in Bengal. The pro-Boer Irish Brigade ballad which Griffith had composed in 1900 suggestively captures this situation of cross-national awareness: 'From land to land throughout the world the news is going round | That Ireland's flag triumphant waves on high o'er English ground'.[30]

NETWORKS OF RESISTANCE

As with present-day bilateral relations between Third World or tricontinental countries, cross-nationalist circuitry was, it is important to recognize, made possible and shaped by worldwide colonial (what we would today term neo-colonial) nexuses of communication and exchange. These took the form of newspapers, the telegraph, new road and railway links, and faster shipboard journeys. Mutual awareness between English-speaking professionals in the different

[27] Aurobindo Ghose, *The Doctrine of Passive Resistance* (1907; Calcutta: Arya Publishing House, 1948).

[28] Aimé Césaire, *Discourse on Colonialism*, trans. Joan Pinkham (1955; New York: Monthly Review Press, 1972), 9–11. Consider also that in Ngugi wa Thiong'o's novel *A Grain of Wheat* (London: HEB, 1967), 73, the Mau Mau or Kenyan 'Movement's' revolutionary hero Kihika holds up the example of 'Mahatma Gandhi, the saint, leading the Indian people against British rule'.

[29] Arthur Griffith, Editorial commentary, *United Irishman* (5 Aug. 1905), 5. The *United Irishman* will henceforth be abbreviated in footnotes as *UI*.

[30] Arthur Griffith, 'Ballad of the Transvaal Irish Brigade', *UI* (24 Feb. 1900), 4. The ground in this case was the besieged Natal town of Ladysmith in South Africa.

regions of the British Raj, for example, was facilitated both by their common educational experience, and by the road, rail, and telegraph networks laid down in the interests of imperial military security and more efficient government.[31] Nationalists in the Indian National Congress, therefore, as also in the early African National Congress in South Africa, were encouraged to think within the broader, cross-regional framework of their colony or potential country, even in some cases of the empire as a whole.[32]

The colonial facilitation of nationalist interconnection may seem an irony, if a subversive one. Yet, clearly, the movement of influence or example, the perception of analogy, could not take place through a mere osmosis of ideas. Such movements required technological, infrastructural, and institutional support, and depended also on the physical shift and drift of individuals between the different regions of the empire. Indeed, although indigenous networks laid down by trade or religious and educational 'pilgrimages', in Benedict Anderson's terminology, existed from pre-colonial times, anti-colonial, cross-nationalist links adapted from and exploited an empire-wide reality: the fact that at official levels, too, the British Empire was both conceived of and operated as a loosely interconnected system, or at least as a series of multilaterally linked, parallel systems. In the words of the historian S. B. Cook, empire formed 'an intellectual and administrative circuit of exchange' based on a 'network of personal ties'.[33] So the Colonial and the Foreign Office, whose staff were already partially pre-selected by being drawn from a narrow socio-economic elite, tended to regard imperial policies which had been developed in relation to one particular colony or dependency as transferable to others (the administrative system of India, for instance, was adapted for use in West and East Africa). This perception was then reinforced by the usual homogenizing effects of imperial

---

[31] See Judith Brown, *Gandhi: Prisoner of Hope* (New Haven: Yale UP, 1989), 10.

[32] Working from his own particular diasporic background, Mohandas Gandhi during his time in South Africa consistently founded cross-regional and cross-nationalist organizations, activist networks, and newspapers (the Natal Indian Congress, the Natal Indian Educational Association, and *Indian Opinion*). See Brown, *Gandhi: Prisoner of Hope*, 47, 49; Judith Brown and Martin Prozesky (eds.), *Gandhi and South Africa* (Pietermaritzburg: Natal UP, 1996). Significantly, the Bengal nationalist Sister Nivedita in *The Master as I Saw Him* (London: Longmans, Green, and Co., 1910), 48, 314, which will be discussed below, observed that the world's speeded-up communications network could be advantageous for the spread of neo-Hinduist truth.

[33] S. B. Cook, *Imperial Affinities: Nineteenth-Century Analogies and Exchanges between India and Ireland* (New Delhi: Sage Publications, 1993), especially 134–5.

governance: the assumption was that colonized others in one space could be ruled more or less as were colonized others elsewhere.[34]

The transference and promotion of high-ranking officials around the empire (Curzon, Cromer, Milner, Lugard, Clifford, etc.) further intensified these cross-border effects, speeding up the interregional spread and adaptation of policy, embedding channels of influence. Such officials might also be accompanied, or their cross-imperial movements repeated, by other, mid-career colonial staff, as well as by newspaper journalists, military men, political activists, scientists, doctors. S. B. Cook summarizes these effects in a discussion of how the long-colonized situation of Ireland, anomalously positioned between Britain and the rest of the empire, was used as a colonial prototype (and later as a nationalist role model). Due to 'the malleability of the imperial administrative structure . . . [and] the ad hoc, experimental and eclectic style of British imperial rule', administrative models and techniques might be readily imported from one imperial unit, such as Ireland, into another, such as India or South Africa.[35]

Drawing from his own experience of cross-imperial travel, W. S. Blunt (1840–1922), the anti-imperialist Tory Radical and supporter of 1880s Egyptian nationalism, was a particularly perceptive contemporary commentator on such intercolonial networks of exchange or, as he put it, 'synchronisms' of attitude on the part of Britain. Noting in *My Ideas about India* (1885) that ex-India officials ruled Egypt in ways that were particularly hard and shrewd, Blunt's opinion was that the common experience of 'despotic', profit-led coercion which connected Ireland, India, and Egypt could effectively promote the spread of the 'art' of 'passive obstruction' between them.[36] Moved by such perceptions Blunt was himself one of the late nineteenth century's most prominent agents and activators of cross-imperial ties. He not only called for self-rule in India, Ireland, and Egypt, in the case of Egypt actively so (and was in 1887 arrested for

---

[34] For further development of this point, see Elleke Boehmer (ed.), *Empire Writing* (Oxford: Oxford University Press, 1998), 192, 500; and *Colonial and Postcolonial Literature* (Oxford: Oxford UP, 1995), 55–9.

[35] Cook, *Imperial Affinities*, 134–5.

[36] Wilfrid Scawen Blunt, *My Ideas about India* (London: Kegan Paul, Trench and Co., 1885), 122, 149; *The Secret History of the English Occupation of Egypt* (London: T. Fisher Unwin, 1907), 263, 219–20. See also his *India under Ripon: A Private Diary* (London: Fischer Unwin, 1909); and Elizabeth Longford, *A Pilgrimage of Passion: The Life of Wilfrid Scawen Blunt* (London: Weidenfeld and Nicolson, 1979).

his support of the Irish National League), but at different times worked alongside, cooperated with, or met prominent nationalist figures: the Indian economic nationalist Dadabhai Naoroji, Lady Augusta Gregory, his one-time lover and one of the moving spirits behind the Irish National Theatre, and also the Hindu revivalist Sister Nivedita during her time in political exile in London. It was entirely appropriate therefore that, in 1907, the Bengali radical Aurobindo Ghose published in his extremist paper *Bande Mataram* Blunt's impassioned pro-Arabi poem 'The Wind and the Whirlwind' (1883), written in support of 'fair rights for all as brothers'.[37]

In an imperial world interconnected through the use of English, ideas of cross-empire solidarity and intraracial exchange also exerted an important ideological hold over white colonial elites.[38] The publication of Charles Dilke's *Greater Britain* (1879, and much reprinted) stimulated a widespread discussion concerning the formation of an Anglo-Saxon brotherhood or imperial federation of settler colonies as a way of binding the burgeoning empire more closely together on the grounds of blood relationship (while simultaneously also overriding and/or sideroading native pressures for self-government). These ideas, endorsed by influential writers like Anthony Trollope, were then further expanded in historical analyses by J. R. Seeley and J. A. Froude (*The Expansion of England*, 1883; *Oceana, or England and her Colonies*, 1886). Even if never practically realized, the constructive possibility of cross-border collaboration within a commonwealth of self-governing colonies was thus raised within settler circles as an issue for debate.

Gaining currency empire-wide, the cross-imperial idea was in these ways made available for annexation by non-white political elites similarly in quest of solidarity and a common vocabulary of rights. Not only W. S. Blunt but also M. K. Gandhi (1869–1948) and Annie Besant (1847–1933), the Theosophist and 1910s agitator for Indian Home Rule, were certainly thinking cross-nationally when in the first decades of the twentieth century they appealed to Queen Victoria's 1858 Proclamation of Empire, India's 'Magna Carta', in

---

[37] Wilfrid Scawen Blunt, 'The Wind and the Whirlwind', *Poems* (London: Macmillan, 1923). See also *The Secret History*, appendix IX, pp. 115–29.

[38] Fredric Jameson, 'Foreword' to Roberto Retamar, *Caliban and Other Essays* (Minneapolis: Minnesota UP, 1989), pp. xi–xii, suggestively remarks how in the late twentieth century a cosmopolitan internationalism continued to be accomplished through the medium of the once-colonial lingua franca English.

order to claim Indian rights to just and equal treatment both in the Raj and across the empire.[39] In the cross-border unity effected by appeals to 1858, they discovered, lay new possibilities for mounting political protest. Partially as an extension of this idea, Annie Besant proposed her ideal of a 'universal brotherhood of man' not entirely contradictorily as the end-goal or 'mighty trust' of an empire 'charged with a religious obligation to bring forth a comity of nations'. Essentially, as Gauri Viswanathan has observed, Besant's 'relational [and inter-racial] model of the commonwealth' conceived of the ideal world confederation of nations as a multiplication of 'one single cellular organism, the British nation, into the far reaches of the globe'.[40] Empire would, in short, give birth to, and be retrospectively justified by, the formation of an international congregation of nations. Irish nationalists, too, placing their emphasis on shared suffering rather than an extension of hegemony, participated in the perception that linked experience created a platform for solidarity. As Maud Gonne, a foremost proponent of this idea, sketched the situation in the Foreword to her autobiography: 'the British Empire [cannot] stand or go without famine in Ireland, opium in China, torture in India, pauperism in England, disturbance and disorder in Europe, and robbery everywhere'.[41] From this it followed that only the resolute refusal of such robbery 'everywhere' could successfully end it.

As the cases of Blunt or Besant suggest, it cannot go without mention that cross-empire link-ups between nationalist elites were moreover facilitated by the both intentional and inadvertent international networking of Europeans who might loosely be called anti-imperial agents: socialists like H. M. Hyndman (1842–1921) of the Social Democratic Federation; the suffragette Sylvia Pankhurst (1882–1960); the libertarian democrat and early campaigner for homosexual self-expression Edward Carpenter (1844–1929); or Theosophists like

[39] Brown, *Gandhi: Prisoner of Hope*, 44; Annie Besant, *India and the Empire: A Lecture and Various Papers* (London: Theosophical Publishing Society, 1914), 31, 35, 112–13.
[40] Viswanathan, *Outside the Fold*, 177–207, in particular pp. 186, 196, 203, 206–7. Based on the ideas of Ernest Renan and Matthew Arnold, Theosophical theories Aryanizing the Celtic race, Viswanathan writes, significantly advanced the making of Indo-Irish analogies and stimulated Irish revivalists like James Cousins.
[41] Maud Gonne, *A Servant of the Queen* (London: Victor Gollancz, 1938), p. i, and see also p. 171. Her own anti-imperial talks were illustrated with magic lantern pictures taken in 'Ireland, India & the Transvaal'. See Anna MacBride White and Norman Jeffares (eds.), *The Gonne–Yeats Letters 1893–1918* (London: Pimlico, 1993), 147.

A. O. Hume as well as Besant. Although they often approached the problem of Britain's expansionist nationalism from very different angles—ranging from materialist theories concerning the international operation of capital to spiritual beliefs in the Unity of Mankind—these freethinking intellectuals, social reformers, and radicals tended to seek solutions for imperial oppressions in an international fraternalism which they to an extent realized practically through travel and political organization. Carpenter, for example, spoke of a 'semen of Democracy' which he figuratively hoped would dissolve socio-political boundaries and establish an empire of humanity for 'the lesser races of the Earth'.[42] Hyndman placed his faith in the 'higher communal life and fraternal intercommunication';[43] the Independent Labour Party leader Keir Hardie looked forward to a progressivist cooperation between nations. Built on a universalist or Christian humanism and a generalized belief in worldwide progress, such beliefs served to reinforce and advance new anti-imperial approaches.

Bernard Porter has convincingly made the argument in *Critics of Empire* that the height of British imperial power and its accompanying jingoism coincided, not accidentally, with a relative dearth of oppositional, anti-imperial thinking in Britain.[44] That Besant, a freethinker of note, leaned on notions of a British-led commonwealth will already have made this plain. Although liberals and reformers may have sought to distance themselves from imperial conquest, the fact of Britain's worldwide empire could not now, at the end of the nineteenth century, be gainsaid. Rather than condemning imperialism on ethical grounds, therefore, the central question was rather how prudently and justly to carry it out in the paternalistic interests of 'civilization'—a matter in which the imperialists had the ideational and imaginative upper hand. Even the liberatory and radical vocabularies of a Sylvia Pankhurst or a Hyndman

[42] Edward Carpenter, 'India the Wisdom-land' and 'Empire', in *Towards Democracy* (London: Swan Sonnenschein, 1905), 460–7. See also Tony Brown (ed.), *Edward Carpenter and Late Victorian Radicalism* (Ilford: Frank Cass, 1990); Chushichi Tsuzuki, *Edward Carpenter: Prophet of Human Fellowship* (Cambridge: Cambridge UP, 1980).

[43] Frederick J. Gould, *Hyndman: Prophet of Socialism* (London: George Allen and Unwin, 1928), 13. See also H. M. Hyndman, *The Awakening of Asia* (London: Cassell, 1919), and his *The Bankruptcy of India: An Enquiry into the Administration of India under the Crown* (London: Swan Sonnenschein, Lowrey and Co., 1886). The spread of worldwide social justice, Hyndman insisted, demanded the decentralization of British India.

[44] Bernard Porter, *Critics of Empire: British Radical Attitudes to Colonialism in Africa 1895–1914* (London: Macmillan, 1968).

tended to echo patriotic imperial idioms and eugenicist assumptions. Hyndman, for instance, who was instructed in the imperial impoverishment of India by, amongst others, Dadabhai Naoroji, firmly believed that England had set the pace for the world's social democratic development.[45] Excepting small critical groupings like the Ethical Societies, of which the moral economist J. A. Hobson and E. D. Morel were members, liberal and socialist anti-imperialists at this time, as Porter pertinently observes, essentially demonstrated the level of their opposition by the degree of their non-involvement: the primary impulse was to reject empire by not dealing with it.[46] Beyond this anti-imperialists tended to attack the more invidious forms of the 'new' imperialism, but did not seek to dismantle imperial structures. As W. S. Blunt well perceived, it seemed that the site where new anti-imperial ideas might emerge was not in Britain, or certainly not in Britain alone. It was in this respect in particular therefore that the 'decontextualized', intermediate, or otherwise transplanted situation of native elites came into its own.[47]

In Rabindranath Tagore's *The Home and the World* (*Ghare Baire*, 1916), Sandip the arch-nationalist criticizes the sceptical moderate Nikhil, a Tagore-surrogate, for being like an 'eternal' pointsman 'lying in wait by the line, to shunt one's train of thought from one rail to another'.[48] Derived from one of India's most hybridized of imperial imports, the railway, and within the medium of another, a novel by a writer who was himself an ideological border figure, both nationalist and internationalist, this metaphor neatly captures that effort of lateral and associative thinking, of moving between and across parallel tracks, which fledgling anti-colonial movements in their different alienated and cross-cultural contexts were having to make at this time. As a way of encapsulating the translational and appropriative methods followed by such movements, Tagore's metaphor attaches to the aforementioned idea of travelling theory (of the critical adaptation of a theory within a different cultural world, often 'from below'). It may also be related to Homi Bhabha's

    [45] See H. M. Hyndman, *England for All* (1881; Brighton: Harvester, 1973).

    [46] Porter, *Critics of Empire*, 94, writes: 'To be an imperial reformer, it seemed, one had to be an imperialist of sorts, and it was among these men less rigid in their anti-imperialism . . . that those ideas were born which could be used to modify and alleviate the effect of the imperialism of the nineties'.

    [47] Rey Chow, *Writing Diaspora* (Bloomington: Indiana UP, 1993), 41–6.

    [48] Rabindranath Tagore, *The Home and the World*, trans. Surendranath Tagore, rev. R. Tagore (1919; Madras: Macmillan India, 1992), 69.

emphasis on the borderline negotiation of cultural meanings, or, as he suggests in 'DissemiNation' and in other essays, on how strategies of resistance and empowerment emerge out of the regenerative interstices between cultural spaces, the pressurized margins marking out domains of difference.[49]

Early ventures in anti-colonial resistance and cross-nationalist interaction offer diverse instances of such interstitial emergence: of how different ideas of resistance might be picked up and developed in cross-border contact zones (like the metropolis), or reinflected and reinforced by being moved across borders and then adapted to local contexts; of the extent to which a liberatory politics represented a cross-hatching of different, often syncretized traditions. The will-to-identity of colonial elites was necessarily being articulated at points of conjuncture between cultures; their politics and writing therefore were always profoundly shaped by both perceptions and experiences of cross-cultural interrelation, solidarity, and dialogue. At the same time, it is important to remember, cross-border allusions and solidarities did not as a rule compromise the (hoped-for) integrity of the nation, or indeed create permanent cross-national political structures. Anti-imperial interaction is to this extent clarified by Emmanuel Levinas's concept of alterity, in which the other—here, the brother or sister nation elsewhere in the empire—is simultaneously recognized as being distant and unknowable, yet as an entity pre-eminently to be taken into account, to be signalled towards.[50]

Separated from the colonial governing elite but also alienated from the mass population by their middle-class status, education, lingua franca, and, in some cases, geographical mobility or educational and bureaucratic 'migrations', early nativist and nationalist intellectuals frequently felt themselves to be more at home in the colonizer's culture than in their indigenous environment.[51] Certainly

---

[49] Homi K. Bhabha, 'DissemiNation: Time, Narrative, and the Margins of the Modern Nation', in his edited *Nation and Narration* (London: Routledge, 1990), 291–322. See also 'Introduction' and ch. 11, 'How Newness enters the world', in *The Location of Culture*, 1–18, 212–35. The first essay reappears in *The Location of Culture*, 139–70. Kumkum Sangari, 'Relating Histories', in Svati Joshi (ed.), *Rethinking English: Essays in Literature, Language, History* (New Delhi: Trianka, 1991), 32, also notes: 'cultural formations produced under the aegis of imperialism have produced specifiable ideological configurations which loop and spread across "national" boundaries'.

[50] Emmanuel Levinas, *Alterity and Transcendence*, trans. Michael B. Smith (London: Athlone Press, 1999). See Chapter 5 for further discussion of Levinas's thinking in relation to cross-national interaction.

[51] Anderson, *Imagined Communities*, 47–65, 114–15.

they tended to find a deeper pool of common experience with other, like-minded colonial nationalist 'pilgrims' than with their own people. The cross-border impulsions of their migratory make-up prompted them therefore to reach beyond cultural and geopolitical boundaries to discover ways of constituting a resistant selfhood. Indeed it has been one of the ironies of native colonial experience across the twentieth century that nationalist writers and intellectuals such as Gandhi or Plaatje rediscovered, or uncovered for the first time—were returned to—their own cultural resources through diasporic contacts made abroad. London, pullulating with secularist, anarchist, socialist, avant-garde, and freethinking circles, as the chapters below in different ways illustrate, thus formed an important meeting ground for Indian, Irish, African, and Caribbean freedom movements.[52]

As David Lloyd has observed of nineteenth-century Ireland, anti-colonial and nationalist elites, finding themselves in peripheral but privileged positions in relation to countries 'marked by a singularly uneven pattern of economic development', grew adept at shifting their dilemmas of self-making around a broad cross-national and cosmopolitan ('cosmo-national' in Nivedita's phrase) landscape.[53] The phenomenon is neatly demonstrated, for example, in the emblematic gesture of cross-border solidarity represented by the (unsuccessful) 1880s efforts to elect the reformist Indian nationalist Dadabhai Naoroji as an Irish Parliamentary Party MP.[54] Elites became acquisitive of modes of self-invention that were at once individualistic and modern, bearing a certain international currency, yet seemingly built on tradition and autochthonous custom. This impulse to borrow and 'reroute' traditions is evident in the parallel late-Victorian efforts in nationalist India and Ireland, both shaped by Theosophical influences, to reconstruct the past as the repository of a lost racial (Aryan) essence *and* as the root of a renewed modern selfhood. No doubt the predominant maleness and overtly masculine ideology of most nationalist/anti-colonial elites in this period also promoted the looking-across to others' methods and strategies.

---

[52] Mulk Raj Anand, 'Why I Write?', in K. N. Singh (ed.), *Indian Writing in English* (New Delhi: Heritage, 1979), 1–9; R. Parthasarathy, 'Whoring after English Gods', in Guy Amirathanayagam (ed.), *Writers in East–West Encounter* (London: Macmillan, 1982), 66; Jonathan Schneer, *London 1900: The Imperial Metropolis* (New Haven: Yale UP, 1999).

[53] David Lloyd, *Nationalism and Minor Literature* (Berkeley and Los Angeles: University of California Press, 1987), 59.

[54] In 1892 he was elected a Liberal MP for Central Finsbury.

The emphasis was on overcoming the effeminization of the colonial subject in the service of a highly idealized national Mother: Mother Africa; Mother India or Durga, 'the *Shakti* of patriotism';[55] Cathleen ni Houlihan in Yeats's eponymous nationalist play (1902). Woman and women's bodies became the sites on which the battle between nationalism and colonialism was fought, on which male elites might parley amongst themselves.[56]

In summary, anti-colonial intelligentsias, poised between the cultural traditions of home on the one hand and of their education on the other, occupied a site of potentially productive inbetweenness where they might observe other resistance histories and political approaches in order to work out how themselves to proceed. Their cross-national contacts created an interstitial place between the cosmopolitan and the parochial in which they were able to lay claim to a till-now-metropolitan discourse of rights and self-assertion. Expressed in their own congresses and conventions, pamphlets and newsletters, this discourse they then made available amongst themselves. In the Janus fashion that Tom Nairn has memorably described as characteristic of nationalisms generally, elites spoke in a voice that bore an 'international resonance' and was thus 'recognizable to another, broader community', yet simultaneously built notions of their own especial racial nature out of essentialized spiritual and mythic resources which they believed the West had left untouched.[57] As the outer-national, diasporic formation of Gandhi's notion of all-India illustrates, they relied on international exchange, and a borrowed second culture, in order, each individually, to assert their own unity

55 Tagore, *The Home and the World*, 162.

56 Major theorizations of the masculinity of anti-colonial nationalisms, and of women's responses to it, are offered in the following, amongst others: Ashis Nandy, *The Intimate Enemy* (New Delhi: Oxford UP, 1983); Marjorie Howes, *Yeats's Nations: Gender, Class and Irishness* (Cambridge: Cambridge UP, 1996); C. L. Innes, *Woman and Nation in Irish Literature and Society 1880–1935* (Hemel Hempstead: Harvester Wheatsheaf, 1993); Anne McClintock, *Imperial Leather: Race, Gender and Sexuality in the Colonial Context* (London: Routledge, 1995); Susheila Nasta (ed.), *Motherlands: Black Women's Writing* (London: Women's Press, 1991); Andrew Parker et al. (eds.), *Nationalisms and Sexualities* (London: Routledge, 1992); Rajeswari Sunder Rajan, *Real and Imagined Women: Gender, Culture and Postcolonialism* (London: Routledge, 1993). Yet resistance to the hypermasculinity of white colonialism was not expressed only in terms of the polar opposites of masculine self-assertion and feminine idealization. Gandhian passive resistance, for instance, implied a refusal to participate in gendered colonial binaries.

57 Tom Nairn, *The Break-up of Britain: Crisis and Neo-nationalism* (London: New Left Books, 1977), and 'What Nations are for', *London Review of Books* (8 Sept. 1994), 7–8.

and singularity, to *think back to* themselves. As Gyan Prakash encapsulates it: 'the unity of the national subject was forged in the space of difference and conflicts', and, we might add, of cross-nationalist interaction.[58]

There is one final point to add to this overview of the channels of cross-border interaction and alternative nationalist thinking available at the height of empire. The interstitial spaces of the turn-of-the-century metropolis where colonial elites met were, as already intimated, significantly activated by the combinatory, syncretizing effects of modernist and avant-garde experimentation (in the forms of Expressionism, Imagism, Fauvism, Dadaism, primitivism, and so on), as well as by the radical new political and religious ideas in circulation. Chapter 5 will examine in more depth how some of these developments, themselves stimulated by the ethnographical explorations and global communications which empire had made possible, prepared the ground for and further stimulated the prevailing interest in alternative systems of cultural reference. The interdiscursivity of modernism, in other words, its layered intersection of diverse aesthetic, spiritual, and political approaches, was informed by—while itself informing—other pathways of cross-cultural, cross-border exchange. The new mystical and spiritualist doctrines of, for instance, mesmerism, Madame Blavatsky's Hindu-based Theosophy, or the modernist W. B. Yeats's Kabbalistic Order of the Golden Dawn, all placed a radical emphasis on the relativistic, multifaceted nature of belief: 'each religion is a different *prism* through which one looks at truth [emphasis in text]', in the words of Maud Gonne.[59] As well as moulding the epistemological and religious questions of any number of writers and artists, this democratic message also made a strong appeal to women and the working classes, as well as to a nationalist seeker such as Gandhi, who was first introduced to the *Bhagavad-gita* by Theosophists in London.[60] In 1912 Ezra Pound commented symptomatically on the new cross-cultural and cosmopolitan modernist order. The West's more intimate intercourse with

[58] Prakash, 'Introduction', *After Colonialism*, 9–10.

[59] Maud Gonne, letter to W. B. Yeats (10 Feb. 1903), in MacBride White and Jeffares (eds.), *The Gonne–Yeats Letters 1893–1918*, 166–7. This new international awareness of the many-sidedness of God, and the potential interconnectedness of all religions, was embodied in the 1893 World Parliament of Religions in Chicago, where Sister Nivedita's guru the Swami Vivekananda presided.

[60] Alex Owen, *The Darkened Room: Women, Power and Spiritualism in Late Victorian England* (London: Virago, 1989).

the Orient, he wrote, which had recently been captured in the translated poetry of the Bengali Rabindranath Tagore (promoted also by
Yeats), was bound to herald an important period of expanded
'world-fellowship'.[61]

Empire, the National, and the Postcolonial, as I have outlined, investigates the political and cultural contexts, mentalities, and literary
textual articulations of some of the anti-imperial and nationalist
movements which came into contact with each other at the height of
the British Empire. To this end it offers a series of critical portraits or
case studies of cross-national awareness, or of negotiation between
imperial and nationalist ideologies. A particularly illustrative instance of cross-national solidarity is explored in the last section of
the present chapter: the Irish nationalist support for the Boer minor-
ity during the Anglo-Boer War (1899–1902). In Irish responses to the
Transvaal's anti-imperial struggle we will see how cross-national cooperation and sympathy between different groups resistant to empire was put on well-publicized international display, and how this
developed and reinforced nationalist formations at home in Ireland.
The pages of the nationalist 'weekly review' the *United Irishman*
(1899–1906), and its successor *Sinn Féin* (1906–7), capture and indeed emblematize the form-giving cross-border contacts which characterize this important anti-imperial moment.

Triangulating the connection of Africa and Ireland with the Indian subcontinent, Chapters 2 and 3, which are interlinked, consider
the cross-border exchanges and negotiations of meaning (especially—though sporadically—with Ireland) which were involved in
the formation of Bengali nationalism in the years 1902–10. While the
spiritually inspired political partnership between the Irish-born Englishwoman Sister Nivedita and the extremist Aurobindo Ghose will
provide a structuring focus across both chapters, Chapter 2 examines
in particular the salient features of the Hindu-nationalist make-overs
in which both were engaged, especially their mutual exchange of Kali
iconography and concepts of self-sacrifice derived from the *Gita*.
Drawing on their key statements of nationalist resistance, Chapter 3
explores in detail both the political and the textual dimensions of
their interdiscursivity, examining in particular the interweaving of
their political careers and their interactive polemical practices.

[61] Ezra Pound, 'Tagore's Poems', *Poetry*, 1.3 (Dec. 1912), 84–6.

Returning to Africa, Chapter 4 will observe how the overdetermined nationalist energies of the black South African politician and writer Sol Plaatje in the period extending from the Boer War to the aftermath of the First World War produced both a pan-nationalist identification with W. E. B. Du Bois's African America, and a silent borrowing from South African Indian, most notably Gandhian, strategies of passive resistance. Once again the accent will be on the nationalist's complexity of engagement with divergent political and cultural discourses, including Tswana oral tradition, Cape liberalism, Victorian ideals of colonial brotherhood, and suffragette and African women's protest. With Plaatje's multigeneric, bricolage writing as a signpost, Chapter 5, finally, will extrapolate the focus on cross-border interaction into the interdiscursive, late-imperial formation that was early twentieth-century modernism. By looking in particular at the salient cross-cultural (Europe–Asia) connections explored in the work of the Anglo-Irish poet W. B. Yeats and the cosmopolitan writer, publisher, and anti-imperialist Leonard Woolf, the chapter will ask whether the cross-border ('cosmo-national') contacts pursued by nationalist elites in the empire might have impinged on metropolitan cultural practices in any significant way.

In a situation where metropolis–margin and cross-national contacts formed a layered and thickly textured web, as Sister Nivedita for one perceived, it will be impossible to do justice to the many and diverse encounters, link-ups, and intersections of interest which took place between movements, communities, political groupings, and individuals in this period. Yet the hope is that these will be sketched in or obliquely suggested nonetheless, especially by way of the interconnections which are outlined through the reappearance of key figures in the different chapters of this book. So it will be discovered that Rabindranath Tagore, a participant in 1905 Swadeshi and a friend of the Hindu mystic and nationalist Sister Nivedita in Chapter 2, re-emerges in Chapter 5 as a catalyst figure in Yeats's explorations in spiritual nationalism. While New Woman ideas make an impact on the young Margaret Noble/Sister Nivedita's thinking about self-representation in Chapter 3, early campaigners for women's rights weave through both Plaatje and Gandhi's political backgrounds in Chapter 4. John Ruskin's *Unto This Last* (1862) was a prominent influence not only on Nivedita, Gandhi, and Plaatje (and on the late nineteenth-century rise of the British working-class movement[62]),

[62] See Lawrence Goldman, 'Ruskin, Oxford, and the British Labour Movement', in

but also importantly on J. A. Hobson, the liberal economist and ally of Plaatje's intellectual mentor Olive Schreiner. And Hobson's anti-imperial ideas were in turn taken up by Leonard Woolf. So, too, as we saw, Theosophy and related spiritualist investigations of the time, which were represented in the figures most notably of Madame Blavatsky and Annie Besant, appear as formative influences, and as forces to be responded to, almost right the way across the book. The nexuses of anti-imperial and anti-establishment thinking which interconnected the empire's many 'outposts of progress' (not excluding London) frequently looped over and doubled up on themselves. In all cases they are far from easy to unravel.

THE IRISH BOER WAR AND *THE UNITED IRISHMAN*

It was during the first year of Anglo-Boer hostilities (1899–1900), when Irish nationalism expressed its strong support for the beleaguered republican Boers, that the disturbance potential as well as the form-giving impact of cross-empire, anti-imperial cooperation was widely demonstrated perhaps for the first time. This was despite the fact that the cooperation was not only short-lived but concentrated within a relatively small group of advanced Irish nationalists (many associated with the secret Irish Republican Brotherhood). As Maud Gonne observed in a letter to her spiritual collaborator and nationalist friend W. B. Yeats, 'rampant' English hostility to the December 1899 pro-Transvaal campaign in Dublin revealed how 'necessary & useful' this campaign was for the reinspiration of Irish nationalism.[63]

Prior to this time there had been expressions of solidarity between anti-colonial nationalisms, such as were exchanged between India and Ireland (as will be seen). Yet these had remained, comparatively speaking, grounded within their respective nationalist contexts. In 1899–1900 the difference was that perceptions of a common oppression shared by the Irish and the Boers produced *concrete* offers of material and moral support from Dublin, as well as military assistance from Irishmen already in the Transvaal. These men, forming themselves into a small Irish Brigade, served with the Boer campaign

---

Dinah Birch (ed.), *Ruskin and the Dawn of the Modern* (Oxford: Clarendon Press, 1999).

[63] Maud Gonne, letter of 11 Oct. 1899, in MacBride White and Jeffares (eds.), *The Gonne–Yeats Letters 1893–1938*, 113. See also *The Collected Letters of W. B. Yeats*, vol. ii, ed. John S. Kelly, Warwick Gould, and Deirdre Toomey (Oxford: Oxford UP, 1997), 471.

in northern Natal under the leadership of Colonel Blake and Major John MacBride: 'the Vierkleur and the Green Flag waved side by side'.[64] Back home, in the aftermath of the subdued and disappointing 1798 centenary celebrations, such displays of transcontinental cooperation proved galvanizing, 'electrifying' in Yeats's description.[65] At the auspicious turn-of-the-century pro-Boer sympathy was embraced as an important and welcome opportunity to ignite nationalist enthusiasm across a broad spectrum of political opinion. Even if in a piecemeal way, the Boer War, nationalist Ireland's surrogate conflict, opened the self-involved enclaves of Irish nationalism to inspiration from beyond the Irish diaspora, if not also to a potentially useful object lesson in armed struggle.

On 11 October 1899, the day of the outbreak of hostilities, Maud Gonne publicly announced the creation of a pro-Boer Transvaal Committee under the slogans 'England's Difficulty is Ireland's Opportunity' and 'Enlisting for England is Treason to Ireland'. A chief object of the Committee was to dissuade Irish soldiers from fighting on the imperial side 'in opposition to the National Will, as servants of our deadly enemy'.[66] Yet, if the Transvaal Committee represented a comparatively narrow fringe of advanced nationalist thinking, the wider front of the pro-Boer cause was demonstrated in the obstructive strategies which Irish MPs adopted at Westminster during parliamentary debates on the war. Within months Michael Davitt had resigned his post as MP in protest at the harrying of the 'small [Boer] nation' by an 'alien' force, and went out to South Africa to report on the war effort.[67] Irish parliamentarians and their direct opponents,

---

[64] In September 1899, not long before the outbreak of the war, Irish nationalists on the Rand led by John MacBride, later a hero of Easter 1916, had organized themselves into a Brigade, and went up to Pretoria to offer their services to the Transvaal Republic. To provide immunity from British charges of treason President Kruger granted to the Brigaders 'burghership' of the South African Republic. MacBride's Brigade later became known as the first Irish Brigade. Contrary to inflated claims in the *United Irishman*, it rarely numbered more than 150 men. Arthur Lynch formed a less prominent second pro-Boer Irish Brigade in 1900. See Donal P. McCracken, *The Irish Pro-Boers 1877–1902* (Johannesburg: Perskor, 1989); *UI* (14 Oct. 1899); IER, 'War Notes', *UI* (4 Nov. 1899), 5.

[65] His actual words were: 'The war has made the air electrical just now'. Letter to W. S. Pyper (22 Dec. 1900), *Collected Letters*, ii. 617–18.

[66] Maud Gonne, 'The Dublin and the Munster Fusiliers', *UI* (23 Sept. 1899), 4–5.

[67] Quoted in Stephen Koss (ed.), *The Pro-Boers: The Anatomy of an Antiwar Movement* (Chicago: University of Chicago Press, 1973), 33–4. Davitt's unambiguously pro-Boer book *The Boer Fight for Freedom* (New York: Funk and Wagnalls Co., 1902), was based on the observations he made as a war reporter for the Irish Parliamentary Party paper the *Freeman's Journal*.

the radical nationalists, temporarily came together therefore on the common platform of their support for the Transvaal's 'strike for liberty'.

Despite the obvious differences of religion and geopolitical context, Irish declarations of solidarity recognized in the Boers a republican people apparently as colonially beleaguered as nationalist Ireland felt itself to be: their culture and language, too, were threatened, their land occupied, their liberty denied. On the basis of these features in common, as well as the fact that the Boers were prepared to defend their freedom with arms, the South Africans' cause might be espoused as virtually coterminous with Ireland's own struggle, a means to 'strike a good and effective blow at the merciless and tyrant power that has so long held our people in bondage'.[68] Indeed, especially given that there were restrictions on political activity at home, the reasons for offering such support became mutually reinforcing. For the advanced nationalist activist the war was in effect a two-tier campaign: both *for* the Boers and *against* England. Or as John MacBride the de facto leader of the Irish Brigade expressed it, the idea of contributing to the Boer struggle with Britain was 'natural', for, 'the policy of . . . all Nationalists is to try and hit England hard whenever they can, as their only chance of getting anything from her'.[69] The opening to Arthur Griffith's 1900 ballad for John MacBride's Brigade (and for the latter's unsuccessful Mayo election campaign) captures the motivation behind this cooperation in a precise linkage: 'For Ireland's cause *and* Kruger's land right gallantly they fight [emphasis added]'.[70] The ballad goes on to proclaim that from the Irish nationalist point of view the war represents a 'wreaking of revenge' on England for 1798, as well as useful preparation for eventually 'driving the tyrant from our shore'. Was it not then almost self-evident that the Irish should fight together with the Boers 'in Freedom's holy cause', to quote from yet another song published in the *United Irishman*?[71] Oom Paul Kruger the unbudging Boer leader

[68] Anonymous (Arthur Griffith?), 'A Call to Arms: To Irishmen in South Africa', *UI* (28 Oct. 1899), 5.

[69] John MacBride, 'Statement of Facts on Behalf of Major MacBride', Fred Allan Papers, National Library of Ireland MS 29819, p. 2. On the same page MacBride also wrote: 'the practice among Irishmen is to unite the Irish race all over the world in the common struggle for national freedom'. A struggle abroad could still be a struggle for Ireland.

[70] Arthur Griffith, 'Ballad of the Transvaal Irish Brigade', *UI* (24 Feb. 1900), 4. Compare Lady Gregory, 'Boer Ballads in Ireland', *Poets and Dreamers*, 72–9, in which the conflict is again repeatedly pictured as a fight for Ireland.

[71] H. S., 'The Boer Woman', *UI* (29 Apr. 1900), 2.

was widely perceived as the cynosure of 'free-loving people through-out the world', a universal signifier of a general and not only a Boer nationalist resistance.[72]

In cities like Dublin and Cork pro-Boer sympathy was for a brief time widespread enough to be depicted as a popular movement (even by today's standards). 'This Transvaal idea has taken hold in Dublin as nothing else has for a long time,' Maud Gonne wrote to Yeats.[73] Especially during the time of the Boer victories in December 1899, as G. A. Lyons has described, women and men wore South African Re-public colours in their hatbands and neckties, and portraits of the Boer Generals were everywhere on sale, as were buttons, pendants, and badges in Transvaal colours.[74] On 1 October 1899 15,000 people turned up on the Dublin Quays before Custom House to cheer the Transvaal flag and to endorse Maud Gonne's anti-enlistment cam-paign. At what turned out to be the culmination of the campaign, a 17 December meeting to protest the Trinity College award of an hon-orary degree to the Colonial Secretary Joseph Chamberlain, support was again vociferous, and concluded with hand-to-hand struggles between pro-Boer supporters and the police. Throughout this time donations to the Irish Transvaal Committee grew steadily.

Pro-nationalist Irish newspapers channelled and reinforced this support. From the beginning of the war the pages of the *United Irish-man*, the unofficial organ of the Irish Transvaal Committee, regu-larly saw the publication of darkly ironic or openly committed 'Recruiting Songs' promoting the anti-enlistment drive.[75] In vigor-ous support of the Boer cause this paper, and to a lesser extent the *Freeman's Journal*, the *Sligo Champion*, and other newspapers around Ireland, outlined points of identification between Irish na-tional history and that of the Boers, in particular their alleged con-tinual struggle against England in the cause of liberty and nationality. Feature essays, 'foreign notes', and commentaries marked out over-lapping debates on embattled national autonomy and the necessary protection of identity, history, and language, so suggesting political

[72] Arthur Griffith, Report, 'The Irish Transvaal Committee', *UI* (2 Dec. 1899), 6.

[73] Letter of 11 Oct. 1899, in MacBride White and Jeffares (eds.), *The Gonne–Yeats Let-ters 1893–1938*, 113.

[74] G. A. Lyons, *Some Recollections of Griffith and his Times* (Dublin: Talbot Press, 1923), 22–35.

[75] Especially after the death of his co-editor William Rooney in 1901, Griffith edited and ran the *United Irishman* more or less single-handedly. He is the assumed author of the majority of the paper's many unsigned reports and notes.

and military strategies, or simply 'energies' or inspiration, worth transferring from one nationalist context to another. As stated by Griffith in the *United Irishman* of 17 June 1899, the experiences which linked the small Boer and Irish nations were 'consistent oppression' and 'systematic robbery' by a powerful Britain, a cruel Goliath figure, active in hypocrisy and interested only in loot. Heaping insult upon injury, Britain had moreover violated 'the white man's tradition' by joining with 'the native races against the brother-white'.[76] Against such villainy manly Boer republicanism was rightly to be defended and supported with arms. Griffith's editorial paints a picture of an unquestioned, although subjectively defined, solidarity.

Importantly, support such as this, pitted against a 'common enemy', was always in the first place self-interested, aimed primarily at *Irish*, not Boer, freedom. Irish Brigade action in this sense represented an appropriated or displaced conflict; essentially it offered a proxy for opposing the empire and consolidating resistance where it was not possible to do so directly at home.[77] In related fashion Gandhi's South African activism, and certainly his pacifist ambulance work at Ladysmith during the Boer War, can be seen in retrospect as preparation or 'homework' for the passive resistance strategies he later activated in India.[78] Although most pro-Boer Irish soldiers had left South Africa by September 1900, and although the lessons in armed and especially guerrilla struggle which they had learned were not at the time adopted by the republican movement,[79] the war's example of successful military surrogacy usefully advanced nationalist pride and self-confidence. Outlining a principle which was also to prove influential during both World Wars, Maud Gonne had defended Irish anti-imperial subversion abroad in a famous 1898

[76] Arthur Griffith, Editorial, *UI* (17 June 1899), 2. See also his indignant 'The English Stirring-up the Natives', *UI* (28 Oct. 1899), 1. An unambiguous suprematism and racism supplied a further point of identification between Irish and Boer nationalisms at this time.

[77] John MacBride, Fred Allan Papers, NLI MS 29817, pp. 113–16, underlines self-interest as part of his justification for supporting the Boers. 'I wanted to organize my countrymen [in the South African Republic] so as to be in a position to strike a blow at England's power abroad when we could not unfortunately do so at home.'

[78] See M. K. Gandhi, *An Autobiography; or The Story of my Experiments with Truth*, trans. Mahadev Desai (Ahmedabad: Navajivan Publishing House, 1958); Balasubramanyan Chandramohan, '"Hamlet with the Prince of Denmark left out"? The South African War, Empire, and India', in Donal Lowry (ed.), *The South African War Reappraised* (Manchester: Manchester UP, 2000), 150–68.

[79] One of the most immediate effects of the Peace of Vereeniging in 1902, and of the humiliating spectacle of Boer defeat, was that advanced nationalist opinion in Ireland grew more sceptical of armed resistance as an anti-imperial weapon.

speech given at Ballina: when other powers closed in on England, she cried, Ireland should be prepared 'and go in for her share'.[80] Or again: 'I always insisted that . . . it was the duty of Irishmen, till Ireland was free, to fight England whenever and wherever they could and use whatever means came to hand.'[81] From 1900 the point she had made could be widely assented to. Displays of pro-Boer opposition and heroics had certainly contributed to boosting the fortunes of anti-British nationalism in Ireland.[82] It also helped reinforce the international and cross-border formations of Ireland's already diasporic nationalism.

The displaced or surrogate dimension of the Irish nationalists' war effort in 1899–1900 therefore underlines one of the key aspects of anti-colonial hand-holding or collaboration: in a phrase, that an overlapping of grievances, ideas, and tactics was adapted in order to strengthen a cause at home. Developments after 1902 bear out this idea of cooperative nationalist self-advancement. Most significantly, the Irish Transvaal Committee of October 1899 formed the kernel of Arthur Griffith's National Council in 1903, which in turn provided the structure for Sinn Féin ('Ourselves') as constituted in 1905. Sinn Féin's emphasis was, as its name suggested, on self-reliance and self-development expressed in non-violent resistance, parliamentary non-cooperation, and the cultivation of local culture and the Irish language.[83] Yet despite such preoccupations, the organization maintained an awareness of nationalist parallels in other contexts, primarily in other European countries, pre-eminently Hungary of the 1860s, Arthur Griffith's chief model, but increasingly once again in the broader British imperial context, including Swadeshi (self-help) protests in India.

Both the *United Irishman* and its successor *Sinn Féin* crystallized in print, in the juxtapositions and parallels of their layout, such cross-border disseminations of ideas and inspiration. Even if the display of these effects remained first and foremost the brainchild of the

---

[80] Quoted in Samuel Levenson, *Maud Gonne* (London: Cassell, 1976), 135.

[81] Gonne, *A Servant of the Queen*, 298. See also *UI* (13 Jan. 1900).

[82] See Alvin Jackson, 'Irish Unionists and the Empire', in Jeffery (ed.), '*An Irish Empire*', 133.

[83] F. S. L. Lyons, *Ireland since the Famine* (London: Weidenfeld and Nicolson, 1971), 247–59. Passive resistance in Bengal (1905–8), too, sought the protection of Indian commerce and industry, and the promotion of Indian labour. By 1905 Griffith had rejected armed opposition not on principle but because he felt it was for the time being practically unsustainable. See Arthur Griffith, 'A National Organization', *UI* (29 Apr. 1899), 3.

almost fanatically dedicated Arthur Griffith, he was clearly acknowledging and encouraging an existing cross-national attention even while at the same time placing emphasis on the need for the nation to have faith in itself. In particular the regular column 'Over the Frontier' which was featured in both papers, carried news-in-brief reports, many drawn from foreign newspapers and agencies, of analogous experiences both of oppression and resistance in countries ranging from Romania to India. Not only political and cultural parallels, therefore, but also creative potentials for nationalist interaction were, one might say, writ large, mapped out in black and white in the paper's pages.

That this was a psychologically heartening if not also a practically productive exercise is indicated by the fact that across the eight years of the *United Irishman/Sinn Féin*'s existence, the 'Over the Frontier' column became increasingly more international in reference. Where it began by referring almost exclusively to the Boer situation, and, failing that, to examples from within Europe, by 1905 Bengal with its apparently parallel movement of self-reliance and national unity became the most regularly cited 'sister' context, both in 'Over the Frontier' and in more detailed news reports. Indeed it would not overdraw the distinction to say that if in 1899 cross-border solidarity was primarily taken to mean the parallel opposition of oppressed nations to imperial injustice (where Britain's autocratic carryings-on were read as a tale of perfidy Ireland had long known about), six years later the predominant concern was with actual points of cross-over, or close cross-nationalist similitudes, such as the development of local industries and the teaching of national history in *both* India *and* Ireland. Bengal's resistance to Britain could therefore be interpreted as a prompt for, or else an affirmation of, Ireland's cause.

The *United Irishman* did not scruple to call the Swadeshi movement 'the Sinn Féin policy in India' (on the basis of which the two countries might think of forming an 'entente cordiale'). Yet it held back from imputing a direct or derivative link to the two nationalist approaches:

the Boer and the Russo-Japanese wars have put a new spirit into the Indian people, and the patriotic Hindus who had for years been preaching to a people whose spirit was subdued, and who regarded the fates as against them, have been transformed, in the people's eyes, from visionaries into statesmen.[84]

---

[84] Griffith, *UI* (16 Sept. 1905), 5; *UI* (23 Sept. 1905), 4. Griffith recognized that Indian passive resistance and boycott also constituted a protest at the Partition of Bengal.

If it did claim some credit for the new defence of tradition and opposition to parliamentarianism in India, it was that Irish nationalism had in some sense prophesied Swadeshi resistance and its 'remaking' of men on the basis of the Irish people's own experience of 'denationalization' and tax drain, and the struggle against these.

Yet, even so, from the perspective of an emergent Sinn Féin which was itself in the process of formulating a policy of national self-development, common interests and parallels of approach with the Indian context were clearly well worth stressing. (And at the same time the colonialist rhetoric of 'civilized' and 'uncivilized' nations that had pertained in 1899 articles supporting the Boers, was now well worth downplaying.) This self-making, it is relevant to remember, was taking place in the immediate aftermath of the Boer defeat in 1902, and of the Afrikaners' steady incorporation into the South African colonial state.[85] The *United Irishman* therefore needed another international cohort with which to claim nationalist solidarity: 'A common enemy, a common purpose, and similarity of circumstances should long ago have led to common action on the part of [these] two peoples.'[86] As if to emphasize the significance of the linkup, a November 1905 report sees the Bengali 'watchword' of ' "Bande Mataram"—"hail to the motherland" ' (originally the refrain of the nationalist writer Bankimchandra Chattopadhyay's 1882 anthem for Bengal)—as inspirationally uniting Indians 'in a common bond' to overthrow Britain's 'social and commercial sway'.[87] Whereas Indians might once have learned from Ireland, Ireland it seems may now draw instruction from 'the cause of India for Indians'.

The *United Irishman/Sinn Féin*'s most exuberant endorsement of India's new spirit of self-assertion appeared with the publication in the inaugural issue of *Sinn Féin* (5 May 1906) of an eight-stanza hymn 'Bande Mataram'.[88] Here, however, the 'Motherland' repeatedly and hypnotically 'hailed' as deity, as in the Bengali anthem (and in the title of Aurobindo Ghose's journal *Bande Mataram*), was Ireland, land of martyrs, 'Gaelic heights', and heroic 'Celts' in the making. The hymn thus built on and sought to absorb into the Irish

---

[85] A revolutionary nationalist Ireland–South Africa link was re-established in the 1970s in the form of underground collaborations between the IRA and the ANC. See for example Simon Hattenstone, 'The Man with No Past: An Interview with Gerry Adams', *Guardian* (30 Apr. 2001), 1–4.

[86] *UI* (14 Oct. 1905), 5.   [87] *UI* (18 Nov. 1905), 5.

[88] 'Rory' (Arthur Griffith), 'Bande Mataram!' *Sinn Féin*, 1.1 (5 May 1906), 3.

context the Bengali 'original and a translation' of the Swadeshi anthem which had appeared in a late issue of the *United Irishman* (and was itself borrowed from the *Gaelic American*).[89] It rang out:

> Hail, Motherland! no bell for these shall toll
> The dead who died for Ireland never pass,
> No history need we other than this scroll—
> Thy grave-scarred bosom shows the noblest roll
> That death raised ever in the patriot grass.

More or less directly juxtaposed with a 'creed' of Indian national unity and brotherhood ('I believe in India, beloved mother of each and all her many children'), the Irishized cross-border citation that is this 'Bande Mataram' forms an elaborate recognition of the symbolic value the newly formed Sinn Féin had invested in nationalist struggle abroad. Significantly, having thus introduced the resonant nationalist cry of Bengal to Ireland, *Sinn Féin* is much concerned in subsequent issues to endorse the rallying force of such a motto or mantra as well as its disruptive impact on the imperial authority (this was something which Sister Nivedita and Aurobindo Ghose, too, were committed to teaching in Bengal[90]). Irish nationalism could hardly have it made clearer that the '[lessons] the Swadeshi movement [preached] trumpet-tongued'—and this hymn mourning recent quiescence yet looking forward to a new dawn—represented lessons also for Sinn Féin: 'not petitions to an alien Government, not appeals to an alien Parliament, but public spirit, cooperation, zeal, and self-reliance build nations'.[91]

---

[89] *UI* (24 Feb. 1906), 5. The *United Irishman* had been proscribed for carrying an article which appeared to support armed resistance.

[90] As Satis Chandra Mukherjee, the editor of the Bengali *Dawn* magazine and an associate of Nivedita put it: 'What Bengali heart is not set beating faster at the sound of the two magic words? When the late Bankimchandra Chattopadhyay in his immortal work—*Ananda Math*, the 'Abode of Joy'—first sang the heart-stirring and soul-lifting song, the opening words of which have furnished Modern Bengal with a battle-cry and a divine inspiration, so to say—could he have dreamt of the transformation—the miraculous and wonderful transformation which the two mellifluous words were destined to work in the hopes and aspirations of his degenerate countrymen? The welkin now rings with *Bande Mataram*. The streets and lanes of Calcutta and of the rest of the province resound with the solemn watch-word. *Bande Mataram* has stirred the hearts of the people to their depths.' Quoted in Haridas and Uma Mukherjee (eds.), *Sri Aurobindo and the New Thought in Indian Politics* (Calcutta: Firma K. L. Mukhopadyay, 1958), p. xxi.

[91] *UI* (11 Nov. 1905), 5.

2   India the Starting Point: Cross-National Self-Translation in 1900s Calcutta

> India is the starting point, and the goal, as far as I am concerned. Let *her* look after the West if she wishes.
>
> (Nivedita, Letter to Josephine MacLeod, 1903)[1]

'FROM ALL POINTS DO THE PATHS CONVERGE': A UNIQUE ENCOUNTER[2]

In the first decade of the twentieth century the largely secret political partnership—if not the underground collaboration—between the Irish-born, English-identified, Bengali activist Margaret Noble or Sister Nivedita (1867–1911), and the Cambridge-educated Bengali intellectual and later sage Aurobindo Ghose (1872–1950), enacted a fascinating international transaction of political ideas, beliefs, and influences. Nivedita—the main focus of this chapter—became after 1898 a Kali devotee, a nationalist radical, and a champion of the Calcutta art movement. Aurobindo was, following his return to India, an increasingly more extremist neo-Hindu nationalist who became, after some years, a spiritual leader.

Even if their interaction was untypical as regards the relative depth of their involvement, it can in many respects be read—as I hope to do both in this chapter and the next—as a cameo of the cultural and political conditions, and the political and textual possibilities, for

---

[1] Sister Nivedita, Letter to Josephine MacLeod (25 Aug. 1903). Quoted in Pravrajika Atmaprana, *Sister Nivedita of Ramakrishna-Vivekananda* (1961; Calcutta: Sister Nivedita Girls' School, 1977), 185 [emphasis in text].

[2] Sister Nivedita, *Studies from an Eastern Home, Complete Works of Sister Nivedita*, 2nd edn., vol. ii, ed. Pravrajika Atmaprana (Calcutta: Advaita Ashrama, 1982), 380. In these chapters the major works of Sister Nivedita from which quotation will be made, will be cited as individual texts. Other references will be to the *Complete Works*, henceforth abbreviated as *CW*. Page citations will be incorporated parenthetically in the text.

anti-imperial cooperation at this critical time in the fortunes of the British Empire. Both figures partook in a strong Mother India idealism and shared an ethic of nationalist manliness. In the intermeshing and cross-referencing of their extremist politics, a cross-cultural interaction took place that had, simultaneously, a cosmopolitan dimension connecting international elites, and an intensely local focus, translating sources of nationalist inspiration imported from elsewhere to match the Bengali context.

Admittedly, most of what mutually involved them took place within the hidden channels of the Calcutta political underground, or through the public yet coded medium of its nationalist or extremist press. The work and the exchanges of opinion they shared, therefore, are for the greater part difficult to trace, being either deliberately obscured, or, very often, unreliably recorded. It is possible however to reconstruct more or less the chief motivations for their involvement—as this chapter will do especially with respect to Nivedita—as well as the background and chronology of their relationship—as in Chapter 3. Through a close reading of their written work it should also be possible to plot the spiritually inspired political partnership, and even more precisely, the anti-imperial interdiscursivity, that they did reciprocally build. Against the charged context of nationalist Bengal 1902–10, which this chapter in part explores, an attentive reading and comparison of their politics and writing across both chapters will give insights into both the circumstances, and the constitutive features and modes, of their transaction, in particular their mutually encouraging political awareness of one another.

To capture the many levels on which their cross-national(ist) and cross-cultural relationship operated, therefore, the discussion will be organized across the two chapters as follows. As well as give some account of the Bengal elite, this expository chapter will consider several of the definitive aspects of Nivedita and Aurobindo's anti-colonial self-making or self-translation, focusing on their different investments in the cross-border nationalism of Bengal. Particular attention will be given to Nivedita's militancy and to her Kali-worship as the culminating sign of her self-assimilation to neo-Hinduism. For, even taking into account Aurobindo's strenuous efforts to 're-nationalize' himself, Nivedita's process of Hinduization was probably the more dramatic make-over, given her Europeanness.[3]

[3] See Rabindranath Tagore's comment on the difficulty for those not born Hindu of gaining entry to Hindu society in *Gora*, trans. Surendranath Tagore (1910; London:

Chapter 3 will explore in more detail how Nivedita and Auro-bindo's interaction in fact developed, that is, both through the medium of their political collaboration and through their various, often interconnected textual practices. By examining their at once distinct and yet linked careers as internationally inspired extremist leaders and organizers, and by drawing on their key statements of in-tention and belief for the years 1902–10, the discussion will consider their overlapping nationalist objectives and interrelated, at times in-tegrated, political strategy, in short, the cross-nationalist textures of their involvement. To expand the concept of nationalisms as existing in interdiscursive contact, other points of cross-national intersec-tion, especially with Irish politics, will be noted as appropriate.

Through a careful decoding of the remarkable Nivedita–Auro-bindo political partnership, therefore, these paired chapters will sharpen the focus on the analogical and interdiscursive nationalist link-ups discussed in Chapter 1, to see how these manifested in prac-tice. Certainly, though emerging from very different cultural and political traditions, and though they also collaborated in several cases as much or more closely with others, Aurobindo Ghose and Sis-ter Nivedita appear to have developed for a time a productive and stimulating 'conversation' which was both shaped by and itself contributed to shaping the cultural contact zone that was elite-dominated nationalist Calcutta.[4] Conducted through the channels of their consciousness-raising speeches, and their prolific, often sub-tly insurrectionary journalism, as well as presumably in private meet-ings, this conversation transacted, tested, developed, and affirmed anti-colonial nationalist and politico-spiritual ideas. In so doing, from what one can judge, it helped lay the ideological ground for the forging of a self-conscious militant politics in 1900s Bengal.

The period of contact between Aurobindo and Nivedita which is the focus of these chapters, ran from 1902 to 1910, with moments of particular closeness and extremist intensity falling in 1905–7 and 1909–10. It was inaugurated by Aurobindo's reading of Nivedita's first book, *Kali, the Mother* (1900), a short collection of musings and

Macmillan, 1924), 25, 335. As will be seen, *Gora* was probably modelled in part on Nivedita's character and experience.

[4] On cultural contact zones see again Mary Louise Pratt, *Imperial Eyes* (London: Rout-ledge, 1992), which relates to early colonial encounter and Patrick Colm Hogan, *Colo-nialism and Cultural Identity* (Albany: State University of New York Press, 2000), 4–10, on more established regions of contact, such as that in 1900s Bengal.

invocations addressed to the Mother, published to raise funds for Nivedita's Calcutta school.[5] This was followed by their subsequent first meeting in Baroda, again in 1902. This was also the year of the Swami Vivekananda's death, within a fortnight of which (the traditional period of mourning), Nivedita had sought a formal separation from Vivekananda's Ramakrishna Order in order to pursue what she now regarded as her political calling. Secret society work on both sides followed these events, which was then galvanized by the outbreak of resistance to Curzon's Partition of Bengal in 1905.

The period ends with Aurobindo's flight from British authority and exile to Pondicherry (a French enclave) to pursue life as a Hindu sage and guru in early 1910, in which process Nivedita was a key helper; and then with Nivedita's death from dysentery in the Himalayas on 13 October 1911. For both nationalists, however, 1905–10 was the period of their most active political involvement in which they mutually supported, encouraged, and helped further to radicalize one another. (It was after his retreat to Pondicherry that Aurobindo Ghose became known by the honorific title, Sri Aurobindo. Following convention, therefore, he will here generally be referred to as Aurobindo. The name Nivedita, the Dedicated or Consecrated One, was bestowed upon Margaret Noble by the Swami Vivekananda on her initiation as his disciple in 1898.[6] I use it not only because it was the name she herself used occasionally as a pen-name, but because it encapsulates her self-defining dedication to Hindu religion and society. Nivedita and Aurobindo Ghose were also the names by which these two figures were known to each other.)

As suggested, the conversation concerning nationalist self-development, manhood, and resistance which Aurobindo and Nivedita, both noted persons of letters, developed in tandem with one another, can be reconstructed from a reading of their key texts. These texts include Aurobindo's two classic and prescient works of resistance theory, essentially his political manifestos: the essays comprising *The Doctrine of Passive Resistance*, first published in *Bande Mataram* (9–23 April 1907); and the development of these ideas in

[5] *Kali, the Mother* (1900; Calcutta: Advaita Ashrama, 1989), *CW* i. 459–504, was first published in London by the 'alternative' publishers Swan Sonnenschein. Page references, to the *CW* version, will be incorporated parenthetically in the text with the abbreviation *Kali*.

[6] See Jayawardena, *White Woman's Other Burden*, 187; Narinder Kapur, *The Irish Raj* (Antrim: Greystone Press, 1997), 20–1.

the more spiritualized *The Ideal of the Karmayogin* (1909–10), written for the journal *Karmayogin*.[7] Nivedita's primary publications are her lengthy reflective biographical study, *The Master as I Saw Him* (1910); the impressionistic and partisan sociological portrait, *The Web of Indian Life* (1904), though this to a lesser extent than *The Master*; and her important radical pamphlet *Aggressive Hinduism* (1905), which she described as her attempt to condense 'the Swami's whole ideal . . . in one message'.[8]

In the most complete account of their relationship he was to give years later, long after her death, Aurobindo revealingly laid stress on the political rather than the spiritual dimension of his contact with Nivedita:

> Then, about my relations with Sister Nivedita—they were purely in the field of politics. Spirituality or spiritual matters did not enter into them and I do not remember anything passing between us on these subjects when I was with her.[9]

His partial denial is interestingly folded into a partial affirmation. This occurs once again, later on in the same retrospective 1946 account, when he observes that, while they were both working as activists in Calcutta, he and Nivedita had little occasion to meet other than at Congress meetings. And yet, 'my collaboration with her was solely in the revolutionary field'.[10] This was a field however which was centrally informed by the intensely involving and often militant Hinduism (a revivalist politics) in which both Nivedita and Aurobindo, as will be seen, participated. Clearly, as these apparent contradictions indicate, their involvement was complicated, its exact links difficult to specify. And yet, even if in some encrypted way, and even if not frequently or before witnesses, the two nationalists

---

[7] Sri Aurobindo, *The Doctrine of Passive Resistance* (Calcutta: Arya Publishing House, 1948), and *The Ideal of the Karmayogin* (1918; Pondicherry: Sri Aurobindo Ashram, 1950). Page references will henceforth be incorporated in the text with the abbreviations *Doctrine* and *Karmayogin* respectively.

[8] See *CW* iii, p. xii. Sister Nivedita, *Aggressive Hinduism* (Madras: G. A. Natesan, 1905); see also *CW* iii. 489–511. Page references to *Aggressive Hinduism*, from the *CW*, will be incorporated in the text with the abbreviation *AH*.

[9] Quoted in A. B. Purani, *The Life of Sri Aurobindo* (1958; Pondicherry: Sri Aurobindo Ashram, 1964), 64. The extended version of *Sri Aurobindo on Himself* (1953), which Purani for the greater part includes, appears as Sri Aurobindo, *Birth Centenary Library*, vol. xxvi (Pondicherry: Sri Aurobindo Ashram, 1972). Henceforth *BCL*. *Doctrine* and *Karmayogin* are collected in *BCL* i and ii.

[10] Quoted in Purani, *The Life of Sri Aurobindo*, 65.

certainly met and cooperated, put their heads together for the political freedom *and* the spiritual predominance of India.

In that both were devout believers in the Advaita Vedanta preached by the Ramakrishna–Vivekananda Order, one could go so far as to suggest that the interconnected nature of their relationship to an extent put into practice, and was at the same time justified by, their ideas concerning the Vedantic Oneness of Spirit, which to them importantly embraced the spirit of the Indian nation. Their political relations, in other words, were highly spiritualized both in content and in expression, and their spirituality bore a strongly political impetus. As Nivedita described what she understood by her guru Swami Vivekananda's Vedanta:

not in the Good alone but also in Evil, in Death as well as Life, in the West and in the East, in fact in diversity of all kinds, is to be read the revelation of Unity. From all points do the paths converge by which the One comes to the vision of man (*Studies from an Eastern Home, CW* ii. 380).

The sense of nationality, she wrote elsewhere, is based on the concept of unity *and* 'inter-relation between the different parts of a single organism'.[11] Such an all-inclusive 'interrelation' was then in effect enacted by her extremist alliance with Aurobindo Ghose.

However we might choose to interpret his obliquities therefore, what Aurobindo's adjustments of the record reveal is not merely that there *was* a relationship with Nivedita to cavil about, important as this fact is. What we also see is that a key feature of the relationship was its participants' awareness of the supposed cultural other (the 'materialist' Westerner, the 'degenerate' Easterner) as a (political and spiritual) co-worker and *interlocutor*, and not as an antagonist, as both colonial and traditionalist attitudes at the time dictated. Importantly for a study of cross-nationalist interdiscursivity (and unlike in the case of her relationship with her guru Vivekananda), Nivedita and Aurobindo Ghose's interrelation operated horizontally: each viewed the other as their equal—literally as their 'ally'— in terms of status, influence, and level of commitment.[12] Despite

---

[11] 'Indian Art', *CW* iii. 4. See also, amongst many other possible references, Sister Nivedita, *The Web of Indian Life* (London: William Heinemann, 1904), 60, 72, 96, 176. The importance to Nivedita of the concept of cooperation and unity within diversity is captured in her repeated use of the themselves linked images of networks, webs, nexuses, and palimpsests. See, for example, *CW* iv. 13–14, 261; *CW* v. 32, 53. Page references to *The Web of Indian Life* will henceforth be incorporated in the text along with the abbreviation *Web*.

[12] Parama Roy, *Indian Traffic* (Berkeley and Los Angeles: University of California Press, 1988), 92–127, examines the economies of identity formation that operated in the mentor

their differences, they met on a basis of politico-spiritual oneness which, remarkably, bridged the conventional race and gender (though, arguably, not the class) divides of the period. Quite how remarkable this was becomes clear in relation to the insularity of many movements of protest in this period. In Britain for example the women's movement or the male-led labour movement tended to remain concentrated in their traditionally separate spheres.[13] In swadeshi-focused Bengal, moreover, conditions were characterized by an increasingly more marked opposition between the British authorities and the *bhadralok* (or emergent middle class).

Within the cross-cultural context of elite Calcutta of course their interrelation was not isolated as a point of contact. Nivedita also built important friendships and cooperations with the moderate nationalist G. K. Gokhale, as well as with the economist R. C. Dutt and the scientist J. C. Bose. Aurobindo Ghose had some (predominantly intertextual) contact with India's other prominent pro-nationalist white woman of this era, the Theosophist leader and later Home Ruler Annie Besant (1847–1933).[14] Like Nivedita, Besant was influentially involved in interpreting Indian culture *back* to colonized India (and like her had some claim to Irish 'roots').[15] The President of the Indian National Congress in 1917, Besant moreover modelled the 1910s Home Rule movement on Irish politics, and her interpretation of an all-embracing and idealized Hinduism showed certain commonalities with Vivekananda's Vedanta. As these various connections suggest, Aurobindo, Nivedita, Besant, R. C. Dutt—and also Tagore, Gandhi, the revolutionary Shyamaji Krishnavarma, etc.—

relationship between Narendranath Dutt (Swami Vivekananda) and Nivedita. Roy tends to place more emphasis on *his* negotiations of national and gender subjectivity in relation to an 'acquiescent' Nivedita, than on *her* investments in the relationship and on her later nationalism, which will be treated here.

[13] See Mary Davis, *Sylvia Pankhurst: A Life in Radical Politics* (London: Pluto, 1999), 5–19.

[14] It is worth mentioning that Aurobindo derived his second name, Ackroyd, from the surname of another high-profile white woman in the cultural history of Bengal, the educationalist Annette Ackroyd, a friend of his father's. However he dropped the name 'before he left England'. See Aurobindo, *On Himself*, 2.

[15] Anne Taylor, *Annie Besant: A Biography* (Oxford: Oxford UP, 1992); Gauri Viswanathan, *Outside the Fold: Conversion, Modernity and Belief* (Princeton: Princeton UP, 1998), ch. 6, 'Conversion, Theosophy, and Race Theory'; Peter Washington, *Madame Blavatsky's Baboon: Theosophy and the Emergence of the Western Guru* (London: Secker and Warburg, 1993). Eric J. Sharpe, *The Universal Gita* (London: Duckworth, 1985), 78–80, claims that Besant's interpretative 1895 translation of the *Bhagavad-gita* profoundly shaped Aurobindo's understanding of Hindu *dharma*.

formed part of that vast, often loosely linked, international *and* cross-nationalist network built now on Theosophist or Fabian involvements, now on shared socialist or nationalist ideologies, which shapes the colonial and yet anti-imperial context to much of this study.

In relation specifically to Besant, however, the figure whose position and role most closely approached Nivedita's, it is the latter's radicalism and, related to this, her self-indigenization which in particular distinguishes her contribution. Vis-à-vis a militant such as Aurobindo, Nivedita's publicly performed self-surrender to Hinduism, and unquestioning belief in the emergence of Indian nationality, would have created a more embedded trust, and a greater potential for collaboration. Though she began her work for and in India some five or six years after Besant, her sense of nationhood was self-consciously India-made, whereas Besant's identification operated through the syncretic fraternity of Theosophy. Nivedita was, Aurobindo recognized after her death, 'practically an Indian in belief, culture and aspirations'.[16] Tagore captures a related perception in his characterization of the arch-traditionalist, Kali-dedicated, and Irish-origin Gora in his 1907 eponymous novel, conceived at a time when he had already become acquainted with Nivedita. In what was clearly intended as a respectful if critical tribute to her, Tagore dramatizes in *Gora* how an outsider may paradoxically become more orthodox than someone born Hindu, in the belief that a strict adherence to doctrine will provide an effective resistance to colonial denigration.[17]

By contrast to this Annie Besant, despite her early radicalism, propagated the idea of self-government *within* the framework of empire, and saw loyalty to the crown as a unifying ideal for India; she at no time openly called for *purna swaraj*, total freedom. Indeed, in so far as she did not join the Indian National Congress till 1913, two years after Nivedita's death, and did so because she had become disillusioned with educational work as a primary force for change, as

[16] Kumari Jayawardena, *The White Woman's Other Burden* (London: Routledge, 1995), 285. To Nivedita Theosophy represented a largely superficial Western occultism, of which her Swami had moreover been critical.

[17] See Tagore, *Gora*; Krishna Dutta and Andrew Robinson, *Rabindranath Tagore: The Myriad-Minded Man* (London: Bloomsbury, 1995), 154; Hogan, *Colonialism and Cultural Identity*, 213–55; Lalita Pandit, 'Caste, Race and Nation', in Patrick Colm Hogan and Lalita Pandit (eds.), *Literary India: Contemporary Studies in Aesthetics, Colonialism, and Culture* (Albany: State University of New York Press, 1995).

had Nivedita some years earlier, one might venture to say that in the 1910s the older Annie Besant was, to some extent, following in the footsteps of Nivedita. India's national customs 'require no apology', Nivedita announced in the important lectures she gave in Madras after her self-imposed exile from India in 1901–2, fully aware of the impact of her words. The nation's unity and spiritual strength were 'self-born', and its future, concomitantly, should be 'self-determined, self-wrought': 'the one central fact is the realization of its own nationality by the [Indian] Nation'.[18] A sign of this studied internality to the culture was Nivedita's care, for example, to address other Indians in her lectures in the collective first person, as 'we'.[19] In *The Web of Indian Life* (1904) or *Studies from an Eastern Home* (1905/1913) she tellingly concentrated on interpreting Indian society from the inside, on its own terms, with respect for its internal coherence: 'That which is Indian for India, I touch the feet of.'[20] (In these ways she adhered to her Swami's injunction never publicly to criticize an already oppressed culture.[21]) In *Gora* Tagore captures the degree of this self-dedication in the central character's rousing words:

We must refuse to allow our country to stand at the bar of a foreign court and be judged according to a foreign law. . . . We must not feel apologetic about the country of our birth—whether it be about its traditions, faith, or its scriptures—neither to others nor even to ourselves.[22]

Nivedita was, not to overstress the point, self-identified with India, which then, as will be seen, led to an identification with the radical

---

[18] This summary combines her two important Madras lectures of 1902, in February ('India Has No Apology to Make'), and November. See *CW* ii. 450–9; Atmaprana, *Sister Nivedita*, 131, 153, 201.

[19] As emphasized by her colleague S. K. Ratcliffe, the editor of the Indian *Statesman*, in his Appendix to her posthumously published *Religion and Dharma* (1915). See *CW* iii. 485.

[20] *Studies from an Eastern Home* (1913), *CW* ii. 145–360, is based on articles first published in the Indian *Statesman* from 1905. See also Nivedita's 19 July 1901 letter to Josephine MacLeod, quoted in Atmaprana, *Sister Nivedita*, 128–30.

[21] Sister Nivedita, *The Master as I Saw Him* (London: Longmans, Green, and Co., 1910), 286. For Aurobindo's agreement with this point, see Sri Aurobindo, *Speeches* (Calcutta: Arya Publishing House, 1948), 37. Page references will henceforth be incorporated in the text along with the abbreviations *Master* and *Speeches*, respectively. Nivedita's non-criticism of India notoriously raised controversy in mission societies in both Britain and the United States concerned about child marriage and the status of widows in India. See her article 'Lambs amongst Wolves', first published in the *Westminster Review* (July 1901), *CW* iv. 509–32, which urges her readers to see the world's peoples as 'clothed with universal humanity'.

[22] Tagore, *Gora*, 23.

movement for national self-determination of which Aurobindo was the underground yet widely acknowledged leader. She and Aurobindo were therefore, one might say, extremist *secret sharers* at a key moment in Bengal's nationalist history. Fiery patriots, prominent and influential workers for *swaraj*, they operated together 'behind the curtain', as he put it, if not always in close proximity, then in regular close contact with one another.[23] It was a closeness they probably achieved with no other like-minded nationalist at this time; their secrecy is a mark of its (asexual) intensity. Despite both being believers in karma, in how individuals were moved by historical currents— 'the Mother works, not we'—both set store by the strategic effectiveness and malleability of their underground roles. Depending on the demands of the Swadeshi movement, they might by way of these roles stand in for one another, they might change positions overnight, and they might escape incognito and under cover of darkness—as indeed in their different ways they did.

As concerns escaping incognito, some comment is appropriate at this point regarding the largely deferential if not unreliable scholarship which exists on both Sister Nivedita/Margaret Noble and Aurobindo Ghose. Inevitably, the reverential inexactness of the critical and the life writing on either subject cannot but hamper any exegesis of their work.[24] Still-current misinterpretations of Nivedita's 'Irishness', for example, represent a symptom as well as a further cause of such difficulties. Understandably, of course, both figures command significant political and spiritual stature in Bengal's national history, a reputation which has had the effect of turning biographical studies into hagiographies. The controversial question of the extent of Nivedita's revolutionary involvement, especially with cadre-based boycott agitation from 1905, for instance, is usually euphemistically

---

[23] Quoted in K. R. Srinivasa Iyengar, *Sri Aurobindo* (Calcutta: Arya Publishing House, 1945), 143. As is observed in Haridas and Uma Mukherjee (eds.), *Sri Aurobindo and the New Thought in Indian Politics* (Calcutta: Firma K. L. Mukhopadyay, 1958), pp. xiii–xliii, according to 1908 government of India reports, Aurobindo, though always careful to avoid the appearance of direct involvement, was seen in official circles as undeniably the nationalist leader of Bengal. Nivedita was almost as influential, and almost equally covert, but her Europeanness gave her a certain immunity from investigation as well as from prosecution. See also Aurobindo, *On Himself*, 15.

[24] See A. M. G. van Dijk, 'Europese Invloeden op het Denken van Sri Aurobindo', unpublished Ph.D. thesis (Utrecht: Rijksuniversiteit te Utrecht, 1977), 292; and Leonard A. Gordon, *Bengal: The Nationalist Movement 1876–1940* (New York: Columbia UP, 1974), 101, for related criticisms of 'disciple-biographers'. A biography of Aurobindo by Peter Hees is eagerly awaited.

and/or apologetically treated. Where interpretations range from protestations of relative innocence, to the imputation that she smuggled known revolutionaries into laboratories run by her physicist friend J. C. Bose (to collect materials for making bombs), the question of her implication offers a test case for the difficulty of establishing the facts of her life in Bengal (even had these not, to a significant extent, been shrouded in secrecy). Nivedita's 1961 biographer Pravrajika Atmaprana claims that her pedagogic and proselytizing work never slipped into outright terrorism. Yet, as will be demonstrated, Nivedita's activities from 1902 *were* in fact 'inextricably mingled', as Lizelle Reymond has said, with those of the Bengali extremists.[25] Another, later (still partisan) biographer Barbara Foxe's judgement is therefore probably the most judicious in this regard, namely, that Nivedita's own statements suggest that 'she saw little hope in the end for any other method [than that of insurrection]'.[26] This would in all probability have led her to collaborate where possible with like-minded activists.

In order to deal with such differences of interpretation and related half-deliberate ambiguities on the part of biographers, the strategy adopted in what follows is to read the different lives against one another's grain, and into each other's silences: to make inferences and deductions by comparing different accounts. So we can say with a fair degree of certainty that, whilst closely watched by the Calcutta police from about 1902/3, and definitely from 1906, as there is evidence to show, Nivedita herself planted no bombs, and perhaps did not overtly incite anyone to do so. Yet at the same time, as the following section will outline further, she was secretly involved with nearly all of the extremist or nationalist groups, or *samiti*, which developed in Calcutta at this time, to the extent that she *directly* liaised with, inspired, and instructed several of the secret societies with which Calcutta was 'honeycombed' from about 1902. This was especially so during the period of government repression following the Swadeshi campaign of 1905–8.[27]

[25] Atmaprana, *Sister Nivedita*, 183–4. Lizelle Reymond, *The Dedicated: A Biography of Nivedita* (New York: The John Day Company, 1953), 279, 282, 336–7, has Nivedita implicated at the highest level.

[26] Barbara Foxe, *Long Journey Home: A Biography of Margaret Noble (Nivedita)* (London: Rider and Co., 1975), 208–9.

[27] Swami Lokeswarananda, 'Sister Nivedita and Indian Renaissance', in A. K. Mazumdar (ed.), *Nivedita Commemoration Volume* (Calcutta: Vivekananda Janmotsava Samiti,

A WARLIKE SPIRITUALITY

The question of Nivedita's militancy is central to an understanding of her political make-up and decidedly advanced nationalism. Certainly, as regards biographical ambiguity, once we develop a more precise image of the ways in which her militancy operated and was accounted for, the outright denial of that militancy becomes the more difficult to make.

It was unambiguously as an advanced nationalist that Nivedita in 1902 first presented herself to Aurobindo Ghose: on the ground of revolutionary extremism, as we will observe again, she sought and indeed found in him a like-minded helpmeet. To her as to him the other's militancy served as a proof of their dedication and a measure of the trust that they might place in one another. It is clear that for both, too, as cultural outsiders to Bengal (Nivedita as a European woman, Aurobindo as an England-returned intellectual), militancy, though no doubt based on conviction, became a mode of de-Anglicization and self-authentication. But not only this. It is also apparent that Nivedita—who was during her London years a Ruskin-inspired utopian, a sympathizer with the Russian anarchist Prince Peter Kropotkin (1842–1921), and an admirer of Mazzini's Young Italy movement—brought a certain inclination towards extremism with her to Bengal.[28] So, importantly, Calcutta did not make a militant of her, but it did, after the break represented by her four years' intense spiritual involvement with her Swami, contribute to making her more militant than she had been before.

From what we can tell, her *practical* participation in the nationalist movement essentially operated at three distinct levels: first, around 1902 and 1905–6 she was instructed by and herself advised moderate Congress nationalists like G. K. Gokhale; second, she had fairly public and open relations with Bengal's extremist protest movement; and, third, she collaborated with the secret revolutionary movement, as is evident from her membership of the (short-lived) Revolutionary Council of Bengal. As regards these second and third levels of activity, it is indicative that at one or other time between 1902 and 1907, the majority of Bengal's prominent activists and

1968), 5. See also Partha Mitter, *Art and Nationalism in Colonial India 1850–1922* (Cambridge: Cambridge UP, 1994), 246.

[28] Gita Srivastava, *Mazzini and his Impact on the Indian National Movement* (New Delhi: Chugh Publications, 1982), 204–5, 220–1, 237, 244–6. For further detail as to Nivedita's various London involvements, summarized in this section, see Chapter 3.

revolutionaries attended Nivedita's well-known Sunday breakfasts, what were in effect extremist 'at-homes'. At least one of these extremists, Barindra Ghose, Aurobindo's younger brother, addressed her as the Mother and Joan of Arc of the Bengal resistance, and she, appropriately Mother-like, called him her 'Bairn'. (It was a name she may also have used of another close nationalist friend, Bhupendranath Dutt, Vivekananda's brother, for whom, following his prosecution for sedition, she stood bail in 1907.)

As further evidence of her involvement, the different sources agree that she recommended to her revolutionary students and contacts more or less the same political readings as her Indian counterparts were themselves translating and drawing inspiration from. These significantly cross-border readings included the histories of other movements of liberation and protest, such as the Land League in Ireland and the Italian *risorgimento*, as well as the anarchist theory of her London contact, Prince Kropotkin, which argued for small group organization and against state rule.[29] Arriving in India armed with relatively advanced political principles, therefore, and fired with 'a burning passion for service', as she told an early audience,[30] it was not too long before she encountered political ideas which chimed in with her own, and which, in the course of subsequent discussion, she to some extent fostered, and was to some extent further encouraged by. She also, throughout the 1900s, contributed her thoughts to the same English language newspapers and journals as did her Bengali extremist counterparts: *Amrita Bazar Patrika, Dawn, New India,* the *Modern Review, Prabuddha Bharat.* She herself therefore entered

[29] Kropotkin's *Mutual Aid: A Factor of Evolution* (1902) laid emphasis on cooperation over competition as a determining factor in the evolution of human society. See Nivedita's 'Chat with a Russian about Russia', *Modern Review* (1901), and 'Review on *Mutual Aid*' (1907), *CW* v. 299–301. Vinayak Savarkar's Marathi translation of Mazzini's autobiography, Lajpat Rai's Urdu life of Mazzini, and Surendranath Banerjee's biography of the same in English, were highly sought after amongst their different language and class audiences. See Srivastava, *Mazzini and his Impact,* 188–9, 238. As the *Times* journalist Valentine Chirol, *Indian Unrest* (London: Macmillan, 1910), 145–6, put it: 'in the literature of unrest one frequently comes across the strangest juxtaposition of names, Hindu deities, and Cromwell and Washington, and celebrated anarchists all being invoked in the same breath.' To Debajyoti Burman, 'Sister Nivedita and Indian Revolution', in Mazumdar (ed.), *Nivedita Commemoration Volume,* 195, Nivedita's 'mental make-up was a synthesis of the Irish Sinn Féin and Russian revolutionary thought'. But, as well as being anachronistic, this probably ascribes too great a settledness to Nivedita's political theory at this time.

[30] Sister Nivedita, 'Influence of the Spiritual Thought of India in England', in 'Lectures and Articles', *CW* ii. 396–400.

fully into the 'honeycomb' of Bengali intellectual life at this time, where such congruences and exchanges of ideas were not only commonplace but themselves made possible further cross-nationalist transaction (as is seen once again in the very different case of Tagore's 1910s interrelation with the West).

By way of a provisional summary, it would seem that Margaret Noble/Nivedita participated from about 1892 in an ongoing radical and radicalizing discussion, located first in London, and then in Calcutta, though suspended or transmuted for a time by her initiation into Swami Vivekananda's Order. For this reason, not surprisingly, she was the obvious choice to take over the editorship of Aurobindo's *Karmayogin*, at his request, once he departed for Pondicherry in 1910. As Aurobindo wrote, 'she had the whole conduct of [the journal]',[31] indeed smoothly slotting into his series of articles, 'The Ideal of the Karmayogin', and contributing on 12 March of that year the final two. What is particularly evident from her last, short article in the series, which is in effect her credo, is how she used her undercover or 'curtained' position cunningly to encrypt her militancy, adapting the words of her Swami's teaching on Indian unity, but flavouring these with the fervour of militant self-surrender, 'I believe that India is one, indissoluble, indivisible. . . . O Nationality, come thou to me as joy or sorrow, as honour or as shame! Make me thine own!' (*CW* iv. 205; *Karmayogin*, 81.)

As the credo reveals, any adjudgement of the extent of her nationalist contribution ultimately comes up against that central situation which it is important to keep in view throughout: that is, the imbrication of spiritual with radical political exercises in extremist Calcutta.[32] So there is no coincidence in the fact that it was Vivekananda's own brother Bhupendranath Dutt who until his exile in 1909 was one of Calcutta's leading revolutionaries, and, next to the less conspicuous Aurobindo, or Barindra Ghose, Nivedita's chief collaborator. As the later scrutiny of their ideological development will track more closely, for both Sister Nivedita and Aurobindo Ghose religion came to be equated with politics: spiritual ideals of, for instance, 'motiveless' action as prescribed in the *Gita* were tightly bound up with militant ideology and strategy. *Dharma*, the right way, the true path, was specifically believed to signify national right-

---

[31] Purani, *The Life of Sri Aurobindo*, 136–7.

[32] See Sumit Sarkar, *The Swadeshi Movement in Bengal 1903–1908* (New Delhi: People's Publishing House, 1973), 488; Sharpe, *The Universal Gita*, 83.

eousness, self-sacrifice to India the Mother, acting in accordance with Her nature. For both extremists, too, Giuseppe Mazzini's ideal of a nationalism *both* centred on the realization of the human spirit *and* interlocked with international brotherhood, gave backing to the mix of India-centred spirituality and cross-national influence which represented such a strong thread in Indian nationalist culture at this time. Aurobindo would on occasion underline Mazzini's approach in his own writing, as when he said: 'our ideal of patriotism proceeds on the basis of love and brotherhood and it looks beyond the unity of the nation and envisages the ultimate unity of mankind' (*Speeches*, 67).

In this context non-involvement with the Bengali militant tendency would have made little sense to a self-made and enthusiastic devotee of Kali such as Nivedita, whose nationalist rhetoric, moreover, whether in speeches or in private letters, was charged with an energy at once aggressive and high-minded. Indeed it is probably in her verbal fieriness that a key piece of the puzzle concerning the degree of her militant involvement lies. Because even if she did not *herself* intend whether by word or by example to incite her acolytes and hangers-on to nationalist retaliation, the sheer force of her revolutionary rhetoric of self-sacrifice would have made an impact not only on those already committed to the movement, but on the still uncertain. It was consistent with her Kali-worship that, although as a mother-figure she herself did not do battle, she wielded those instruments she was best suited to, her pen and her voice, with a ferocious and inspiring dedication. Already in 1901, in a private letter to her friend Josephine MacLeod, to whom she was generally less guarded than with others, Nivedita had written fervently, and explicitly, of her plans for India:

We want the slow-growing formative forces put well to work. Do not think I can be forgetful of the planting of trees, the training of children, the farming of land. But we want also the ringing cry, the passion of the multitude, the *longing* for death. And we cannot do without these [emphasis in text].[33]

Filled with the spirit of the *Gita*'s warrior ethic—Nivedita concluded the letter—India must 'strike the blow on the instant of heat'.

Some four years later, at the height of the Bengal Resistance, she remained equally convinced, and equally combative, as she said in *Aggressive Hinduism*:

[33] Quoted in Atmaprana, *Sister Nivedita*, 128–30.

Aggression is to be the dominant characteristic of the India that is today . . . aggression and the thoughts and ideals of aggression. Instead of passivity, activity; for the standard of weakness, the standard of strength; in place of the steadily yielding defence, the ringing cheer of the invading host. (*AH* 492–3)

Could India's radical youth, exposed to such language, have remained unmoved, merely satisfied with the day-to-day drudgery of a passive resistance such as Tagore came to support? Nivedita's unequivocal call to 'India's sons' to 'seize the battlements' (*AH* 504) left in no doubt where she placed herself in the debate concerning the limits of a defensive and submissive politics, and where she wanted to take her collaborators and followers.

THE CROSS-MESHED CALCUTTA CONTEXT

It is important now to begin to fill in the socio-economic and (especially) interdiscursive contours of the Bengal which Margaret Noble first encountered on 28 January 1898 and which so profoundly reshaped her life. What was the cultural and political topography of the Calcutta to which Aurobindo Ghose, too, bore his revolutionary mission in 1902, of the city where he would experience both the illuminations and the frustrations that led eventually to his permanent exile from British India? Following the relatively unexpected declaration of Curzon's Partition on 19 July 1905 a vociferous *bhadralok* discontent exploded across the capital of the Raj. To quote Tagore, a powerful chemistry ignited 'the ashes of lifeless Bengal' into 'suddenly [speaking] up: "Here am I".'[34] What were the constituents of this chemistry? What had fomented beneath the surface of the province's inertia, as described by Aurobindo amongst others, to produce the apparently self-generated protest of 1905–8?[35]

Probably the two most important factors contributing to the patriotic electrification of Bengal were, first, the cultural and literary renaissance which flourished amongst the English-educated professional

[34] Rabindranath Tagore, *The Home and the World* (*Ghare Baire*), trans. Surendranath Tagore, rev. R. Tagore (1916/1919; Madras: Macmillan India, 1992), 115.

[35] The term Bengal as used throughout this chapter refers to that administrative and cultural unit under the Raj which was unified by a language, Bengali, in the process of being standardized by the Bengali elite, as Mrinalini Sinha outlines in *Colonial Masculinity* (Manchester: Manchester UP, 1995), 3, 24. There was a fittingness as well as a logic to this first province of British India, where the keystone of its economic and political domination lay, becoming the seat of extremist resistance to Britain.

intelligentsia from the 1880s, featuring the work of, amongst others, Bankimchandra Chattopadhyay, Michael Madhusudan Dutt, and Romesh Chandra Dutt. Second, there was the psychological and economic effect on this elite of the colonial 'bleeding' of the province's resources. To deal with salient aspects of the Calcutta Renaissance first, the Bengali *bhadralok* or middle-class elite, its self-awareness sharpened by the standardization of the Bengali language and by its early experience of a colonial education, had developed an influence and authority that extended well beyond the confines of the province.[36] As in the related case of Bombay, therefore, any significant shift in its frameworks of value and belief, any ripple of discontent, had the tendency rapidly to radiate outwards to other regions within the Indian Empire. (This dominant intellectual position did much moreover to encourage the potentially lethal conflation, by the *bhadralok* themselves, of Bengali with Hindu nationalism, which Aurobindo's as well as Nivedita's work demonstrates.[37])

As a number of writers on India including Nivedita have observed, the expansion of the imperial communications system combined with the diffusion of a colonial education in English, helped activate and facilitate the spread of the national concept in India in a fundamental way.[38] Across the length and breadth of the subcontinent, in fact, English-speaking professionals from different language backgrounds, their interactions speeded up by the expanding railway and telegraph network, were able now to participate in political and cultural debates, and to confer on issues of perceived national importance. English in India, as Aijaz Ahmad writes, became '*the* language of national integration and bourgeois civility'. A Western education

---

[36] See, for example, Mukherjee and Mukherjee (eds.), *Sri Aurobindo and the New Thought*, pp. xvi–xvii; Sumit Sarkar, *Modern India, 1885–1947* (1983; New Delhi: Macmillan, 1989), 108; Anil Seal, *The Emergence of Indian Nationalism* (Cambridge: Cambridge UP, 1968). Sarkar's *Modern India* repeats but also brings up to date his earlier book *The Swadeshi Movement*'s material on the Bengal Resistance. On the study of literature in colonial India, see Rajeswari Sunder Rajan (ed.), *The Lie of the Land* (New Delhi: Oxford UP, 1992); Gauri Viswanathan, *Masks of Conquest* (New York: Columbia UP, 1989).

[37] Their consolidation of an image of a pure 'Hindu' India with a pedigree extending back into a heroic past, obviously had the deleterious effect of labelling other Indians, Muslims in particular, as foreigners, as India was to discover to its cost across the twentieth century.

[38] See *Web*, 102–3, 294. Modernity in the form of modern science and an increasingly more 'globalized' technology, Nivedita observed, produced the perception of cultural relativity, which allowed one to measure and appreciate one's own national strengths against others (*AH* 498–9).

in English brought an understanding of world political developments, 'without which', the historian Sumit Sarkar also reminds us, 'it would have been difficult to formulate conscious theories of nationalism'.[39]

The spread of the English language and of an English literary education, in other words, created the conditions of possibility for a cross-border transaction, such as with Ireland, such as with Nivedita, to emerge. Vivekananda himself implicitly acknowledged this informing fact of cultural interdiscursivity in the dual stress he placed on India-wide 'man-making' on the one hand, and, as we will see, the usefulness of the new communications networks for conceptual exchange between people, and peoples, on the other. An intellectual synthesis, he and Nivedita believed, was required in order to conceptualize and keep pace with the new technological unification of the world.[40]

Paradoxically encouraged therefore by the spread of Western learning, elite Bengali nationalism in the later decades of the nineteenth century found probably its most powerful stimulus in the efflorescence of nationalist literature in the vernacular, most notably the historical retrieval work of Bankim and the young Rabindranath Tagore's rural lyricism. This cultural national movement moreover coincided, not accidentally, with the various forms of neo-Hinduist revival which also emerged across these decades—revival generated around the figures of the mystic Sri Ramakrishna Paramhansa (1836–86); the Swami Dayananda of the fundamentalist movement the Arya Samaj, based in the Punjab; and Ramakrishna's successor, Nivedita's guru the Swami Vivekananda, who established the Ramakrishna Mission at Belur near Calcutta in 1897.[41] Vivekananda's approach, with its emphasis on the glories of the past as against the degeneration of present-day India, but also on the need for a 'man-making' and modernizing social reform reinforced by self-help, proved highly influential. In a context where Indian crafts and industry, as well as religious beliefs, were being steadily eroded by European infiltration, each one of these nodes of neo-Hinduist revival drew compelling attention to the importance of the traditional and

---

[39] Aijaz Ahmad, *In Theory* (London: Verso, 1992), 73–94, especially p. 75; Sarkar, *Modern India*, 66.

[40] See, for example, *Master*, 314; Santwana Dasgupta, in Mazumdar (ed.), *Nivedita Commemoration Volume*, 106.

[41] Rajat Kanta Ray, *Social Conflict and Political Unrest in Bengal 1875–1927* (New Delhi: Oxford UP, 1984), 141–2; Sarkar, *Modern India*, 71–3, 106–11.

the local (the swadeshi) as against the foreign. 'Indians,' Aurobindo urged, 'it is the spirituality of India . . . that will make us free and great' (*Karmayogin*, 20–1). Or, to quote Nivedita: India should evict its colonial 'robbers' and 'go back to where she was before. . . . Anything else will do little good and much harm.'[42]

As was typical for emergent anti-colonial movements founded on nationalist principles elsewhere in the world, including in Ireland, the cultural movement in Bengal was thus distinguished by its turn to a romanticized, pastoral past and a yet unblemished spiritual essence in order to mould a coherent identity in the present: an identity, that is, independent from industrialized Europe in its traditionalism and inner 'truth', yet also modernizing.[43] In Ireland, too, the retrieval of old Irish laws, as well as research into the Irish language, had contributed to generating the cultural nationalism of the 1880s and 1890s. As a further characteristic of the paradoxical or double-faced aspect of nationalism, it was also typical that these efforts of reawakening in Bengal were significantly enabled by European scholarship, such as that of the Oxford professor of comparative philology F. Max Müller (1823–1900), as well as by suprematist ideas concerning the superiority of ancient Aryan culture which were based in part on the Sanskritic excavations of the Orientalists.[44] A Western presence was thus central to Bengal's self-making renaissance, as to its cultures of dissent. As the writer Nirad Chaudhuri, himself a child of *bhadralok* culture, once acerbically observed, in spite of its asseverations to the contrary, the Anglicized elite of Renaissance 'Upper India' converted Hinduism into a self-authenticating 'nationalistic myth' largely interpreted through the lens of English books.[45] So we

[42] Atmaprana, *Sister Nivedita*, 128–9. On India's perceived 'degeneration' and the compensatory preoccupation with Hindu glory, see Tapan Raychaudhuri, *Europe Reconsidered* (New Delhi: Oxford UP, 1988).

[43] Partha Chatterjee, *Nationalist Thought and the Colonial World: A Derivative Discourse?* (London: Zed, 1986); Tom Nairn, *The Break-up of Britain: Crisis and Neo-nationalism* (London: New Left Books, 1977).

[44] Nirad C. Chaudhuri, *Scholar Extraordinary* (London: Chatto and Windus, 1974); R. W. Neufeldt, *Friedrich Max Müller and the Rg Veda* (New Delhi: Oxford UP, 1980); Johannes H. Voigt, *F. Max Müller* (Calcutta: Firma K. L. Mukhopadhyay, 1967). See also Javed Majeed, *Ungoverned Imaginings* (Oxford: Clarendon Press, 1992); Vishnawath Prasad Varma, *The Political Philosophy of Sri Aurobindo* (London: Asia Publishing House, 1960), 173, 213. Van Dijk, 'Europese Invloeden', 310, suggests that Aurobindo's thinking about the high culture of classical India was distinctly influenced by Max Müller's *India, What can it teach us?*

[45] Nirad Chaudhuri, *Thy Hand, Great Anarch! India 1921–1952* (1987; London: Hogarth, 1990), 33, 210, 675.

see once again how the ground for cross-national exchange may be laid within the make-up of early anti-colonial nationalism itself. The receptiveness to European influence, including theories of nation-statehood and Enlightenment individualism, created an atmosphere within the Bengali elite that made not only *possible* but *permissible* the two-way transaction of ideas between intellectuals such as Aurobindo and Nivedita. It was within this at once revivalist *and* Europe-informed context that they felt able to discuss and formulate strategy.

Following on from this, it is moreover worth remarking that without Bengal's acceptance of Western knowledge, whether reluctant or otherwise, Margaret Noble in her first years in India would probably have felt far more alien (and therefore less empowered) than she did. It is again paradoxical, one might also note, that her political shift after 1902 brought her significantly *more* in line with Calcutta's intellectual syncretism. Her move from the numinous unknowability of her guru's neo-Hinduism, and (back) towards the political radicalism of Prince Kropotkin, Mazzini, and others, effectively assimilated what she understood of Vedantic Oneness to a more widely shared and internationally familiar concept of nationalist unity and strength. She used to her advantage, therefore, and in this way underwrote, the several cross-national sources of political influence experienced by nationalist Bengal.

But Bengal's cross-cultural self-construction is most signally embodied perhaps in the fact that the neo-Hinduism, or unified and purified Advaita Vedanta,[46] of Nivedita's guru, the Swami Vivekananda—also an important spiritual authority for Aurobindo —was initially developed and consolidated in the United States and Britain (see *Karmayogin*, 12–13). Vivekananda's vivid and to some extent simplified presentation of his ideas to wide acclaim at the 1893 World Parliament of Religions in Chicago dramatically demonstrated this acquired 'otherness' of his belief.[47] Revealingly, therefore, on her arrival in India, Nivedita later wrote in *The Master as I Saw Him*, she was struck by the difference between the Hindu 'world religion' which the Swami had represented to the West, based on the relativity of all truths, and the explicitly parochial Vedanta he

---

[46] As captured in Vivekananda's all-embracing catch-phrase for his non-dualist belief, 'The Many and the One are the same reality'.

[47] See Elleke Boehmer, *Empire Writing: An Anthology of Colonial Literature 1870–1918* (Oxford: Oxford UP, 1998), 192–8; Sharpe, *The Universal Gita*, 68–70.

preached at home, which sought the regeneration of India in the worship of the Mother Kali (*Master*, 21, 23, 31, 47, 49). Indianization must come before universalism, he repeatedly said, as also did Aurobindo in *The Ideal of the Karmayogin* some while later (*Web*, 395). In Europe, Nivedita sums up, Vivekananda's thought attached to 'no special form', whereas in India he was constantly preoccupied with the country's revival (*Master*, 201–8, 218).

And yet, if the Swami was both 'world-moving' and 'nation-making' (*Master*, 292), these interests, though apparently mutually exclusive, were reconciled in the area of India's spiritual expansion, that is, through the infiltration of other religious cultures by its re-generated harmonizing spirit. In this way, Vivekananda believed, as did his devotees Nivedita and Aurobindo, Mother India would eventually become both the heartland and the means of the world's spiritual union. In a nutshell, to the extent that cosmopolitanism had become a vehicle for neo-Hinduist nationalism, so too nationalism might one day become a channel towards a Hinduized internationalism.

Along with its neo-Hinduist Renaissance, the *second* crucial element shaping nationalist sentiment in Bengal was what Aurobindo referred to as the 'one great fact . . . the terrible poverty of India and its rapid increase under British rule', that is to say, the 'drain' represented by British economic imperialism.[48] The most prominent author of the drain theory of imperialism in India was the Bombay businessman and later British MP (for Central Finsbury), Dadabhai Naoroji (1825–1917). Others, too, however, contributed to its development and dissemination, amongst them the Bengali scholar and writer R. C. Dutt (1848–1909), the friend of Nivedita and author of the influential *The Economic History of British India* (1902); the British socialist (and contact of Nivedita) H. M. Hyndman (1842–1921); and W. S. Blunt (1840–1922), the pro-Egypt radical whose *My Ideas about India* (1885) is unmistakably informed by Naoroji's thought.

Exhaustively backed up by statistics, the drain theory was propounded from the early 1870s by Naoroji and his cohorts in countless pamphlets, committee reports, journalism, and parliamentary

---

[48] Sri Aurobindo, 'The Man of the Past and the Man of the Future', in Mukherjee and Mukherjee (eds.), *Sri Aurobindo and the New Thought*, 3. Sarkar, *Modern India*, 24–42, 86–8, gives a lucid overview of the 'drain' of wealth within the different interlocking sectors of the economy.

speeches.[49] To Indian moderates, British radicals and liberals, and Indian extremists alike, the case and its supporting evidence were overwhelmingly persuasive as a defence of the economic and political rights of the Indian people. The theory held, in sum, that the cost to India of British colonization was, contrary to imperial rhetoric, to the vast benefit of Britain, and the extreme disadvantage of India (to the tune of about £30 million annually). India had since the late eighteenth century been steadily 'bled' of its industrial, agricultural, and fiscal wealth, along several channels: enormous military expenses, import–export imbalances including duties on British goods, debt farming, and 'Home Charges' in the form of interest on development loans and remittances, as well as an extremely unfavourable exchange rate (officials' salaries and pensions were paid in sterling in Britain).[50] This drain was then further exacerbated by a 'moral drain' of administrative expertise through the exclusion of Indians from government, or, to quote Naoroji himself: 'the evil of foreign rule involved the triple loss of wealth, wisdom and work'.[51]

Even taking into account its oversights—for example, concerning comprador economics—the drain theory of wealth was at once sophisticated in its detail yet devastatingly direct in its critique. It sharpened the political awareness of an entire post-1870s generation of Indian intellectuals who, themselves victims of drain and unhappy about their loss of position within the province's oversubscribed rentier economy, were understandably receptive to such theories of exploitation. Given Britain's monopoly over economic life in Calcutta, the overprofessionalized *bhadralok* sector was in fact almost completely without opportunity for industrial and commercial self-development, or indeed for amassing the resources necessary for such development. In this context drain theory offered a sufficiently broad base from which to mount a protest to the more taxing elements of colonial rule.[52] One of the planks of Aurobindo's argument

[49] Dadabhai Naoroji, *Poverty and Un-British Rule in India* (London: Swan Sonnenschein and Co., 1901). See also the earlier work, *The Poverty of India* (London: Vincent Brooks, Day and Son, 1878).

[50] See H. M. Hyndman's synopsis in *The Bankruptcy of India: An Enquiry into the Administration of India under the Crown* (London: Swan Sonnenschein, Lowrey and Co., 1886), 41. Hyndman acknowledges the importance to this work of Naoroji's analyses. See also S. B. Cook's summary in *Imperial Affinities* (New Delhi: Sage Publications, 1993), 84.

[51] Naoroji, *Poverty and Un-British Rule in India*, 56, 283.

[52] Drain theory also sharpened grievances within the Civil Service over its racially determined inequalities, a campaign spearheaded by the moderate Surendranath Banerji. See

for an organized, defensive resistance to imperialism, for instance, was his claim that Congress politics could not staunch 'the murderous drain by which we purchase the . . . exquisite privilege of being ruled by Britain': only an 'entire and radical change of the system' would bring improvement (*Doctrine*, 11–13; 36). And when Nivedita reported on the 1907 famine, or on the punishing rigours of jute production in Bengal, she attributed these difficulties to the colonial agricultural economy, skewed to meet the needs of a foreign market—in short, to drain.[53]

However, as Sarkar amongst others underlines, the shift of the Bengal intelligentsia into an increasingly more ardent patriotism was not a cultural or a socio-economic movement alone, nor was it, moreover, only Bengali in provenance. Strong feelings about racial discrimination in India at large, as well as more widely in the Indian diaspora (most notably in South Africa), formed another important catalyst for nationalism both in the province and elsewhere in the subcontinent.[54] Across the Indian Empire, intellectuals, politicians, and community leaders felt aggrieved that the rights of imperial citizenship for Indians, as laid down in the Queen's Proclamation of 1858, had not been observed, whether under the Raj or in the wider empire. Such grievances kept memories of the Mutiny or 1857 Rebellion and the Ilbert Bill controversy of 1883 painfully alive.[55]

India-wide anti-colonial sentiment and the concomitant rise of nationalist self-assertion were also encouraged by such international developments as British setbacks in the Anglo-Boer War (1899–1902), the insurrectionary movement in Russia, and the Japanese victory of 1905, as well as by resistance activity closer to home, such as B. G. Tilak's inauguration of the patriotic Shivaji and Ganpati festivals in Maharashtra, and, during the 1896–7 famine, his moderately successful 'no-rent' or boycott campaign modelled on the National Land League in Ireland.[56] There was again that important sense, which we have noted before and will again, of a movement benefiting

Ray, *Social Conflict*, 141, 150–1; Sarkar, *Modern India*, 23, 67–8, 109; Sinha, *Colonial Masculinity*, 5–7.

[53] See her 'Glimpses of Famine and Flood in East Bengal' (*Modern Review*, 1906–7), *CW* iv. 445–505; 'The Relation between Famine and Population', *CW* v. 185–6; 'Lord Curzon on Famine in India', *CW* v. 200.

[54] Sarkar, *Modern India*, 81–2, 109.

[55] Rozina Visram, *Ayahs, Lascars and Princes* (London: Pluto Press, 1986), 7.

[56] Also important was his widely influential interpretation of the *Gita* as a revolutionary manifesto. Sarkar, *Modern India*, 53–4.

from, and participating in, a groundswell of liberatory feeling that extended more broadly than the confines of its own particular geopolitical or 'national' space.

These different but often overlapping forms of grievance and discontent were then ignited by the Indian Universities Act of 1904, which aimed at inhibiting nationalist education in Bengal, and finally set blazing by 1905 Partition, a measure more or less openly designed to split nationalist politicking in the province. The extremism, as it was called, which now sprang to the foreground of Bengali political life, prominently adopted self-help and strenuous passive resistance as its policies. Swadeshi, boycott, national education, local justice—these were Aurobindo's watchwords of the time. For over two years Swadeshi nationalism defined itself in open opposition to the moderate politics of so-called prayer and petition of the Indian National Congress.[57] As Aurobindo's uncompromising message spread through elite Bengal, to be met by frequently vicious repression, extremist opinion began to feel ever more strongly that only the most forthright modes of self-development and resistance would enable India to achieve the goal of full independence.

INTERDISCURSIVITY: OF KALI AND THE *GITA*

Cross-border diffusions of patriotic sentiment; the English language and Orientalist scholarship as the channels for such diffusion: through these means, as we have begun to see, an environment emerged in Bengal in which interdiscursive cross-over and mingling might take place. Here, political debates, sometimes held in English, juxtaposed references to ancient scripture with allusions to Mazzini, or the history of Ireland was cited in newspaper reports in both English and the vernacular commenting, for instance, on Civil Service agitation. In Nivedita's work certainly Kali is companioned by Prince Kropotkin; for Aurobindo both Charles Parnell and Krishna provide models of right action.

Yet it was of course not only within Bengal that tendencies towards a cross-nationalist traffic of ideas were developing. Indeed it is useful to remind ourselves that a cultural contact zone, especially where marked by colonialist divisions, may remain relatively

---

[57] As it was described in Aurobindo's systematic critique of Congress gradualism, 'New Lamps for Old', published in the pages of *Indu Prakash* (Aug. 1893–Mar. 1894). Quoted in Varma, *The Political Philosophy of Sri Aurobindo*, 166.

unselfconscious and inert unless contact is broadly *seen* to be and *experienced* as enabling, unless it is activated in certain ways. The *bhadralok*'s transactive nationalism was significantly informed by the internationalized political context of empire, itself moulded by nationalist influences disseminating from such places as Ireland, Japan, the United States, South Africa. In relation to Nivedita and Aurobindo, these influences will be examined in the next chapter. Yet in a general sense, too, there had to be at least the general perception of creative juxtaposition and interchangeability for one nationalist movement to be interpreted as an example for another. 'The first condition of intra-imperial analogies and exchanges' was the recognition that the colonial experience in one place could be 'relevant to that of other places under British rule'.[58]

In India (as in Ireland) one of the most important media for constructing such perceptions of analogy was the English and the vernacular press, to which both Nivedita and Aurobindo contributed. As Howard Brasted has found, Indian newspapers in the late 1870s and 1880s, such as the *Bengalee* or the *Hindu*, widely saw Japan and also Ireland—the latter with its experience of grinding famine, its wasting drain—as India's cohorts in the East and the West. The Irish struggle for Home Rule, for example, was carefully followed through its different phases, and not only in India. Van Dijk suggests that Aurobindo may have picked up ideas of boycott and passive resistance from newspaper reports on Ireland which he read as a student in both London and Cambridge.[59]

As regards Aurobindo and Nivedita *together*, that is, their interdiscursive partnership and the conditions of its possibility, what is from the outset noteworthy about their contact, even from as early as 1902, is that it is made up of two or more apparently counterintuitive cultural cross-overs. It performs an *interbraiding* of lines of resistance derived from their different cultural and political traditions. The word *interbraiding* is used advisedly here, as signifying crossings upon crossings. In other words, what is particularly fascinating about the interdiscursivity between Nivedita and Aurobindo

[58] See Cook, *Imperial Affinities*, especially pp. 26, 134–5.

[59] Howard Brasted, 'Indian Nationalist Development and the Influence of Irish Home Rule, 1870–1886', *Modern Asian Studies*, 14.1 (1980), 37–63. Van Dijk, 'Europese Invloeden', 236–7, suggests that Aurobindo in England may not have been unaware of Indian newspaper reports also. The *Gaelic American*, which was secretly disseminated amongst revolutionary Bengalis from the late 1900s, further underlined and reinforced the parallels between the Indian and Irish contexts.

is that the influences they share and exchange in several cases origi-
nate with the, on a superficial level, non-conventional partner or
source.

So we find not only that Nivedita the foreigner to India was on 25
March 1898 initiated by Vivekananda as a *Hindu brahmacharini* or
probationer nun (for which he was obliged to invoke a long-forgotten
law to circumvent her outsider or *mleccha* status); and not only that
the 'England-returned' Aurobindo was groomed during the near
fourteen years of his *English* education for the elite and European-
dominated Indian Civil Service. That is, we find not only that the
young Margaret Noble, Irish-born, female, and of a dissenting background, was in imperial class terms probably located further outside
the establishment than the brahmin, almost-white-but-not-quite
Aurobindo. What we *also* find is that in 1902 Aurobindo read and admired Nivedita's first book *Kali, the Mother* (1900) for its complex
though plainly expressed understanding of the contraries of destructive energy or *shakti* which the goddess embodied. We find therefore
that Nivedita's Kali in certain important ways helped shape the neo-
Hinduist Aurobindo's understanding of the Mother, that defining
figure in Bengali revolutionary thought.

From Nivedita's standpoint, the adoption of Kali as the avatar of
her worship, which had occurred within a year of her arrival in India,
was clearly part of her attempt to authenticate herself as a Hindu, as
were her lectures to Bengali audiences on the complexities signified
by the Mother, again within a year of arriving. This self-authentication comes into critical focus at the end of this chapter. To speak here
in broader terms, the goddess Kali, signifying 'the loss of all things
and [of] the condition to which one is attached', became for her the
symbol of a total engagement with India, with both its poor and dis-
possessed, *and* with its revolutionaries.[60]

For his part Aurobindo wrote of his first encounter with Nivedita:

She had heard of me as one who believed in strength and was a worshipper
of Kali, by which she meant she had heard of me as a revolutionary. I knew
of her already because I had read and admired her book *Kali, the Mother*. It
is in those days that we formed a friendship.[61]

Her thinking as reflected in the book and related speeches clearly cor-
related with his own. In the pages of *Kali, the Mother* Kali was the

[60] Hogan, *Colonialism and Cultural Identity*, 240.
[61] Purani, *The Life of Sri Aurobindo*, 64–5.

terrifying manifestation *both* of destructive deity *and* of nationality (a concept which particularly attracted him). She was a goddess whose devotees, burning with the flame of renunciation, became embodiments of her will, her 'incarnation of the sword', as Aurobindo hoped his own followers might become (*Kali*, 493–4).

An impressionable as well as an admiring reader, therefore, Aurobindo was at this time himself still preoccupied with efforts to revise and re-Indianize his identity after the long period of his 'denationalization'. Perhaps encouraged by Nivedita, it is significant that he would from now on increasingly invoke the vengeful Divine Mother in his own political writings. His responsiveness to Nivedita's impassioned work had of course already been primed by his 1890s study of his literary and nationalist mentor, the writer Bankimchandra Chattopadhyay. Yet Nivedita's little book as it were condensed and packaged the complex Divine Mother concept for general consumption—a fact which Aurobindo evidently recognized and then built upon. Even if this happened within the context of the far wider cultural and political upsurge across Bengal, for which Kali became a prominent symbol, Nivedita, so Aurobindo's response suggests, was centrally instrumental in the deity's promotion. Or, as P. B. Ghosh goes as far as to say, 'Kali, through Nivedita, became an ideal of self-sacrifice' within Bengali nationalism. 'Nivedita who was as politically conscious [as Aurobindo or Vivekananda]', writes Kumari Jayawardena, 'chose Kali to fire Indians into action'.[62]

At their first meeting, therefore, not only did Aurobindo's identification with a deity Nivedita *herself* had elevated, signal to her his radicalism. But, equally, that elevation (and her association with Vivekananda's nationalist mission of 'man-making') confirmed for him her political commitment and trustworthiness. In this context it is telling that from 1902, the year of their meeting, both began openly to cite Kali as part of their advocacy of what was called Aggressive Hinduism. Nivedita, for instance, after her politically motivated break with the Ramakrishna Order, transposed Kali's thunderbolt emblem into her banner as a fighter for India's freedom.

With respect to Aurobindo again, there is no reason to believe that his theory of small-group revolutionary organization dedicated to the worship of Mother India, which he developed in the blueprint pamphlet *Bhawani Mandir* (*Mother Temple*, 1905), and based on his

[62] P. B. Ghosh, in Mazumdar (ed.), *Nivedita Commemoration Volume*, 97; Jayawardena, *White Woman's Other Burden*, 191.

reading of Bankim's *Anandamath* (1882), was not also inspired by Nivedita's (and Vivekananda's) example and writing.[63] The pamphlet's central focus on Mother-worship as tied in with Hindu expansionism can be read as suggesting this. Significantly, too, Aurobindo laid stress on the political rather than the religious purpose of these temples or *maths*; correspondingly, we remember, it was later the political over the religious side of his relationship with Nivedita that he emphasized. A spiritualized politics was clearly more important for him at this stage than a world-remote spirituality, a prioritization which again coincided with Nivedita's own recent change of direction from piecemeal reform as part of spiritual devotion, to outright political radicalism. Viewed in this light, that judgement towards the end of his life concerning his largely political 'relations' with Nivedita, represents when read in context perhaps the highest valuation possible.[64] At the time, too, there was clearly no question about the regard in which he held her, as was confirmed when, within a year or so of their first meeting, she was invited on to the five-member Revolutionary Council Aurobindo set up in Calcutta to coordinate advanced nationalist activities.

In short, it is possible to suggest that Aurobindo's concept of India as a Divine Being, the Mother to whom Her sons owed the gift of their strength, was, at the very least, reinforced by his reading of Nivedita: '[Kali] waits for worship that she may give strength', he wrote, along similar lines to those of his British collaborator (*Karmayogin*, 5). Nivedita's self-sacrificing extremism, focused on Kali, in all probability therefore gave definition and support to Aurobindo's own, and prepared the ground for their clandestine cooperation from 1902. Significantly, while he had had in the 1890s the experience of seeing 'a living presence in an icon of Kali', it was not until 1904, that is after his encounter with Nivedita, that he first adopted a Kali mantra for his yoga.[65] 'If it is strength we desire', he

---

[63] Modelled on the *maths* of *Anandamath*, Bankim's 1882 reinterpretation of the 1770s Sannyasin Rebellion, Aurobindo's Mother temples were to be schools run as monastic retreats for the training of patriots or *karmayogins* devoted to Kali. See Ray, *Social Conflict*, 140–1, 165; Purani, *The Life of Sri Aurobindo*, 62, 66–7. Rakhal Chandra Nath, *The New Hindu Movement 1886–1911* (Calcutta: Minerva, 1982), 17, observes that Vivekananda's ideas on manliness and Kali were probably indebted to Bankim.

[64] Purani, *The Life of Sri Aurobindo*, 64–7, 225–66; Srivastava, *Mazzini and his Impact*, 244–5.

[65] Ashis Nandy, *The Intimate Enemy* (New Delhi: Oxford UP, 1983), 91; Aurobindo, *On Himself*, 16, 19, 32. In a vision he had in Baroda Aurobindo was instructed by

wrote in *Bhawani Mandir* (1905), 'how shall we gain it if we do not adore the Mother of strength? She demands worship not for Her own sake, but in order that She may help us and give Herself to us.'[66] Or again, a few years later:

the sap that keeps [patriotism] alive is the realization of the motherhood of God in the country, the vision of the Mother, the perpetual contemplation, adoration and service of the Mother.[67]

On one level of course it is perhaps not so surprising that their meditations on this important deity bore the mark of one another's work: Nivedita and Aurobindo were among the more prominent commentators on the Mother in the English language in Bengal.

If, therefore, Sri Ramakrishna Paramhansa embodied to Aurobindo the unified spirituality that was Bengal's inner strength, and if the seer's successor Vivekananda was believed to direct that strength and, significantly, give it a masculine emphasis, then from Aurobindo's perspective Sister Nivedita could be said to have played a key role in helping to give practical definition to that potent spirituality.[68] She was, granted, a lesser authority, and yet with her correlative emphasis, for example, on the Mother's need for an aggressive Hinduism, she clearly represented to him a potentially important political helpmeet.[69]

To turn back now to Nivedita herself, she would, from the time of their first meeting, come to associate herself more closely with the warrior ethic (as opposed to that of the nun or mystic) which Aurobindo for his part had strenuously espoused for some years, based on the teachings of the *Gita*. This, then, was the direct impress on her of the encounter with Aurobindo. Indeed, Indian nationalist adaptations including Aurobindo's own of the Hindu sacred text the

Ramakrishna and Vivekananda to worship the Mother. Yet he conceded having learned of Vivekananda's patriotism mainly through Nivedita.

[66] Purani, *The Life of Sri Aurobindo*, 80.

[67] *Bande Mataram* (Sept. 1907). Quoted in Srinivasa Iyengar, *Sri Aurobindo*, 150. See also Sri Aurobindo, *The Mother* (Calcutta: Arya Publishing House, 1928). This also appears in *BCL* 27.

[68] As Aurobindo says in *The Ideal of the Karmayogin*, 12, 23, 26–30, Ramakrishna and Vivekananda, the great resisters, together represented a synthesis of divine learning and 'life'. See also Purani, *The Life of Sri Aurobindo*, 80; Roy, *Indian Traffic*, 92–127.

[69] The critic S. K. Kshirsagar, in Mazumdar (ed.), *Nivedita Commemoration Volume*, 168, goes so far as to say that, on the basis of her pro-nationalist embodiment of her Swami's ideals, Nivedita formed a *trimurti* or holy triumvirate with Ramakrishna and Vivekananda.

Bhagavad-gita, present another powerful if more generalized instance of the confluence or cross-hatching of different religious and other discourses within a liberatory politics (not only in Bengal, but in nationalist Maharashtra also). Here, too, as in the case of *Kali, the Mother*, a text furnished the site for an influential cross-border and cross-nationalist interdiscursivity.

As Eric Sharpe has pointed out in his extensive study *The Universal Gita*, the *Bhagavad-gita*, several times translated in Europe, had until the final decades of the nineteenth century provided the focus for an almost exclusively Western philological and theological discussion concerning the make-up and advocacy of a universal humanity. In these discussions F. Max Müller, the editor of the *Rg Veda* (1845–62), had again acted as a key commentator and facilitator. This Europeanized *Gita*, in effect a Western construction, was the version which many Indian nationalists first encountered. Both Gandhi and Aurobindo, to quote only two examples, first read the *Gita* in English translation (Sir Edwin Arnold's influential *The Song Celestial* (1882) in Gandhi's case, and just possibly in Aurobindo's).[70]

With the rise of nationalist interest in purified tradition and past custom, however, stimulated by Ramakrishna and then Vivekananda's reinterpreted Vedanta (as well as by Western Theosophy's focus on Hindu belief), the *Gita* was as it were brought home and taken up as an India-centred text. Read as a lesson in 'purposeless' or selfless devotion (*bhakti*) to the Indian Motherland, it was this *Gita* which provided nationalists and especially extremists with at once the intellectual and the emotional justification they required for their demanding political commitment. Nivedita appropriately called the text the 'gospel of the Indian Revival' (*Web*, 234, 237), and, in *The Ideal of the Karmayogin*, Aurobindo drew on its authority to appeal for the spiritual strengthening and moral cleansing of India in the nationalist cause: 'The recurrent cry of Sri Krishna to Arjuna insists on struggle; "Fight and overthrow thy opponents"' (*Karmayogin*, 15–16).

A text that had been processed by Europe thus provided not only a medium for cross-cultural mediation, but a channel of self-differentiation from Europe, and itself came to do service as a symbol of nationalist self-sacrifice. Popularized and politicized, the *Gita* of the

---

[70] Judith Brown, *Gandhi: Prisoner of Hope* (New Haven: Yale UP, 1989), 25–6; Sharpe, *The Universal Gita*, 68–9, 79–80.

1900s also reflected the close interaction between political radicals and religious revivalists that characterized the period, with both groups reading the text as a call to arms. Significantly, following government repression in the final years of the decade, Bengal's spiritually inspired radicals would become polarized either as revolutionaries (for example, Bhupendranath Dutt, Vivekananda's brother), or as mystics and religious devotees (Sri Aurobindo himself). That link of spirituality and politics again points to how the invocation of time-honoured religious texts, or of traditional symbols like Kali or Krishna, formed an important part of an exercise in self-rooting by a freshly politicized though often culturally alienated elite.

So far I have mentioned iconic texts and shared symbols, as well as newspapers, as conduits for and instruments of cross-national and anti-colonial exchange. Another of these interdiscursive conduits in the 1900s Bengali nationalist context was the colony–metropolis journey by ship. Though not strictly speaking a discursive medium of cultural transaction as such, it was a conduit that was possibly even more powerful in the immediacy of the contact which it created. In a word, the shipboard journey allowed for the making of cross-national (cross-border) connections between groups and individuals, as well as for the formation of cross-national*ist* perceptions. So, in a segue that is now becoming familiar, it, too, contributed to defining the contours and content of emerging anti-colonial and nationalist ideologies.

As Indians began more frequently to travel to the metropolis for their education or on political missions, it was the case that not only Britain's relations with its most populous colonial possession, but also India's understanding of Britain became crucially informed by the impressions, proximities, and in rare cases close relationships forged on board ship.[71] The shipboard journey—its seeming suspension in time, the seclusions as well as the interactions it made possible, its determining direction of travel, either towards England the seat of colonial government, or back home—created if not conditions of receptivity to outside influence, then at the least an objective distance permitting the reassessment of a political situation, or a reconsideration of what might be learned from elsewhere. As Chapter

[71] Antoinette Burton, *At the Heart of the Empire* (Berkeley and Los Angeles: University of California Press, 1998), examines in depth the gradual increase of travel by Indians to Britain in the late nineteenth century.

4 will show, one of the key texts of early South African black nationalism, *Native Life in South Africa* (1916) by Solomon Plaatje, too, had a seagoing genesis. Also like Mohandas Gandhi's *Hind Swaraj* (1909), *Native Life in South Africa* was written on board ship between Cape Town and London on a mission to petition on behalf of South Africa's oppressed.

In his pathbreaking discussion of how a transnational circulation of ideas and alliances shaped the formation of black modernity, Paul Gilroy in *The Black Atlantic* appropriately chooses as his organizing symbol of this intercultural and intertextual enterprise 'in motion' the ship on its transatlantic journey.[72] Gilroy's perhaps too exclusive focus, as we briefly saw in Chapter 1, is on the making of the Black Atlantic's compound cultures. Yet, just as his concept of 'outer-national' identity construction can, with certain modifications, be mapped on to (indeed, can be seen to rise out of) South Asian and South African contexts also, so too is the image of the ship or the journey by ship as a channel of transnational or cross-national communication, adaptable here. The important point to make however is that the shipboard journey in these contexts did not only bring cultures into relationship. It also consolidated *for the duration of a journey* the *already* interrelated; hence, once again, my preference for the term cross-national as designating entities *in* interconnection. How the ship confirmed prior interrelations is seen for instance in the fact that the Swami Vivekananda used his 1899 voyage by ship with Nivedita from Bombay to London to continue with and advance her induction into Vedanta and a Hindu-centred religious consciousness. He also clearly took advantage of shipboard proximities, as *The Master as I Saw Him* suggests, to further inculcate in her the imperative of remaking Indian identity in a sterner and stronger mould (even while steering clear of invoking nationalism as such).

A seasoned all-India and world traveller, whose image as a self-consciously martial neo-Hindu guru was crystallized before Western audiences, the Swami, one might say, was viewed by the majority of his followers including Nivedita, and to an extent by Aurobindo, as himself a figure signifying international synthesis. His mission throughout, Nivedita insistently stressed, was the marriage of ancient knowledge and the rationality of modernity as expressed in science (*Master*, 23, 56–7, 126). A national education in science,

[72] Paul Gilroy, *The Black Atlantic* (London: Verso, 1993), especially pp. 4–5, 16–17.

Vivekananda believed, should be made organic, continuous with local cultural habits. The aim of his Ramakrishna Order was 'to effect an exchange of the highest ideals of the East and the West, and to realize these in practice' (*Master*, 202). India therefore should 'embrace' 'the whole modern development' (*Master*, 203).

Opting whether by chance or design, or a mixture of the two, for a teaching environment that was itself in motion, the ship, it was tellingly this message of cross-cultural transaction and synthesis that the Swami developed for Nivedita as they themselves travelled between continents. On the same Bombay-to-England journey, again tellingly, Nivedita worked on writing up her own self-acculturating or self-translating bridge text, *Kali, the Mother*. There were distinct practical considerations involved in so doing, such as her concern to have the manuscript ready for publication in London. Yet the distance from India, the country which had such an emotional hold on her, and—at the same time—the closeness to one of that country's foremost spiritual authorities, who was also her beloved guru, clearly freed Nivedita into engaging at a high level of sophistication with Bengal's political syncretism, as embodied in the figure of Kali. Her position of being suspended between continents certainly acted with a distinct stripping and cauterizing effect on her prose, producing the strangely unlocalized and disembodied intensity that distinguishes *Kali, the Mother*.

Whatever her motivations, the exercise of shipboard writing was sufficiently productive to set a precedent for Nivedita. She later wrote parts of her personal study of Vivekananda, *The Master as I Saw Him*, a highly subjective and again curiously uncontextualized gospel of his thought, while travelling in 1907 between Bombay and London.[73] The book was moreover to a large extent based on the shipboard notes of the 1899 journey which recorded, as she wrote, 'the greatest occasion of my life': the journey with the guru had given her 'one continuous impression of his mind and personality' (*Master*, 230–1).

It is evident that shipboard travel provided for Nivedita and her Swami a space that was at once sufficiently intimate and removed from the world to allow reflection upon, as well as an ongoing reinforcement of, the cultural and religious interbraiding of their activities. Here they were able to gain a perspective on neo-Hinduism

---

[73] Foxe, *Long Journey Home*, 193.

not only as specific to India's present needs, important as this was, but as a religion with a wider spiritual resonance also. Chiefly through the medium of the Swami's teaching and Nivedita's books, the ship became a platform from which they might project their vision of the worldwide and world-integrating spread of Hinduism upon the future. The journey was a channel both for her current and the world's prospective Hinduization, even while that Hinduization itself was seen as creating potential channels between cultures.

In the seaborn(e) *The Master as I Saw Him* Nivedita set herself up, appropriately enough, as Vivekananda's 'witness' and 'thought-reader' (*Master*, 125, 128–9)—explicitly as a conduit for the wisdom and the training that he was imparting via her to 'all the Indian generations': 'For I knew that here I was but the transmitter, but the bridge, between him and that countless host of his own people, who would yet arise, and seek to make good his dreams' (*Master*, 254–5).[74] In the difficult process of writing *The Master as I Saw Him* and its several spin-off texts (including, arguably, *The Web of Indian Life*) across the next ten years of her nationalist activism, Nivedita continued in this role as a 'bridge'-builder, working between pockets of radical and reformist opinion both in India and in the West. Her work of transmission was therefore both a consolidation of the deeply informing East–West circuitry which the shipboard journey had contributed to putting in place, and a further enactment of the international or intercontinental exchange of ideas for which, Nivedita was convinced, India, especially the Aryan highlands, had historically always been the setting.[75]

'SHE IS IN ME AS SHE IS IN YOU': NIVEDITA'S KALI-WORSHIP[76]

Nivedita's Mazzini- and Mother-inspired militancy probably formed one of turn-of-the-century Calcutta's more pronounced instances of

---

[74] As the transcriber of his message Nivedita in effect became one of the chief keepers of the Swami's spiritual flame. She wished to be, she further commented, the vessel for him 'to pour his own mind and thought into'. Quoted in Reymond, *The Dedicated*, 241. Even the Swami's intensely personal and reverential verse 'The Voice of the Mother' (1898), from lines spoken in reverie on Kali, was written down, collated, and later published by Nivedita. See *Master*, 207, 232–4; *Kali*, 493–4.

[75] Atmaprana, *Sister Nivedita*, 220.

[76] This was Nivedita's response when her Brahmo Samaj friend Surendranath Tagore questioned her about her apparent adoration of images. See Reymond, *The Dedicated*,

cross-cultural and cross-nationalist interbraiding. Indeed it is possible to say that Nivedita's interdiscursivity both demonstrated and dynamically embodied Bengal's locally constituted yet internationally derived extremism, which her collaboration with Aurobindo Ghose then further put into practice. The most eloquent sign of this cross-nationalist self-translation, no doubt, was her identification with Kali, the widely hailed avatar of Bengali *shakti*, or national energy; the 'shameless, pitiless' Mother goddess of destruction whom, as we saw, Aurobindo also upheld (*Master*, 218–19).[77]

To Aurobindo as to Nivedita, Kali became a politicized symbol of religious oneness and devotion. As a deathly and death-defying figure, she could be made to signify the absolute imperative of self-dedication to the nation, an uncompromising, 'non-cringing worship' (*Kali*, 472; *Master*, 207–8, 223). In order to obtain a closer understanding of what was on Nivedita's part an extraordinarily rapid embrace of indigenity in the form of Kali-worship, the aim in what follows will be to look at the impulses behind this total dedication, in particular at its cross-national *and* nationalist determinants.

At a time of deep personal depression in New York State in September 1900 Nivedita received from the Swami Vivekananda, under the aegis of Kali the Terrible, a (to some extent fittingly) paradoxical blessing: to be both mistress *and* servant to India; both a leader in reform and a social helper. He was clearly well aware of and wished to draw out that impulse in her which, within months of meeting him, had prompted her desire 'to make myself the servant of his love for his own people'.[78] A year or so before, on 13 February 1899 in Calcutta as part of her consecration as a *brahmacharini*, Nivedita had revealingly chosen to lecture on Kali and Kali-worship as a strategy with which to break through her Bengali audience's possible wariness regarding her foreignness—and, at the same time, to defy the Brahmo Samaj's modernizing secularism.[79]

Already at this early stage of her religious pilgrimage, acceptance of the Mother's fearsome otherness, as espoused by Sri Ramakrishna and his disciple Vivekananda, seems to have represented to Nivedita

---

184. Elsewhere Nivedita distanced herself from the so-called 'beastly' rites of Kali-worship, defending a reverence for images as a way of seeing God. *CW* ii. 432–5.

[77] Tagore, *The Home and the World*, 107, 91. See also Karan Singh, *Prophet of Indian Nationalism* (London: George Allen and Unwin, 1963), 32.

[78] Atmaprana, *Sister Nivedita*, 15, 80, 118–19.

[79] See 'Kali and her Worship', and 'Kali-Worship', *CW* ii. 418–38.

a sufficiently ambitious self-surrender, a leap of faith outside 'the accustomed perspective' which was required, so she wrote, if 'one's conception of the world were to be made inclusive of the view-point of foreign peoples' (*Master*, 45, 198, 211). As a form of compensatory reification—the paradoxical elevation of what inspires the deepest feelings of fear and disgust—the bloodthirsty Kali might also have embodied certain personal feelings of revulsion as well as of inadequacy which India's alien cultural reality could early on have evoked in her. Self-dedication to her created a point of entry into Bengali religious consciousness that was potentially at once publicly and personally persuasive, reconciling Nivedita's feelings of cultural insecurity by wedding them to compellingly contradictory traditional forms as well as to modern nationalist aspirations. 'Though Thou Slay us, *yet* will we trust in Thee', was the motto of Kali's children, as Nivedita wrote both in her first Kali lecture and in *Kali, the Mother*, inadvertently perhaps citing the travails of Job (*Kali*, 473; *CW* ii. 427).

Differently put, the goddess Kali, whose terrors were so specific to Hindu culture in Bengal, became to Nivedita, again paradoxically, at once the focus of her self-lowering before Mother India, *and* the chief point of intersection for the anti-colonial and nationalist impulses she derived both from within Bengal and from outside it, in particular the anti-materialist values she had acquired during her years in London. In adopting Kali as a nationalist symbol and as her personal myth, she could in effect modernistically hybridize—and at the same time neo-Hinduize—the deity within its own cultural heartland, as is evident for example from the cloying language of the Victorian nursery prayer that she uses in the final intercessionary sections of *Kali, the Mother*.[80] An added advantage was that, in thus indigenizing herself while syncretizing or hybridizing Kali, as will be seen, she also eventually achieved the emotional autonomy from her guru which they both had sought: she made the ultimate self-dedication, of her love for him, on the altar of India's freedom.

In commentaries on Nivedita it is now almost habitual to attribute the remarkable phenomenon of her self-sacrifice to India and the Mother with reference to her 'Irish blood' and the bonds of sympathy

---

[80] It is significant that her chief confidante Josephine MacLeod once reassured her with these words: 'Your message of Kali is *your own* and Swami had nothing to do with it [emphasis added].' Quoted in Foxe, *Long Journey Home*, 106.

that this must have forged.[81] However, as will be suggested below, her efforts to enter 'into the circle of [her] Master's energy' (*Master*, 128–9), must have represented far more complex a process than an explanation based on conformity to racial or national inheritance suggests—especially an inheritance that did not, or not at first, affect her nationalist politics in any significant way. This qualificatory reflection on Nivedita's Kali-worship will therefore deliver an important caution as regards any tendency, such as is explored in this book, to attribute a solidarity between colonized peoples or nationalist leaders primarily to their common experience of oppression, or indeed to racial commonalities (such as a so-called common spirituality in the cases of Ireland and India). As we will observe, Nivedita's complicated identification with Kali shines far more light on her self-construction than on her background, not only on how she experienced Hinduism and her relationship to India, but also on her habitually sublimated feelings for her much-loved Swami (for whom, even after his death, she said she would sacrifice everything).

Nivedita represented her origins in a lecture at the Hindu Ladies Social Club in Bombay in 1902 as having been 'born and bred an English woman'.[82] At this time she had been a *brahmacharini* for as much as four years. Earlier, indeed within a day of her initiation by her Swami, while still transported by what had been one of the most moving experiences of her life, her sense of national belonging had been unshaken. She had shocked him by speaking of the 'passion and loyalty with which [she] regarded the English flag'.[83] As she herself

---

[81] Nivedita is uncomplicatedly identified as an Irishwoman in the following: Moni Bagchee, *Sister Nivedita: A Study of the Life and Works* (Calcutta: Presidency Library, 1956), 117; Ganesh Devi, 'India and Ireland: Literary Relations', in Joseph M. McMinn (ed.), *The Internationalism of Irish Literature and Drama* (Gerrards Cross: Colin Smythe, 1992), 301–2; Foxe, *Long Journey Home*, 12–14, 87, 125; T. G. Frazer, 'Ireland and India', in Keith Jeffery (ed.), '*An Irish Empire*' (Manchester: Manchester UP, 1996), 78–83; Kapur, *The Irish Raj*, 20–1; Reymond, *The Dedicated*, 3, 269, 282; Roy, *Indian Traffic*. Amruta Rao, *Sister Nivedita and Dr Annie Besant* (New Delhi: APC Publications, 1996), p. ii, typically observes that, as her two women subjects had ' "Irish" blood flowing in their veins', they were therefore the more interested in resisting the imposition of foreign rule. And yet Besant, for one, was born in London, and had only one Irish grandparent; Nivedita identified herself as English. The assumption however is pervasive. In the words of Inderpal Grewal, *Home and Harem* (London: Leicester UP, 1996), 9, 66–7, Irishness, as also for the less problematically Irish Margaret Cousins, made these women 'more receptive to anti-English and colonial movements'.

[82] Foxe, *Long Journey Home*, 12–14, 87, 125.

[83] This and the following quotations in this paragraph are taken from *Notes of Some Wanderings with the Swami Vivekananda* (1913), *CW* i. 286–7.

later openly recognized, this patriotic loyalty initially lent considerable bias to her thinking: it was 'the blindness of a half-view' which,
during their pilgrimage across the north of the subcontinent following her initiation, she and the Swami both worked 'with infinite pain'
to wear down. And yet, even as she was becoming more aware of race
hatred under the Raj, she continued for some time to hold to the
views concerning the superiority of British civilization and its
benefits for India which she had carried with her from London along
with her social radicalism. What she later called her 'island' mentality repeatedly sabotaged the Swami's stern lessons in the relativity of
cultural values (*Master*, 46), to the extent that he was one day impelled to cry out, 'Why do you insist on comparing this country with
[your own], what is suitable here with what is done there? Really,
patriotism like [yours] is sin.'[84]

From this it is more than evident that Nivedita was at this stage culturally schizophrenic, 'divided to the vein'.[85] A different perspective
on this dividedness—now in fact introducing an Irish element—is
captured in her descriptive sociological study *The Web of Indian
Life*, in which she observes that 'terrible pictures of the Hindu rou-
tine' 'embittered my English childhood', and initially also poisoned
her expectations of India. At the same time, she notes, the 'Celtic'
traits of a well-developed orality, a striving for the infinite, and a love
of freedom particularly endeared India to her (*Web*, 5, 105, 169). She
could also however be openly and severely critical of Ireland, in particular of what she saw as its historical backwardness and irrational-
ity, expressed as sectarianism.[86]

It is possible that the Protestant, Northern Ireland-born Margaret
Noble may have received from her maternal grandfather, an Irish nationalist, a strong impression of Ireland as a model of nationalist
self-determination and that this model was reawakened by her experiences in India. Her whole family certainly was broadly nationalist in sympathy, although her parents lived in England for the greater
part of their adult lives. During Margaret's own time spent working

---

[84] Quoted in Reymond, *The Dedicated*, 116. For Nivedita's early-1900s views on the
empire's benefits, and how colonization might stimulate India into 'self-activity' (and
Britain itself into the redeeming work of social service), see the October 1900 Sesame Club
lecture, 'New Interpretations of Life in India', *CW* ii. 439–49.

[85] Derek Walcott, 'A Far Cry from Africa', in *Collected Poems* (London: Faber, 1992),
17–18.

[86] The Irish, she wrote in a Unionist voice, lost two great chances of 'schooling', the
Roman occupation and the Protestant Reformation (*CW* v. 113).

as a teacher in London (1890–8), as we will see again, she reputedly had contact with nationalists in the Home Rule movement: her English patriotism aside, this fact is not as unlikely as it first seems when seen in the context of her background Irishness.

However, that her tendency to identify with India was chiefly attributable to her Irish 'blood' or cultural disposition must remain questionable even in the light of these details. This is especially so if we consider the other avenues for self-expression and feeling-in-common that India offered to the independent-minded and questing Margaret Noble. In her study of colonial women's work in the subcontinent, Kumari Jayawardena, for example, helpfully suggests that to Margaret Noble as to the other white women missionaries, Theosophists, and mystics who travelled, worked, and lived in India, the region offered freedoms of religious, social, and cultural exploration, obviously predicated on imperial hierarchies, which were not then available to women in England.[87] These freedoms were further enhanced within the situation of cultural symbiosis they developed in conjunction with native elites. That is to say, Nivedita's status as an educated, middle-class white woman mapped on to the interests of the Bengali intelligentsia within whose confines Swadeshi resistance tended to remain concentrated. So, while the educated European Margaret Noble for her part was always better socially equipped to deal with the professional elite of Calcutta than with a broad-based mass movement, the elite, too, had its status and modernizing ambitions confirmed in its acceptance of her.

That said, the assumption that her Irish background predisposed her to radicalism and a responsiveness to Indian nationalism does cooperate with the identity constructions which Nivedita and her Indian supporters themselves entertained. These were used, crucially, as justifications for the close involvement of a *mleccha* or foreign woman in the nationalist cause. Her so-called 'Celtic blood' and hence Aryan disposition were aspects of Nivedita's make-up which Vivekananda in particular was concerned to underline, as when, after a deliberately lengthy delay following their London meetings, he invited her to come to work for India in the country itself. Her 'Celtic blood' became for him the stamp of her appropriateness in relation to these plans. In a frequently cited letter of 29 July 1897 he wrote:

[87] Jayawardena, *White Woman's Other Burden*, 183–94. See also Roy, *Indian Traffic*, 126–7.

Let me tell you frankly that I am now convinced that you have a great future in the work for India. What was wanted was not a man but a woman; a real lioness, to work for the Indians, women especially. India cannot yet produce great women, she must borrow them from other nations. Your education, sincerity, purity, immense love, determination and above all the Celtic blood make you just the woman wanted.[88]

In the face of what he problematically saw as India's degeneracy reflected in the subjection of Indian women, he, too, was concerned to develop cross-national sympathies to promote the country's modernization—but sympathies, necessarily, with nations and assertive women of the right patriotic temper.[89]

Concerning his own alignment with the Mother and strong mother figures, it is noteworthy that, before he became the Swami Vivekananda (meaning, 'having the joy of spiritual discrimination'), Narendranath Dutt had strongly resisted submission to *his* guru Ramakrishna's Kali-worship. It was part of his capacity to entertain contraries that he seems also to have been acutely aware of the significations of violence, suffering, and excess, those extremes of hate and love symptomatic of the *Kaliyuga* (the present age of confusion) which the goddess continued to embody in the culture at large. Revealingly, throughout his time as a spiritual leader, Vivekananda generally chose to accentuate the goddess's aspect as Mother, India itself, over her other divine attributes.[90]

Against this variegated backdrop, therefore, to a devotee and follower such as Nivedita, believing, as she once wrote to Tagore, that nationalism should represent an acceptance of everything Indian, Kali would have appeared as doubly the medium and the sign of her self-surrender (whether as an Irish or as an Englishwoman). Kali was the goddess of extremes, but she was also the extreme Other, even within the otherness of the Hindu religion. To identify with her, in other words, was to give up everything of the past. So, in response to Vivekananda's repeated instruction during her probationary year to 'Hinduize' herself—'*You have to forget your own past, and to cause*

---

[88] Quoted in, amongst others, Atmaprana, *Sister Nivedita*, 30–1; Bagchee, *Sister Nivedita*, 117.

[89] Gayatri Spivak, *In Other Worlds* (London: Routledge, 1987), 241–68, has spoken of how the polarized investments in Bengali female iconography opposed the faithful and subordinate wife to the fearsome and dominant Kali.

[90] P. B. Ghosh, 'Kali: The Vision of Nivedita', in Mazumdar (ed.), *Nivedita Commemoration Volume*, 96–7; Roy, *Indian Traffic*, 101–7.

it to be forgotten. You have to undo even its memory [emphasis in text]'—Nivedita chose first and last to turn to Kali: 'I set myself therefore to enter into Kali worship, as one would set oneself to learn a new language, or take birth deliberately, perhaps, in a new race' (*Web*, 395; *Master*, 211).

The metaphor of being reborn as an Indian through the excesses of the Mother obviously gives a revealing insight into Nivedita's attempt at a wholesale adoption of a new spiritual and cultural identity. But it also sheds light on something that was perhaps more deeply embedded than this quest for a make-over—a more secret and even more complex desire to transcend or to escape personal or libidinal identity entirely. In their role as identificatory symbols, she importantly wrote, the gods and epic heroes functioned as 'perpetual Hinduizers' (*Web*, 124). Tied in with her new birth as a Hindu, was, arguably, the acquisition of 'impersonality', a displacement of personal desire 'for the welfare of many', as Vivekananda himself said when laying out for the devoted Margaret Noble the terms of any future commitment to India.[91] In the guru's case, too, the impersonality of Kali's ego-denying worship seems to have been one of the main sources of his attachment to the goddess. This is confirmed if we are to read any psychological significance into the timing of his deliberate switch from Shiva to Kali-worship. It was on their 1898 pilgrimage, which took in Amarnath and Kshir Bhawani, the central shrines to Shiva and Kali in Kashmir, that Vivekananda rededicated himself to the goddess, significantly after weeks of confused appeals for attention from his smitten disciple. Gravely depressed by her guru's apparent indifference to her, Nivedita was at the time advised by him to do likewise, to give herself wholly to the goddess (*Master*, 164–7).

Nivedita's feelings for her Swami, in spite (or even perhaps because) of his status as a monk, were during these early months unambiguously passionate and obsessive, even if usually suppressed. Since arriving in India, it seems, she had repeatedly relied on what she called 'emotionalism' to make appeals to him, and been painfully withstood. As he advised, in lines which she later recorded:

---

[91] Reymond, *The Dedicated*, 49, 63. Reymond reminds us that, not long after their first meeting in London, when Margaret Noble first expressed her desire to unite her life with Vivekananda's in order to work for India, his immediate response was to lay down a sexual boundary with the protestation, 'I am a monk'.

The heart must become a burial ground,
Pride, selfishness, and desire all broken into dust,
Then and then alone will the Mother dance there!

(*Master*, 231–2)

In her spiritual biography of the Swami, which is around the point of this quotation highly textured with similar hints and partial references to the effort of repressing her feelings, Nivedita's own final comment on her period of 'bewilderment' and illusion-breaking was: 'I understood, for the first time, that the greatest teachers may destroy in us a personal relation only in order to bestow the Impersonal vision in its place' (*Master*, 139). Differently but also tellingly, she wrote in *Kali, the Mother* that the image of the goddess was 'not so much a picture of the deity, as the utterance of the secret of our own lives' (*Kali*, 472).

Nivedita's personal relations with the Swami have drawn relatively little critical commentary, no doubt once again for reasons of religious decorum.[92] Yet from her own account, as we see here, it is more than clear that impersonality or self-abasement became a way of processing an initially troubling, and never entirely stable or problem-free emotional and (probably) sexually charged devotion to Vivekananda the charming man as well as the charismatic guru. For instance, after hearing him lecture in New York in 1900, she spoke of experiencing an orgastic 'great trembling' in which she appeared to 'cast off' the fragments of her former life. Despite the alienating shock of their experiences in Kashmir, she continued from time to time to feel the 'great salt tides' of personal love for him 'rise' in her.[93] In this tortured situation perhaps Kali-worship alone adequately

[92] Jayawardena, *White Woman's Other Burden*, 188–9, 283, pauses briefly on the subject of the personal relationship between Nivedita and Vivekananda, noting its aspects of mutual dependence and friendly teasing, and instances of obsession. See also: Reymond, *The Dedicated*, 128–9, 150; Romain Rolland, *The Life of Vivekananda*, trans. E. F. Malcolm-Smith (Mayavati: Advaita Ashrama, 1947), 152. In *Notes of Some Wanderings* Nivedita spoke of the loss of her imperialist preconceptions, the 'veritable lion in the path', as a 'terrible' experience. Yet all the signs suggest that it was the leonine form of the Swami itself that probably caused her (she whom he called a lioness) the fiercest of terrors—of loss of self-control, and of the loss of his support. Roy, *Indian Traffic*, 92–127, writes insightfully about the erotic charge that the Swami's presence stimulated in other Western women also, though it is clear that Nivedita was the most personally involved of his followers. The Swami did not escape censure from his fellow monks for his receptiveness to Western women, as noted in Amiya Sen, *Swami Vivekananda* (New Delhi: Oxford UP, 2000), 42.

[93] Quoted in Jayawardena, *White Woman's Other Burden*, 283, and Reymond, *The Dedicated*, 196–7, respectively.

displaced—and yet simultaneously signified—the intensity of her commitment, and continued to do so after his death. She was later to speak of her early years in Calcutta as demanding a deeply painful change to her mind's 'centre of gravity'—by which she could not have meant only the shift in her Anglocentric opinions.[94] (Indeed it may be that her wordy, much reiterated regard for the 'Hindu Wife's' role of service and self-sacrifice, as in *The Web of Indian Life*, operated along with Kali-worship as an encrypted expression of her dedication to Vivekananda as much as it did as anti-imperial special pleading.)

In *The Master as I Saw Him* Nivedita percipiently wrote that 'hidden emotional relationships' formed 'the channels along which ideas are received', and that her relation to the Swami, as to the Mother, had necessarily to become one of deferential daughterhood instead of a link between co-worshippers (p. 131). Kali, in other words, required a deep, often disturbing, and constantly demanding subservience—a relationship which then in a sense released Nivedita into partnerships of greater equality with fellow devotees like Aurobindo. British commentators at the time, it is worth recalling, saw Kali-worship as a disgusting and bloodthirsty cult based on 'primitive superstition',[95] and progressive Indians such as the Tagores criticized Nivedita for her apparently barbaric adoration of an image. Against the background of such associations, and the sheer intensity of emotion signified by Kali-worship, the terms of Julia Kristeva's analysis of *abjection* (the state of being 'not yet one', 'not quite another') offer a final synoptic insight into Nivedita's self-abnegation.[96] Caution must of course be exercised when positing resemblances between heterogeneous traditions and rituals where in fact none might exist. Yet in this case the analogies are so distinct as to provide some scope for a theorization of Kali as Nivedita's abject, especially if we take into account the interpenetration of European and Indian traditions which Nivedita herself, in part through her worship, attempted to effect.

Kristeva describes abjection as a condition of 'total unfamiliarity' isomorphic with the pre-verbal self. It is associated with the stage in

[94] Sister Nivedita, *Notes of Some Wanderings*, CW i. 287.

[95] Sir Alfred Lyall, 'Introduction', to Valentine Chirol, *Indian Unrest* (London: Macmillan, 1910), pp. vii–xvi.

[96] See Julia Kristeva, *Power of Horror: An Essay on Abjection*, trans. Léon S. Roudiez (New York: Columbia UP, 1982), 5, 179. Further page references will be incorporated in the text.

development *before* unconsciousness, inevitably identified with the feminine and with the body's internal processes, in which all is rejected yet unrecognized, 'catastrophic' and repellent yet still proximate to the self. Abjection therefore is ambiguity 'above all', 'a composite of judgement and affect, of condemnation and yearning' where the divides between love and hate, for instance, do not exist or break down; where one and other combine or recombine (pp. 9–10). In terms of relationality it thus compares in certain respects with Levinas's account of the self's turn to the supremely alien other, of being for the other. From the place of abjection, Kristeva suggests, derive the rituals of defilement and purification in religion, and it is in certain figures of the sacred—such as Kali, I would suggest—that its ambiguities may be both introjected, and expelled (p. 11).

To turn now to Kali, quintessentially contradictory in nature, Mother and Destroyer, garlanded with the decapitated heads of her victims, fearsome to those who resist her, comforting to those who seek union with her—her worship would fundamentally have signified to the yearning outsider Nivedita/Margaret Noble that loss and transcendence of (her feminine, British) self which she hoped to find in Vedantic neo-Hinduism and, some years later, in the Bengali nationalist movement. The act of abandoning herself to this cruel and forbidding, yet all-embracing, figure clearly meant establishing kinship with something that was completely alien and yet in some sense of the self. By bathing in her 'radiance' (*Master*, 172) all boundaries were broken down (between cultures, between self and other); all distinctions between good and evil disappeared. The Mother, as Nivedita saw her, was in all and was all-in-all. Henceforth she, the worshipper, might feel the dust of India 'burning' in her body.[97]

In 1900, after a further period of depression about her as-yet-unfulfilled mission in India and unsatisfactory relationship with her guru, Nivedita received a valedictory (and indeed final) blessing from him: 'if I made you, be destroyed. If Mother made you, live!' (*Master*, 278). As the performative injunction suggests, Nivedita, by casting herself upon the Mother, was able to explore both spiritual and political ways of filling the void created by his inexorable and continuing withdrawal from her—and also perhaps by the inevitable erosion of her British identity. From this experience, too, she extracted concepts of service and love that were at once supremely abjective

---

[97] Reymond, *The Dedicated*, 147.

and yet constitutive of a new impersonal self: strength of character she now defined not as the fear of pain, but as its embrace (*CW* v. 89). As in the case of Aurobindo, who like Nivedita grew up a cultural orphan, the cult of the Mother from this point on became synonymous with the love of the nation. The term *mother* itself developed a symptomatic multivalency in her writing (as a referent for strength, essence, authority, spirit, and so on). In sum, by means of Kali-worship Nivedita was able to perform first an asexualizing surrender to her guru's unifying and self-emptying neo-Hinduism, and then, a few years later, as will be examined in the next chapter, a self-consecration to the revivalist politics that he had in part inspired.[98]

---

[98] In the terms of Judith Butler's theory of gender performativity, as in *Gender Trouble and the Subversion of Identity* (London: Routledge, 1990), Nivedita's Kali-worship could be understood as an overtly asexual demonstration (both bodily and textual) of a sublimated heterosexual devotion to Vivekananda—one which existed in ambivalent yet symbiotic relationship with his own disavowal of Ramakrishna's homoerotic advances. The inadequacy of Western terminologies of sexuality when applied to non-Western subjects, however, must circumscribe the persuasiveness of such a reading.

3   'But Transmitters'?[1]: The Interdiscursive Alliance of Aurobindo Ghose and Sister Nivedita

> In a subject nationality, to win liberty for one's country is the first duty of all, by whatever means, at whatever sacrifice.
>
> (Aurobindo Ghose, *The Doctrine of Passive Resistance*, 1907)

> The true seer is he who carries his vision into action, regardless of the consequences to himself, this is the doctrine of the *Gita* repeated again and again.
>
> (Sister Nivedita, *The Web of Indian Life*, 1904)[2]

By the early 1900s the political ideals and aims shared by Aurobindo Ghose and Sister Nivedita were set fair to bring their work into closer alignment. True, for the good reason of preserving secrecy, alignment in this case did not always mean direct, one-to-one collaboration, but it did signify a roughly coordinated cooperation (one that became increasingly more organized from 1905). Certainly it signified an awareness of the *potential* of such organized political and ideological cooperation, an alliance which might be expressed both on paper and in fact.

For both activists, admittedly, the period of their revolutionary involvement was relatively brief if intense, punctuated by long periods without contact, and bouts of ill-health. Both suffered serious 'brain fever' in the second half of 1905, the time of the mass outburst of the Swadeshi movement (it was typhoid in his case, malaria and

---

[1] Sitting at Vivekananda's feet on board ship to England in 1899, taking notes for what would later become *The Master as I Saw Him*, Nivedita wrote: 'I knew that here I was but the transmitter, but the bridge, between him and that countless host of his own people, who would yet arise, and seek to make good his dreams.' Sister Nivedita, *The Master as I Saw Him* (London: Longmans, Green, and Co., 1910), 253.

[2] Aurobindo Ghose, *The Doctrine of Passive Resistance* (1907; Calcutta: Arya Publishing House, 1948), 66; Sister Nivedita, *The Web of Indian Life* (London: William Heinemann, 1904), 234–7. As before, page references to Aurobindo's and Nivedita's major works will henceforth be cited in the text alongside the designated abbreviations.

meningitis in hers). Advanced nationalism at this time moreover tended to be concentrated within different cells of activity, in particular the *samiti* or national societies which shared members and would have been aware of each other's activities, yet did not necessarily overlap. So both Nivedita and Aurobindo probably had more direct and more regular contact with, for instance, Barindra Kumar Ghose, Aurobindo's younger brother and emissary to Calcutta, and Nivedita's political acolyte, than with one another.

Yet, although not physically occupying the same office or attending the same meetings, their behind-the-scenes work did draw Aurobindo and Nivedita together as co-workers and, not to stretch the point, compatriots. Whereas the previous chapter drew out some of the distinguishing contextual features and informing symbols of their cross-national(ist) interaction, this biographical and textual critical chapter will concentrate on plotting the historical and intertextual course of what is known of their partnership. Within the timespan of their early years followed by the period of their connection, the focus will be in particular on their cross-nationalist interlinkings or interbraidings *in text*—the traces of their relations, in other words, as these may be detected in their writing as well as in their political work. This will involve, therefore, examining their own particular disposition towards cross-border or cross-national links. Right across the concentrated 1902–10 period, in fact, Nivedita and Aurobindo contributed to the same like-minded journals on related issues to do with Hindu revival and self-realization, and their intertextual awareness of one another was safeguarded and promoted rather than hampered by the anonymity they attempted to preserve. The lines of their cross-referentiality on both religion and politics, indeed of their demonstrable interdiscursivity, therefore tie them together, as do the shared if largely silent pages of their collaborative history.

AUROBINDO GHOSE IN ENGLAND: 'THE SPIRIT ALONE THAT SAVES'[3]

Born in 1872, Aurobindo spent his early childhood within the shadow cast by his mother Swarnalata Bose's depression, and under the ban against learning his mother tongue, Bengali, imposed by his

---

[3] Aurobindo, *Karmayogin*, 5.

Anglophile father, the civil surgeon Krishnadhan Ghose.[4] In 1879 Krishnadhan took Aurobindo and his two elder brothers to Britain where the boy began that thirteen-year period of garnering academic successes in English educational establishments that he would later call his denationalization.[5] After first receiving private tuition with the Drewett family in Manchester, he attended St Paul's School in London (1885–90), and in 1890 won both a classics scholarship to Cambridge, and a place to sit for the prestigious Indian Civil Service (ICS) examinations, which had been open to Indians for little over a decade.

Yet, if England began by making of him a classics scholar in its own mould, his time in Cambridge (1890–2) by contrast shaped and quickened his still highly theoretical patriotism. He became involved in the Indian debating society the Majlis (founded 1891), as well as, in 1892, a 'still-born' secret society, the Lotus and Dagger, dedicated to the freedom of India.[6] As we will see again, his extra-mural life during these years reveals an informing interest in movements of self-determination in other lands, in particular, from what can be gathered, a responsiveness to nationalist developments in Ireland, and to the influence of the Italian spiritual nationalist Giuseppe Mazzini (1805–72). He also read widely in the histories of the successful modern republican and nationalist movements of the Netherlands, France, and America.[7] Throughout this time, moreover, his father, despite his imperial sympathies, kept him supplied with articles clipped from the *Bengalee* which foregrounded British injustices in India.[8]

---

[4] The following contribute different (sometimes overlapping) details to the biographical sketch of Aurobindo Ghose: A. B. Purani, *The Life of Sri Aurobindo* (1958; Pondicherry: Sri Aurobindo Ashram, 1964), which includes a version of 'Sri Aurobindo on Himself' (1946), 225–66; Sri Aurobindo, *On Himself, Birth Centenary Library*, vol. xxvi (Pondicherry: Sri Aurobindo Ashram, 1972); also: A. M. G. van Dijk, 'Europese Invloeden op het Denken van Sri Aurobindo', unpublished Ph.D. thesis (Utrecht: Rijksuniversiteit te Utrecht, 1977); Leonard A. Gordon, *Bengal: The Nationalist Movement 1876–1940* (New York: Columbia UP, 1974), 101–34; K. R. Srinivasa Iyengar, *Sri Aurobindo* (Calcutta: Arya Publishing House, 1945); Ashis Nandy, *The Intimate Enemy* (New Delhi: Oxford UP, 1983), 85–100; Karan Singh, *Prophet of Indian Nationalism* (London: George Allen and Unwin, 1963); Vishwanath Prasad Varma, *The Political Philosophy of Sri Aurobindo* (London: Asia Publishing House, 1960). As well as *Sri Aurobindo on Himself*, the original source for many of these biographical studies is: Sisirkumar Mitra, *The Liberator: Sri Aurobindo, India and the World* (New Delhi: Jaico, 1954).

[5] Sri Aurobindo, *Speeches* (Calcutta: Arya Publishing House, 1948), 42.

[6] Aurobindo, *On Himself*, 4.

[7] Van Dijk, 'Europese Invloeden', 296–7.   [8] Gordon, *Bengal*, 105.

Some of Aurobindo's political reference points therefore coincided with those of the twenty-something Margaret Noble, who, during the period that he was in Cambridge, the early 1890s, was teaching in Wimbledon in the company of Ruskin-inspired socialists and other radicals, and, it is possible, attending pro-Home Rule 'Free Ireland' meetings.[9] Like him, Margaret Noble during these early years was growing receptive not only to nationalist ideas as such, but to the insights and inspiration that might be derived from the experience of anti-imperial activists located in different though related contexts, that is, to the potentials of cross-national exchange.

The most overt signs of Aurobindo's fledgling radicalism however lay, first, in his new interest in learning Sanskrit and his native Bengali, till now unmapped terrain, and, secondly, in his apparently strategic reluctance to join the ICS. The evidence once again is contradictory, yet it appears that he may in part deliberately have had himself disqualified for the ICS riding test whilst otherwise passing the examinations with distinction.[10] Despite the wishes of his father, despite the long-term direction of his studies, he seemingly did not wish to work for the empire as one of its few non-white favoured sons.

Having perforce become what postcolonial criticism describes as a mimic man, by the time he arrived back in India in 1893 to begin work in the (non-Raj) Baroda Civil Service, he was ready to re-authenticate or re-Indianize himself.[11] Learning and imitating both from Orientalist and Bengal Renaissance cultural sources, studying Indian history, he aimed to reconstruct his identity as an Indian and a Hindu. In *The Ideal of the Karmayogin* he later described this process as the colonized person's winning back of the 'kingdom' of himself, as claiming his 'inner swaraj': 'what we have to take from the West we shall take as Indians' for 'by a European strength we shall not conquer' (*Karmayogin*, 8–9, 20–1).

Amongst the influences which helped produce this change of heart, it is significant that Aurobindo's school and university years

[9] Her biographers once again do not agree on this matter.

[10] Singh, *Prophet of Indian Nationalism*, 42. Gordon, *Bengal*, 105–6, however, points out that this may be a redemptive reading after the event, as Aurobindo in fact twice failed to turn up for the riding exam, and twice petitioned for a re-test. Even so, while one of his priorities may have been to disguise his incompetence at this activity, he seems also to have used this incompetence to 'escape [the ICS] bond'. Aurobindo, *On Himself*, 4.

[11] He had been offered the job in the independent princely state following a meeting in London in 1892 with the Gaekwar, Maharaja Sayaji Rao.

coincided with Dadabhai Naoroji's two political campaigns for election as a British MP, which would have included powerful speeches about Britain's 'bleeding' of the Indian budget. Naoroji's London home, as Gandhi later noted, was an open port of call for Indian students at this time: it was here that the nucleus of early Congress leadership was formed. Aurobindo's two elder brothers, one of whom, Manmohan, was gaining attention as an Aesthete, certainly visited.[12] Elsewhere in the capital, too, lively political discussion groups to do with both India and Ireland were springing up, in which the maverick Home Ruler Frank Hugh O'Donnell, and his Bengal CS brother, C. J. O'Donnell, among others, were influential.[13]

As this suggests, another key moulding force upon a receptive mind such as Aurobindo's emerged out of contemporary Irish politics. Irish agitation at the time took the predominant forms of National Land League resistance (from 1879), led by Michael Davitt and Charles Stuart Parnell, and of the ongoing parliamentary campaigns for Home Rule (which came to points of crisis with the Bills of 1886 and 1893). As we noticed earlier with the interpellation of Nivedita as a worker for India on the basis of her perceived Irishness, the Irish struggle was already at this stage being taken as a pre-eminent model for anti-colonial resistance elsewhere in the empire, by Indians and others. Davitt himself called his country a 'nursery' of ideas of land reform and nationalization.[14] 'A common history of oppression', Nehru later observed, produced in the two countries a pool of nationalist ideals and strategies from which both might draw. As Aurobindo and Nivedita's joint work for India will again demonstrate, this pool included an overriding preoccupation with those areas perceived to be untouched by colonial history: spiritual life (ritual, beliefs, daily observances); other cultural activity (located in the space of 'the home' instead of 'the world'), and the pre-oppression past.[15]

[12] Mohandas Gandhi, 'Foreword' to R. P. Masani, *Dadabhai Naoroji: The Grand Old Man of India* (Mysore: Kavyalaya Publications, 1957), pp. vii–viii. See also Sumit Sarkar, *Modern India, 1885–1947* (New Delhi: Macmillan, 1989), 88–9.

[13] Howard Brasted, 'Irish Home Rule Politics and India 1873–1886', unpublished Ph.D. thesis (Edinburgh: University of Edinburgh, 1974), and the article based on the thesis, 'Indian Nationalist Development and the Influence of Irish Home Rule, 1870–1886', *Modern Asian Studies*, 14.1 (1980), 37–63.

[14] Brasted, 'Irish Home Rule Politics', pp. iv–vi.

[15] Nehru quoted in Ganesh Devi, 'India and Ireland: Literary Relations', in Joseph M. McMinn (ed.), *The Internationalism of Irish Literature and Drama* (Gerrards Cross: Colin Smythe, 1992), 330. See also Inderpal Grewal, *Home and Harem* (London: Leicester

In the taciturn third-person autobiography he collaged together towards the end of his life, Aurobindo was to deny that the programme of the Bengal Resistance as regarded swadeshi and boycott was conceived along the lines of Irish Sinn Féin.[16] And yet, whilst in the 1900s he may not necessarily have closely followed Irish developments, in the 1880s and 1890s he was unmistakably affected by Irish nationalist politics such as they were developing in London and in Dublin. Even at the time of the Swadeshi movement he to an extent contradicted these later protestations, so tacitly accepting the evidence of etymology embedded in his own deployment of the word *boycott*.[17] Most notably in *The Doctrine of Passive Resistance* (1907), he openly sets up the Ireland of Parnell with its no-rent campaigns and obstructionism (or boycott) as a leading example both of organized passive *and* active resistance (pp. 27–8, 30–1, 42).

It is indeed almost impossible that the student Aurobindo, when exposed to the news of the ongoing Irish struggle for self-determination, would not have found such images resonating deeply with his own developing ideas concerning adequate responses to colonial occupation and the possibilities for creating a redemptive spirituality in his homeland.[18] More practically, the Irish example also taught much about the moral effectiveness of obstructionism and recalcitrance as political weapons. Aurobindo had read Matthew Arnold on the Celtic mind, and this too will have reinforced his sense of there being an embattled yet productive spiritual commonality or 'psychic subtlety' which connected Ireland and India. As we see in the article 'In Either Case' in *The Ideal of the Karmayogin* (pp. 17–23), the history of nations in Aurobindo's view obeyed a law of inevitable progression from a state of slavery to one of freedom. On this scale Ireland and India were evidently linked both as regards their

UP, 1996); Wayne E. Hall, *Shadowy Heroes: Irish Literature of the 1890s* (Syracuse, NY: Syracuse UP, 1980). Of course various African, African-American, and Caribbean liberation movements, too, have since resourced cultural life-ways and artifacts as offering the means of mental decolonization.

[16] Purani, *The Life of Sri Aurobindo*, 230.

[17] The term *boycott* is taken from the name of the British Army officer, Achill landowner, and evicting agent against whom the policy was first applied during the Land League campaign. See, for example: R. F. Foster, *Modern Ireland 1600–1972* (Harmondsworth: Penguin, 1988); Robert Kee, *The Green Flag*, ii: *The Bold Fenian Men* (Harmondsworth: Penguin, 1989), 77–86; F. S. L. Lyons, *Ireland since the Famine* (London: Weidenfeld and Nicolson, 1971), 168; Noel McLachlan, 'The Path Not Taken: Michael Davitt and Passive Resistance', *TLS* (12 Feb. 1999), 14–15; T. W. Moody, *Davitt and the Irish Revolution* (Oxford: Oxford UP, 1981).

[18] Van Dijk, 'Europese Invloeden', 231–42.

subordination and as regards their reliance on alternative psychic or religious modes of self-expression.

Three poems on Ireland which Aurobindo wrote during the 1890s convincingly reveal that its history furnished him with symbols of national struggle through which to encode his hopes for Bengal. What is particularly telling perhaps is that, as these texts show, the only nations Aurobindo ever addressed as 'Motherlands' were India and Ireland.[19] The poems—'Charles Stuart Parnell, 1891' and 'Hic Jacet—Glasnevin Cemetery', two lyrics produced in England on the eve of his return to India and first published in *Songs to Myrtilla* (1895); and the longer, more explicitly idealizing and combative 'Lines on Ireland, 1896' written in Baroda—all three take their keynote from the recent dishonouring of the (to Aurobindo) tragic hero and potential 'deliverer' of Ireland, Parnell.[20] As we read across the poems the 'contemned' though still starlike son of Ireland, Parnell, is built into a figure for Aurobindo's own unfulfilled nationalist questing, while Parnell's motherland Ireland becomes a symbol for the nation brought low.

At the same time, however, in his capacity as a 'high spirit' and 'fount of power', Parnell is also set up by Aurobindo as a paragon of nationalist resistance under its more positive and world-changing aspects. As a 'glass of patriots', an ideal model, his is a battle relentlessly waged, with cunning over force, enacting that principle of fated action (the movement over and above the leader) which Aurobindo would later also derive from his reading of the *Gita*. In both 'Hic Jacet' and 'Lines on Ireland' the at once prototypical and exemplary status of 'Erin' seen from the point of view of other 'enslavèd nations', is unambiguous. This again underlines the extent to which Aurobindo's political conditioning as a patriot was from the start cross-nationally informed and potentially interdiscursive.

'That which once has been may be again,' Aurobindo predicts in 'Hic Jacet', looking forward to the time when the 'bleeding' Erin,

---

[19] Van Dijk, ibid. 296, makes the same observation.

[20] Sri Aurobindo, *Collected Poems and Plays*, vol. i (Pondicherry: Nolini Kanta Gupta, 1942), 10–16. See also Elleke Boehmer (ed.), *Empire Writing* (Oxford: Oxford UP, 1998), 325; and the discussion of the poems in Devi, 'India and Ireland', 306. As regards Parnell, the international mentor to nationalist movements including that in 1900s Bengal, it is worth remembering possibly his most famous line, now a commemorative motto inscribed on his statue in O'Connell Street in Dublin: 'no man can set a boundary to the march of a nation'. Quoted in Nicholas Mansergh, *Nationalism and Independence* (Cork: Cork UP, 1997), 151.

downtrodden by 'alien masters', may again be raised up as a triumphant Kali-like figure 'armed with clamorous thunder', '[t]errible and fair'. 'Lines on Ireland, 1896', written a few years after his 1893–4 *Indu Prakash* series 'New Lamps for Old' criticizing Congress policies of conciliation, is even more open about that country's dynamic force of cross-national influence and inspiration. In a situation where, post-Parnell, even Ireland has been reduced to 'beggar's weeds', Aurobindo appeals to the 'brave example' of the 'mighty genius': when 'alien oppression maddened has the wise', 'pupils of thy greatness shall appear, | Souls regal to the mould divine most near'.

Cambridge, it would appear therefore, built in Aurobindo a tendency towards Indian patriotism. But if this was a period of preparation, the years in Baroda, during which he worked in several government departments before becoming a lecturer in French and English at Baroda College, can be regarded as his time of true practical as well as intellectual apprenticeship as a nationalist. In order to 'feel' his way back into Hinduism (*Speeches*, 74), he not only pursued his study of indigenous Indian languages, now including Marathi and Gujarati, but translated, amongst others, Kalidasa and Bhartrihari, as well as writing his own Vedantic lyrics and long historical poems of heroic action such as *Baji Prabhou*. It was also while working at Baroda College that he married (in 1901). The most prominent traces of his largely unremarked-upon relationship with his wife Mrinalini Bose are three letters (the first of 30 August 1905) in which he justified to her important new political decisions (such as his taking leave without pay to devote himself to politics).[21]

As expressed in the 'New Lamps for Old' essay series, Aurobindo's especial concern in Baroda was with India's 'crying weaknesses' encapsulated in the ineffectuality and gradualism of the Indian 'Un-National' Congress: what in *The Doctrine of Passive Resistance* he would still be calling Congress's 'tinkerings and palliatives' (*Doctrine*, 11–14). The 'New Lamps' essays were particularly eloquent and hard-hitting in their indictment not only of British domination as such (of its unimpressive mundanity rather than its much vaunted superiority), but of its psychic effects—its restriction of Indian potentialities and consequent mental colonization, its creation of brown sahibs or 'serf[s] masquerading as heaven born[s] . . . trained

[21] Singh, *Prophet of Indian Nationalism*, 49.

to the fixed idea of English superiority and Indian inferiority' (see also *Doctrine*, 11–19):

Hence we do not care to purchase an outfit of political ideas properly adjusted to our natural temper and urgent requirements, but must eke out our scanty wardrobe with the cast-off rags and threadbare leavings of our English masters.[22]

Aurobindo's response to the situation was implicitly to set himself up, once the quintessential mimic man, as a model of cultural resistance. For the repair or indeed the complete disposal of these 'cast-off rags', he strenuously urged from this time on Indians should turn not to the British but to their own capabilities (as he of course was attempting to do). They should address their inadequacies by reawakening a sense of manhood and pride in themselves; essentially they should make themselves anew by reviving the heroic spirit of the past. (Such aims again intersect with African and Caribbean nationalist—especially negritude—writings from later in the twentieth century.) The 'New Lamps' essays were followed by a second 1890s series on the spiritualized politics and revisionist historical work of Bankim. Collected as *The Renaissance in India* (1923), these essays located in Bankim's patriotic writing further means of combating the Westernization of the older generation of Bengali nationalists.[23]

At around the same time that the Swami Vivekananda was taking his message of Indian regeneration to the West, therefore, Aurobindo, too, was beginning to advocate a reviving masculinity as the antidote to the nervous imitativeness of nineteenth-century educated Bengal. With his Europeanized heart hungrily seeking such knowledge as might be made dynamic for India, it was inevitable that he would also feel a strong attraction to the beliefs in dynamic Oneness and the Divine Energy of Kali held by Ramakrishna and his disciple.[24] It was further predictable that any activist similarly concerned to awaken India's soul by channelling the forces of revival which Bankim, Ramakrishna, and Vivekananda had roused—such

[22] Aurobindo, 'New Lamps for Old' 5, *Indu Prakash* (30 Oct. 1893). Or, as he said in *Speeches*, 36–7: 'We went to school with aliens, we allowed the aliens to . . . draw our minds away from all that was great and good in us. We considered ourselves unfit for self-government and political life.' Following the publication of the second essay in the 'New Lamps' series, Aurobindo was asked to reduce the force of his critique.
[23] Sri Aurobindo, *The Renaissance in India*, trans. Rameshwar De (Chandernagore: Prabartak Publishing, 1923).
[24] Srinivasa Iyengar, *Sri Aurobindo*, 41, 44–5.

as the energetic newcomer to Bengal, the soon-to-be-renamed Margaret Noble—would strongly recommend themselves to Aurobindo as a co-worker.

THE YOUNG MARGARET NOBLE: 'THE OCEAN THROUGH AN EMPTY SHELL'[25]

The Irish Protestant family into which Margaret Noble was born on 28 October 1867, in Dungannon, Co. Tyrone, seems to have been, on both sides, moderately nationalist, and in support of Home Rule, at certain times openly so.[26] In particular her Hamilton grandparents, with whom she spent a considerable part of her childhood while her father was training as a Wesleyan minister in England, were vigorously anti-Unionist—though this political thinking did not at first noticeably impinge, as we have seen, on the imperialist views of their granddaughter.

Margaret and her sister attended secondary school in Halifax, in England, which constituted for her, as for many other educated young Victorian women, her training as a teacher—in her case for positions in Keswick (1884–6), Wrexham (1886), and Chester (1889). During these years she became interested in the innovative (child-centred) teaching methods of Froebel and Pestalozzi, and involved herself in social and charity work. Based on these new methods, she started in 1890, together with a colleague, a girls' school in Wimbledon, and, in 1892, branched out to set up her own school in the same area. The Ruskin School as it was called significantly reflected another important influence on her at the time, one which laid the foundation for her later political morality, her belief in the generation of

---

[25] The full quotation, elaborating Nivedita's sense of being a 'transmitter', is: 'Let My will flow through thee, as the ocean through an empty shell' (Kali, 493).

[26] This biographical account is based on an intercutting and comparative reading of the three most authoritative lives of Margaret Noble/Sister Nivedita: Lizelle Reymond's controversial The Dedicated: A Biography of Nivedita (New York: The John Day Company, 1953), which though unreferenced, and novelistic in style, claims to draw on interviews with people Nivedita knew; the subjective Pravrajika Atmaprana, Sister Nivedita of Ramakrishna–Vivekananda (1961; Calcutta: Sister Nivedita Girls' School, 1977), which extensively sources Nivedita's own writing; and Barbara Foxe, Long Journey Home: A Biography of Margaret Noble (Nivedita) (London: Rider and Co., 1975), now regarded as the most reliable source, though heavily dependent on Atmaprana. Moni Bagchee, Sister Nivedita: A Study of the Life and Works (Calcutta: Presidency Library, 1956), exaggerates Nivedita's revolutionary ties throughout, but is nonetheless useful for highlighting, along with Reymond, those political details that Atmaprana's book leaves blurred.

value through independent work.[27] Her sympathy for Ruskin and for the Arts and Crafts movement doubtless also prepared the ground for the connections she was to make with socialists and other radicals like the anarchist Peter Kropotkin (around 1891, and during her 1900s visits to London), H. M. Hyndman of the Social Democratic Federation, and the radical journalist W. T. Stead (the last two both in 1901). She was also drawn to the writing of the American Transcendentalists and of Walt Whitman, whose ideal of 'communion' between the nations of the globe later harmonized with her Swami's message for the West.[28] Her first newspaper articles, which date from these London years, criticize working-class poverty and express support for women's education, though chiefly as an enhancement of their nurturing role in the home.[29]

As again for other late Victorians, Margaret Noble's growing social and political awareness was accompanied by an increasingly more vexing spiritual crisis, in which the structures of Christian belief, whether high or low church, no longer she felt provided an adequate refuge or answers to her gropings after 'Truth'. It was while enduring this crisis, exacerbated by two serious disappointments in love, that she began to attend various discussion circles in London, including the Sesame Club, with which the former vicereine of India Lady Ripon as well as Thomas Huxley and Bernard Shaw were associated. In February 1895, at one of these meetings, she first encountered the Swami Vivekananda, fresh from his lecturing successes in America, and was struck not so much by the originality but the 'strangeness' and 'dignity' of his religious philosophy of the all-pervasive One (*Master*, 21). His combination of mystical conviction with rational lucidity also excited her, as did the comparative reach of his thinking, such as when he urged, as he had at Chicago two years before, that the time had arrived when nations should exchange their ideals 'as they already were their commodities' (*Master*, 6). From this time on her attention became unshakeably fixed on travelling to India in order, she hoped, to experience his philosophy at first hand.

---

[27] Partha Mitter, *Art and Nationalism in Colonial India 1850–1922* (Cambridge: Cambridge UP, 1994), 246, 254–60. See also E. P. Thompson, *William Morris* (London: Merlin Press, 1977), 692–8.

[28] See Foxe, *Long Journey Home*, 96, 113, 125.

[29] Nivedita's later focus on women's issues would always be mediated via her commitment to Indian nationalism.

Yet it was not until the middle of 1897 that Vivekananda formally invited Margaret Noble to come to India and work for Indians, specifically for the education of Indian women. As we saw, he was probably apprehensive about both the degree of her passionate intensity and her possible reactions to the subcontinent's strangeness. India, he felt, required workers motivated by a fully India-centred consciousness. However, once in Calcutta, Margaret Noble was initiated into the Ramakrishna Order within the relatively short period of a month, on 29 March 1898, after which she embarked on what she called her pilgrimage of sorrow through northern India with the Swami and two other of his Western women disciples, Mrs Bull and Nivedita's soon-to-be-confidante Josephine MacLeod. During her ensuing year of acclimatization and instruction, Nivedita established a small girls' school in Bosepara Lane (November 1898), involved herself in plague relief, and had her initiation as a *brahmacharini* confirmed (February 1899). In June 1899 she left with Vivekananda on a joint fund-raising tour of America via England.[30]

Observing the joy she was obtaining from following her guru, Rabindranath Tagore is said to have observed towards the end of this probationary year: 'There is no doubt that Nivedita has found the object of her inner devotion.'[31] In the United States, however, when Vivekananda embarked on a lecture tour independent from her own, Nivedita again suffered a period of intense anguish at the distance he was putting between them. It is from this time that we can date her growing efforts to transmute her feelings into a broader resolve to work politically for India.[32] Her letters, and the various literary, journalistic, and lecturing activities that involved her between 1900 and 1902, the year of her return to Calcutta and of the Swami's death, all point to this fact. In the space created by his increasing retreat from the world in part due to ill-health, she worked out, once back in England, a process of reconciling her still-troubled devotion to him with a still-unformed commitment to India's betterment, as she saw it. She would now be involved only in what was 'Indian for India', as she said in the important letter to Josephine MacLeod of 19 July 1901.[33] Or, as she also put it, underlining the cross-border political pilgrimage

---

[30] Like *Kali, the Mother*, some of Nivedita's later publications, including the 1907 *Cradle Tales of Hinduism* (*CW* iii. 145–360), were produced as fund-raising ventures for the Ramakrishna Mission and her school.

[31] Quoted in Reymond, *The Dedicated*, 174. [32] See Ch. 2.

[33] Atmaprana, *Sister Nivedita*, 128–30.

she was by now making: 'I have identified myself with the Idea of Mother India, I have become the idea itself.'[34]

Significant factors which contributed to this process of radicalization included the political (and cross-national) connections that she was able to form or to reaffirm in London with W. T. Stead and Prince Kropotkin, amongst other prominent figures, as well as with various progressive Indian students and in particular the economist and writer R. C. Dutt. It was R. C. Dutt, another reader and admirer of her recent publication *Kali, the Mother*, who now suggested that she begin the close study of Hindu culture (viewed on its own terms) that became *The Web of Indian Life*. Another influential factor was her attendance at the Congress of the History of Religions as part of the 1900 Paris Exhibition, and her work there with the sociologist Patrick Geddes. Through this work she gained valuable insights into how imperialism fuelled by capitalist forces fostered worldwide poverty, and how economic forces thus linked nations, though in unequal relationship. She also at this time met the brilliant but by the West still disparaged Bengali biological physicist Jagadis Bose, for whom she would shortly partially ghost and edit such works as *Response in the Living and Non-Living* (1902) and *Comparative Electro-physiology* (1907).

One of the consequences of these shifts in her attention and acquaintance was that, back in India in 1902, even as she re-established her school for girls (now with the help of Christine Greenstidel), she began to forge important contacts with moderate but dedicated nationalists such as Surendranath Banerji and G. K. Gokhale, and the Brahmo Samaj Tagore family, as well as with radicals like Aurobindo Ghose. (Again she was working *between* groups holding different political convictions, in a lateral, 'cross-border' way.) Gradually but steadily she came to the conclusion that organized political resistance, passive at first but active if necessary, needed to be employed against the British presence in India if cultural pride and national self-sufficiency were to be (re)generated.

The point of resolution for her came at last when, to quote her own words, she formally put herself at a distance 'far outside [the Swami's] course'[35]—that is, when she decided to transfer his teachings directly into the arena of nationalist politics, and was consequently obliged

---

[34] Reymond, *The Dedicated*, 262–3.
[35] Quoted in Foxe, *Long Journey Home*, 126.

to take formal leave of the Ramakrishna Mission. Although political in motivation, this was however a decision that aimed for consistency with Vivekananda's spirituality. While he had always insisted that the Mission avoid any connection with politics, he had at the same time instructed her in the importance of fostering national pride and self-interest. This she now intended to activate in practice. His emphasis on national 'manliness', as she wrote, would henceforth equate for her with nation-making—just as he himself (she believed) had suggested it might.

In later reconstructions of his thinking, most notably in *The Master as I Saw Him*, Nivedita would always underline the intensity of what she understood as the Swami's devotion to the spiritual-cultural entity of the Indian nation. Her own vehement language in the book—the repeated use of words like 'passion' and 'love' with respect to him—transmits the force of his 'great spiral of emotion . . . [of] love of soil' (*Master*, 69–70). Partially of course her interpretation of the Swami as a half-unconscious nationalist involved a retrospective justification of her own change of direction. But Aurobindo, B. C. Pal, and others, too, saw not only Vivekananda but his mentor Sri Ramakrishna as nationalizing forces.[36] Their joint message of spiritual reawakening, and Vivekananda's specific warnings concerning the spirit-deadening effects of Western materialism as well as of Asian submissiveness, to them entailed an exhortation to nationalist self-assertion alongside and in spite of modernization. As Nivedita wrote:

Throughout those years in which I saw him almost daily, the thought of India was to him like the air he breathed. True, he was a worker at foundations. He neither used the word 'nationality', nor proclaimed an era of 'nation-making'. 'Man-making', he said, was his own task. But he was born a lover, and the queen of his adoration was his Motherland. (*Master*, 64–5)

National self-respect thus rested on man-making,[37] and man-making (or, more precisely, son-making) demanded devotion to the

---

[36] Around the turn of the century, as we saw in Chapter 2, n. 65, Aurobindo had a vision in which both Ramakrishna and Vivekananda instructed him to worship the Mother. See Gordon, *Bengal*, 110.

[37] It is characteristic of the nationalist iconographies of Nation-Mothers and sons, that Nivedita, the 'daughter' to the guru, eventually became a surrogate mother to the Bengali nation's sons, such as Barindra Ghose, through a process of first serving them as their helpmeet. Anne McClintock, *Imperial Leather* (London: Routledge, 1995), 353–88. See also n. 92 below.

Mother. So far indeed had Nivedita travelled along the path towards seeing Vivekananda as the epitome or 'living embodiment' of nationality (one that could only be fully realized outside the orbit of his religious following), that she was ready to withdraw from his Mission within a mere two weeks of his death on 4 July (*Master*, 73, 310). As she powerfully expressed it at the time:

Is it not by taking the *national* consciousness of the women, like that of the men, and setting it toward greater problems and responsibilities [than those of her school], that one can help? . . . I think my task is to awake a nation, not to influence a few women.[38]

As a way of beginning to awaken that nation while also securing her new 'edge' or distance from the Mission, as she put it, Nivedita soon after set out on a transregional speaking tour of the subcontinent. This took her to a number of important cities, including Aurobindo Ghose's Baroda, where she delivered lectures on *shakti* and the Unity of Asia, and, in a discussion with the Gaekwar, the ruler, appealed for organized and directed resistance to the empire.[39] At the start of her Baroda visit her old friend R. C. Dutt and Aurobindo Ghose, both now of the Baroda Civil Service, met her at the train station. In the plain-spoken style he was to come to value, Nivedita introduced herself to Aurobindo saying she had heard 'I was a worshipper of force, by which she meant that I belonged to the secret revolutionary party like herself'. It was at this point, in a spirit of mutual interest (though probably not at this stage, despite what he seems to imply, on a basis of actual revolutionary party membership), that their conversation about nationality, in effect their cross-nationalist contact, began.

As was earlier seen in brief, the potential for cooperation seems to have presented itself to both Nivedita and Aurobindo from the outset. She saw in him a gifted intellectual who bore rich funds of historical and spiritual knowledge which he might (and indeed already had begun to) devote to the service of his people. And Aurobindo would have discovered in the slightly older Nivedita both a keen political sense of India's oppression, and a background of considerable experience in organizing schools and contributing to political groups. During this first period of contact Nivedita is said to have given him a copy of Vivekananda's *Rajayoga*, so confirming her

[38] Quoted in Reymond, *The Dedicated*, 264–5.
[39] Purani, *The Life of Sri Aurobindo*, 64–5.

Mother- and India-centred credentials. 'Count on me,' she is reputed to have urged, giving him her hand, 'I am your ally.'[40]

A JOINT 'CRY FOR BATTLE'

As I suggested earlier, we are in possession of relatively little verifiable detail about the actual encounters other than the first that took place between Aurobindo and Nivedita. In what follows however it is possible to plot the dates and the interlinked progress of their key nationalist activities in order to arrive at a fairly clear picture of the (loose) interbraiding of their commitments for the years 1902–10.

As Nivedita may already have known, from 1901 or 1902 Aurobindo had begun to train and send out from Baroda as a type of advance guard a number of young revolutionaries, in particular Jatindra Banerji (Jatin), a soldier in the Baroda army, his own younger brother Barindra Kumar Ghose, and, not long thereafter, Bhupendranath Dutt, Vivekananda's younger brother. Their objective was to establish in centres around Bengal (Dacca, Khulna, Midnapur, Rangpur), but especially in politically inert Calcutta, national societies or *samiti* (as alternatives to Congress). These would be centred on intellectual or cultural activities (such as in Ireland in the 1890s), but secretly dedicated also to revolutionary propaganda, and the recruitment and physical training of militants.[41] It is likely that Aurobindo himself initiated these young 'emissaries' as he called them by means of a revolutionary oath made with a sword and a *Gita* in hand. He had himself been given the oath not long before by the Tilak-led revolutionary movement in Maharashtra.[42]

Prominent *samiti*, or those important to Aurobindo and Nivedita, included the Dawn Society associated with the *Dawn* magazine run by Satis Chandra Mukherji and concerned primarily with plans for national education and some political training; the influential and successful Anusilan Samiti founded by Jatin and Barin with the Calcutta-based lawyer Promotha Mitter; the Young Men's Hindu

---

[40] Quoted in Rakhahari Chatterjee, 'Nivedita and Contemporary Indian Politics', in A. K. Mazumdar (ed.), *Nivedita Commemoration Volume* (Calcutta: Vivekananda Janmotsava Samiti, 1968), 220–1.

[41] Gordon, *Bengal*, 112; Purani, *The Life of Sri Aurobindo*, 63–8, 225–66; Sarkar, *Modern India*, 123.

[42] Aurobindo, *On Himself*, 15. Eric Hobsbawm, *Primitive Rebels: Studies in Archaic Forms of Social Movement* (1959: Manchester: Manchester UP, 1963), 167–8, comments on the indigenous content of these Bengali nationalist rituals.

Union; and the Bande Mataram Society to propagate patriotism and raise money for Aurobindo's later journal of the same name.[43] Their '[springing] into existence' doubtless kept the new lines of contact between Baroda and Calcutta alive, and, we will see, gave shape to the triangulated relationship developing between Nivedita, political Calcutta, and Aurobindo. As Aurobindo wrote, he was soon to travel to Calcutta 'personally to see and arrange things myself', yet, even when not geographically proximate, the various parties seem to have remained in regular touch through 'a network of runners'.[44]

From around 1902–3, and until the Surat split in 1907, Aurobindo's ultimate aim was to capture Congress and turn it into an instrument for coordinated political action: it was an aim he shared with Nivedita. But in the interim he sought to organize the emergent extremist movement in the Raj capital under the umbrella of a self-appointed central council of five. Comprising Promotha Mitter, Jatin, C. R. Das, Surendranath Tagore, and Nivedita, the objective was that this secret Revolutionary Council act as an executive coordinating committee for Calcutta's scattered national societies, with Aurobindo as its undercover leader. The plan had been in part sketched in the revolutionary pamphlet *Bhawani Mandir* (1905).[45]

The Revolutionary Council in the event did not achieve its aims and was later unobtrusively disbanded. Yet many of the individual young men's societies and study groups made an important contribution to political life in Calcutta during these years. Whether through the medium of their local history and craft workshops, readings from the *Mahabharata* and the *Gita*, physical training programmes, or social work, the groups wove strong nationalist aims together with more occasional cross-national interests.[46] It was Nivedita's networking yet stabilizing role as a facilitator and teacher that to a significant extent ensured this success. By 1903 she, the Hinduized Englishwoman, had securely established herself as a rallying point within nationalist Calcutta. Giving talks, personal advice, and

[43] Foxe, *Long Journey Home*, 168–9; Haridas and Uma Mukherjee (eds.), *Sri Aurobindo and the New Thought in Indian Politics* (Calcutta: Firma K. L. Mukhopadhyay, 1958), p. xxiii; Purani, *The Life of Sri Aurobindo*, 63.

[44] Purani, *The Life of Sri Aurobindo*, 64–5.

[45] Ibid. 230; Singh, *Prophet of Indian Nationalism*, 58–60. In *The Doctrine of Passive Resistance*, 10, Aurobindo continues to be exercised at the lack of a strong central authority in Bengal.

[46] Sarkar, *Modern India*, 119, describes the *samiti* movement as 'one of the major achievements of the *Swadeshi* age'.

editorial help, stimulating political discussion and teaching history, encouraging physical training and local arts and crafts, she was animatedly involved in *samiti* work at almost every possible level. Her Sunday breakfasts—'extravagant in brown bread and Quaker oats'—became a fixture on the political calendar and provided an important occasion for making contacts.[47] She was, wrote her fellow journalist S. K. Ratcliffe, 'at the call of almost any group' which appeared 'sincere'.[48]

To them she recommended herself through the unstinting enthusiasm and sincerity of her self-dedication, confirmed with the publication of her sympathetic, indeed partisan, study *The Web of Indian Life* in 1904. In the case of the Anusilan Samiti, for instance, whose leadership dovetailed with that of the proposed Revolutionary Council, she was allegedly so highly trusted as to be invited to give training in anarchist and insurrectionary theory alongside coaching in Indian history. More certain is the fact that she donated to the Society a literally cross-national collection of nearly 150 books including some of the classics of radical Bengal: works on 'the Irish Revolution, the History of the Mutiny, the History of the Dutch Republic, the Lives of Mazzini and Garibaldi', as well as histories of the American and French revolutions, and the writings of R. C. Dutt and Naoroji.[49] As this suggests, her sense was fundamentally that comparative and evolutionary historical study '[sharpened] one's own sense of nationality'; that the interdiscursive, in effect, focused the local and particular. In *The Master as I Saw Him* she comments that a country must needs advance itself through a knowledge of the ideals of other nations (p. 40).[50] Essentially her politics comprised a continuously adaptive realization, on the ground, of both international and local discourses of nation-centred self-development and resistance.

A further important level of political engagement lay in her indefatigable journalism. Throughout these charged years, Nivedita like Aurobindo wrote prolifically, especially on politico-religious topics, for such newspapers and periodicals as *New India*, the *Modern Review*, the *Statesman*, and the *Times of India*, as well as the Dawn

[47] Nivedita quoted in Reymond, *The Dedicated*, 280.

[48] S. K. Ratcliffe, 'Appendix', *Religion and Dharma*, CW iii. 484.

[49] Rakhahari Chatterjee, 'Nivedita and Contemporary Indian Politics', in Mazumdar (ed.), *Nivedita Commemoration Volume*, 220–1; Atmaprana, *Sister Nivedita*, 183.

[50] See also Bagchee, *Sister Nivedita*, 73–4; Reymond, *The Dedicated*, 285.

Society's eponymous paper. The funds from this work were channelled in part into the Bosepara Lane school though also into *samiti*
activity. Throughout Nivedita's chief object was to promote, as her
colleague Aurobindo was doing at a greater distance, and at a higher
level of confidentiality, 'national-consciousness': 'India', she wrote,
'must become obsessed by this great conception [of nationality]'.[51]
A believer in 'Dynamic Religion' and therefore in proactive political
conversion, as she often explained, she was therefore energizing and
applying by means of her tireless nation-making work the nationalist message as well as the comparative cross-national links that her
reading materials and discussion groups, too, were promoting. In
these years she also became increasingly interested in Buddhism,
which she interpreted as a force for democratization contained
within Hinduism.

With the mention of her fierce and—for the Calcutta authorities—
disquieting 'national-consciousness', the inevitable question of the
extent of her extremism again arises. It is worth rehearsing this question one more time, in context, as it reflects sharply her simultaneous
and interlinked nationalist/cross-national involvements. The emphasis Nivedita placed on the importance for an activist of training
and technique, as well as her informed support for aggressive revolt
in those cases where other strategies of self-determination had failed,
do suggest she was associated with the Bengali revolutionary element by more than just implication. She is said to have asked her revolutionary friends, like Barindra Ghose, not to tell her of their more
advanced activities, and once (in 1910) refused to give up her revolver
for a terrorist mission. She did however carry that revolver. In 1907,
she compromisingly arranged for Barin to work as an assistant in the
Presidency College laboratory run by her friends Bose and the Professor of Chemistry P. C. Ray, where, as she could not but know, he
would have access to bomb-making materials. On the basis of this
evidence one commentator writes that Nivedita was in fact an important 'brain' behind Bengali terrorism, and that it was she who in
1906 prompted Aurobindo to move to Calcutta on a permanent
basis.[52] Here, as the head of the newly founded Bengal National College and underground editor of *Bande Mataram*, he might more
easily lead the extremist movement.

---

[51] Atmaprana, *Sister Nivedita*, 201; Reymond, *The Dedicated*, 277, 298.
[52] Swami Lokeswarananda, in Mazumdar (ed.), *Nivedita Commemoration Volume*,
18.

The crux of the matter must finally be whether the 'aggressive Hinduism' she professed lay at the heart of her nationalist project, or whether it represented its outer limits. As the next section's discussion will again emphasize, the stirring 1905 pamphlet *Aggressive Hinduism* was intended as in many ways a summation of her hopes for India (her 'last will and testament'), as well as being a distillation, as she wanted, of her Swami's thought.[53] In its pages she does not mince her words concerning the extent of a nationalist's commitment to India. Indians, she writes, must be absolute for the Mother: young men, as she also urged in a 1904 speech in Patna, should unflaggingly direct themselves to the national 'cry for battle'.[54] As this helps to suggest, her politics were *in theory* highly spiritualized, comparative, intertextual, and *therefore* extremist, but *in practice* opportunistic, localized, and cautious. Though a self-professed Hindu, she also, we must remember, remained a white woman under the Raj, and so it would have been deemed either inappropriate or dangerous for her to take a more frontline position. In the end perhaps the wonder is how *openly* radical she in fact was. Fundamentally, for five years from 1902, her political involvement represented a partially latent and secretive but always potentially inflammable and inflaming form of active resistance.

As for Aurobindo, who was soon to take leave without pay from Baroda to further his political work, the conviction that in certain circumstances aggression was required to withstand state aggression, was rarely in doubt. Where an established government lays 'a moral as well as a legal ban' on other means of protest, he wrote, remembering lessons learned from the Irish Land League in the 1880s, 'the answer of violence to violence is justified and inevitable' (*Doctrine*, 29–30). Consequently he was during these years under almost constant surveillance from the colonial government. As had become well-nigh customary by 1907, the time of the quoted statement, the recourse to violence was morally and emotionally supported by the *Gita*-derived ethic of pursuing a given action without a thought for self, without shrinking from bloodshed: 'The morality of the Kshatriya [or warrior] justifies violence in time of war, and boycott is a war' (*Doctrine*, 86; see also *Karmayogin*, 28–30). Having asserted this, however, Aurobindo did for some time believe, certainly until

[53] 'The aim of his whole life was, as he had said to me, in Kashmir, "to make Hinduism aggressive, like Christianity and Islam" ' (*Master*, 202). See also CW iii, p. xii.
[54] Quoted in Atmaprana, *Sister Nivedita*, 168.

1907, that for a variety of reasons, including India's lack of self-confidence and the absence, in fact, of totalitarian state coercion, the nation was not yet ready to take this final militant step.

In spite of their widely ramifying nationalist interests, the popular outbreak of resistance to Partition in 1905 took Bengal's extremists by surprise. It is a fact which testifies to their relative distance from the masses, their ambitions to raise 'the people' notwithstanding. Yet, in so far as this action to a marked degree fulfilled their dreams for the mobilization of Bengal, leaders like Aurobindo and Nivedita quickly adapted themselves to the new rhythm of events. History, as Aurobindo believed, worked out its own laws, and individuals should adapt accordingly (*Speeches*, 122). Boycott, or non-cooperation with the government, with its positive accompaniment of Swadeshi or national self-reliance, was inaugurated at a mass meeting in Calcutta on 7 August 1905 'to attract attention to our endless grievances', in the words of Surendranath Banerji,[55] and, importantly, to teach, as Aurobindo perceived, how the regeneration of India might come from within (*Speeches*, 19). As importantly, Swadeshi resistance brought extremism into the forefront of political debate, and this in turn stimulated the formation of new *samiti* and volunteer corps. Both in his organizational work with these societies and in his still-undercover journalism, Aurobindo now concentrated on popularizing the idea of violent resistance should the demand for a more extreme response arise.

Nivedita, too, made adjustments in the direction and focus of her *samiti* work to fit in with the new goal of *swaraj*, or national freedom by means of non-cooperation. Once again she acted as a key link-person and coordinator, putting people in touch with one another, helping traders and manufacturers organize lines of supply. Writing on swadeshi she recommended disciplined, well-directed effort supported by organized propaganda in order to promote the distribution and sale of goods (*CW* iv. 284). At national and provincial Congress meetings both she and Aurobindo now associated themselves openly with, and motivated the action of, the extremist wing, Nivedita at Benares at the end of 1905 (when Aurobindo had typhoid), and Aurobindo at Barisal in April 1906 (when she was indisposed). Both independently believed that Congress should begin to

---

[55] Rajat Kanta Ray, *Social Conflict and Political Unrest in Bengal 1875–1927* (New Delhi: Oxford UP, 1984), 152–4.

inculcate a concept of spiritualized nationality. By writing briefs and petitions, by trying to persuade the moderate Gokhale of the value of boycott, Nivedita in fact probably covertly scripted the entire extremist text such as it emerged at Benares.[56]

In March 1906 the Calcutta inner circle comprising Barindra Ghose and Jatindra Banerji founded the revolutionary Bengali paper *Yugantar* with Bhupendranath Dutt as the named editor, although overall editorial control was probably Aurobindo's. With its motto an invocation from the *Gita*, to re-establish 'the kingdom of righteousness', the paper was launched from Nivedita's house.[57] This was followed by the launch in August of the English-language *Bande Mataram* (the title the Swadeshi movement's cry of 'Hail Mother' taken from Bankim's *Anandamath*). Nominally edited for a time by B. C. Pal, *Bande Mataram* from the outset once again had Aurobindo as a powerful presence 'behind the curtain'. By way of his unsigned editorials and other contributions he now began more plainly to lay out his nationalist and revolutionary vision for Bengal, in effect to become 'the teacher of the whole nation'.[58] However, like Nivedita, he was even at this stage elaborating his themes relatively covertly, from within the heart of the underground.

All this was to change with the paper's eventually unsuccessful prosecution for sedition in 1907 for having published articles from the itself prosecuted *Yugantar*, and with Aurobindo's subsequent formal resignation from Baroda. Already at the conflict-ridden Calcutta Congress of December 1906 Aurobindo had emerged as one of the foremost extremist theorists. But it was the revelation following prosecution that he was the source of the stirring eloquence behind *Bande Mataram* that lifted him into prominent public view. At Calcutta he, Tilak, and others had succeeded in forcing a resolution supporting *swaraj* through Congress. A year later, at Surat, this resolution would irreparably split the moderates, under the leadership of Pherozeshah Mehta, from the extremists.[59]

During the build-up to Surat, and into 1908, extremism in Bengal came ever closer to erupting into what Sumit Sarkar has characterized

[56] Foxe, *Long Journey Home*, 191–2; Amruta Rao, *Sister Nivedita and Dr Annie Besant* (New Delhi: APC Publications, 1996), 185 ff.

[57] Foxe, *Long Journey Home*, 192; Purani, *The Life of Sri Aurobindo*, 232; Eric Sharpe, *The Universal Gita* (London: Duckworth, 1985), 77–83.

[58] Srinivasa Iyengar, *Sri Aurobindo*, 143, 136. The essays comprising his *Doctrine of Passive Resistance* appeared in *Bande Mataram* in April 1907.

[59] Purani, *The Life of Sri Aurobindo*, 229, 103.

as the third and final stage of nationalist resistance, which Aurobindo himself in his *Doctrine of Passive Resistance* had anticipated.[60] Beyond non-cooperation sustained by self-help, the first
stage, and beyond active resistance or a concerted attempt to damage
the state without direct confrontation, the second stage, lay political
violence, a last resort in the face of continuing repression. With
police bannings and deportations now the order of the day, and with
the return of *samiti* members from military training abroad, the situation in Calcutta was rapidly growing more volatile. In May 1907 the
first extremist bombs exploded, bringing about a police clampdown
which would eventually remove both Aurobindo and Nivedita from
the Calcutta political stage.

Within two months of the bombs, having drawn notoriety for
standing bail for the prosecuted Bhupendranath Dutt, Nivedita left
for England. In January the following year a combined religious
school and bomb-factory was set up in the Maniktala suburb of Calcutta (again demonstrating the link of spirituality and politics which
characterized the period). Barindra Ghose, amongst others, was
centrally involved in this endeavour. Within months however almost
the entire Maniktala group would be exposed for its mismanaged
Muzafferpur assassination attempt on a District Judge. Aurobindo
was arrested on suspicion on 5 May 1908, and was then tried for con-
spiracy at Alipur. Full acquittal followed his year's imprisonment.[61]

Nivedita's exit from the Calcutta nationalist stage at this charged
time invites conflicting interpretations. From the time of her 1906
illness she had been taking a noticeably more passive political role,
devoting herself to her writing and work for the revival of Indian art.
Her justification for a 'retreat' on the grounds of health thus has a
clear validity. However the suddenness of her decision to leave
equally persuasively suggests that she was consciously seeking to escape the fraught situation, or even that political leaders had asked
her to opt for voluntary exile for their mutual safety.

Related to this, a further theory presents itself, one which takes
greater account of her still-fervent nationalism. In the context of the
repression as well as the gradual migration abroad of the Bengal resistance, it may be that Nivedita returned to London to continue as

[60] Sarkar, *Modern India*, 97–8; 112–15.

[61] Singh, *Prophet of Indian Nationalism*, 102, 192, records that Barindra Ghose confirmed not long before his death that Aurobindo was *the* leader of the secret party of violence in Bengal, despite the CID's inability to prove his involvement at the time.

before with her political work but via a safer although still effective (cross-national) route. As Debajyoti Burman notes, following the suppression of all extremist papers in Bengal, one of Nivedita's tasks could well have been to help set up alternative publication venues, for *Bande Mataram* in Geneva or London, for instance.[62] Building on her many journalistic and other contacts, this work would have required her to solicit support from India's radical supporters and other potential helpmeets, including Indian revolutionaries abroad like Shyamaji Krishnavarma and Vinayak Savarkar, the leaders of India House in London.[63] On a fund-raising lecture tour of America in early 1909, Nivedita certainly did make contact with Indian nationalists in exile, including once again Bhupendranath Dutt,[64] and in London she renewed her connections with Prince Kropotkin and W. T. Stead, as well as meeting with other pro-India sympathizers including the Irish MP William Redmond, W. S. Blunt (whom Aurobindo had published in *Bande Mataram*), the Irish nationalist and ex-Baroda CS C. J. O'Donnell, and Keir Hardie (who had himself recently returned from India chanting 'Bande Mataram' as he disembarked as a gesture of solidarity). In short, during her time away Nivedita in all probability continued, with India's interests at heart, to work within cross-national networks, perhaps now even more literally so than before. It is also revealing that on her return to Calcutta in mid-1909, she seems uncharacteristically to have operated for a time under an assumed name in order to avoid renewed police attention. In that same year, in May, Aurobindo was released from Alipur gaol.

[62] Debajyoti Burman, 'Sister Nivedita and Indian Revolution', in Mazumdar (ed.), *Nivedita Commemoration Volume*, 201–2.

[63] India House (established 1905) was the radical Indian student centre in the heart of Highgate in London. Mutual connections and identifications linked its members with Nivedita, including Hyndman and Peter Kropotkin, and Veer Savarkar's widely shared admiration for Mazzini's nationalism. It was from India House that, in July 1909, Madan Lal Dhingra launched his surprise assassination of the high-ranking civil servant Sir Curzon Wyllie. Nivedita was sailing back to India at this time and in all likelihood was not implicated in the incident in any way. Yet it is not beyond the bounds of speculation that she advised people associated with India House as to the growing impossibility of undertaking extremist action in India itself. See Rozina Visram, *Ayahs, Lascars and Princes* (London: Pluto, 1986), 102–12. I am indebted to Leena Dhingra's unpublished University of East Anglia creative writing thesis on Madan Lal Dhingra.

[64] Debajyoti Burman, 'Sister Nivedita and Indian Revolution', in Mazumdar (ed.), *Nivedita Commemoration Volume*, 202; Kumari Jayawardena, *The White Woman's Other Burden* (London: Routledge, 1995), 193.

It was now, during the period of quiescence following the near-total suppression of the Bengal resistance, that Nivedita and Aurobindo reached their point of most direct even if understated contact with one another. As Aurobindo later wrote: 'I began [now] to make time to go and see her occasionally at Baghbazar.'[65] Both no doubt felt wearied by the years of tension as by the police surveillance to which they were both still subject. They probably also missed the presence of many of their co-workers of previous years. In consequence both began to move deeper into the spiritual dimensions of their nationalist belief or *dharma*. They would have agreed, as their journalism of this time certainly does, that the nation must be developed as first and foremost a spiritual entity. Aurobindo, for example, had been inspired in prison by a vision of Krishna.[66] Nivedita was furthermore practically concerned to protect from compromising political associations her work for the Calcutta art movement and as Jagadis Bose's assistant. As Aurobindo again commented, in words that cast something of a retrospective light on the extent of her former involvement: 'There was no question *at the time* of danger to her, in spite of her political views [emphasis added]'.[67]

Yet, to be sure, though necessarily less openly committed, the work of the two radicals continued during these later years to be expressed as different forms of nation-building. Aurobindo established the papers *Karmayogin*, in English, and *Dharma*, in Bengali, repeating the pairing of *Bande Mataram* and *Yugantar* in order to continue to comment upon and to direct the process of national growth. It was in *Karmayogin* for instance that he published the essays later collected as *The Ideal of the Karmayogin*, a work considerably more concerned than previously with the spiritual self-realization of the nation though still in support of a *Gita*-inspired unflinching resistance to Europe. As for Nivedita, though she remained the director of her Bosepara Lane school, her energies were now mainly channelled into what Aurobindo called 'the revival of the aesthetic mind of India', namely the nationalist art movement which was at this point centred in Calcutta.[68] As she asserted in her cultural criticism, perhaps thinking back to the experience of Revival in Ireland, art needed

[65] Purani, *The Life of Sri Aurobindo*, 64–5.
[66] Srinivasa Iyengar, *Sri Aurobindo*, 182; Varma, *Political Philosophy*, 167.
[67] Purani, *The Life of Sri Aurobindo*, 64–5.
[68] Sri Aurobindo, *Views and Reviews* (extracts from *Arya* 1915–20) (1941; Madras: Sri Aurobindo Library, 1946), 65–6. See also *Karmayogin*, 28–30.

to grow out of a national struggle, and in turn had the power to give wing to the 'free spirit' of the nation.[69] The colonial authorities clearly saw this activity as less of a threat than before. In 1910 Nivedita was visited socially by the vicereine Lady Minto.

Yet this work remained political, even if only by implication. In July 1909, not long after his acquittal, Nivedita tipped off Aurobindo about a rumour of his possible deportation, advising him to continue his work 'from outside'. His 'Open Letter to my Countrymen' was his pre-emptive official response, which he himself called 'a last political will and testament' (*Speeches*, 170).[70] As part of its programme for a future the course of which he might no longer be in a position to direct, the Letter reiterated the importance of self-help alongside self-determined resistance and boycott, and again stressed the need for national unity. Unusually, however, Aurobindo now suggested to his followers to negotiate their political action on the right side of the law; by the beginning of 1910, again reflecting current political trends, he was urging them to suspend all terrorist activity. As other articles in *Karmayogin* were also making clear, he was coming close to stepping out of the historical vanguard, which he called *kala* or Zeitgeist, altogether, in order to hand over to others less mystically preoccupied than he now was: 'When a man seems to have rejected his work, it merely means that . . . Kali leaves him for another' (*Karmayogin*, 71–6).

Neither Nivedita nor Aurobindo however had as yet formally laid down their leadership positions within Bengali nationalism. That moment came willy-nilly for Aurobindo when, in February 1910, he was forced to flee to the French colonial enclave of Chandernagore following a message from a *Karmayogin* staff member that its offices were to be raided. He had, it appears, once again courted unwanted attention by referring to a recent terrorist murder as 'daring'.[71] It was claimed at the time that Nivedita helped him to escape and that she visited him in Chandernagore before he left for Pondicherry in April 1910. Aurobindo himself denied these charges. Remembering what we already know of his other euphemistic references to their relationship, it may be however that his denial of her involvement was an

[69] Sister Nivedita, 'Indian Art' (articles from the *Modern Review*, 1907), CW iii. 3–90; Mitter, *Art and Nationalism*, 255; Reymond, *The Dedicated*, 332.

[70] Aurobindo, 'An Open Letter to my Countrymen', first published in *Karmayogin*, 6 (31 July 1909). See also *Speeches*, 166–90; *On Himself*, 62.

[71] Burman, in Mazumdar (ed.), *Nivedita Commemoration Volume*, 202.

attempt to deflect pressure from her, in particular given the high-risk position of *Karmayogin* editor he had assigned to her 'in [his] absence'. Whatever the case, he himself, in exile, was now free to absorb himself in the life of the spirit. In this realm, he had come firmly to believe, India's path to independence and its gift to humanity lay.[72]

Nivedita's brief editorial stint on the *Karmayogin* was to be her final task as nationalist inspirer and understudy to the Bengal resistance. On 12 March she used it, interestingly, to write her own credo, in effect her valediction to active nationalist politics but rededication to 'Nationality'. The short piece of prose fittingly appeared as the conclusion to Aurobindo's series of essays, *The Ideal of the Karmayogin*. 'I believe', she wrote,

that India is one, indissoluble, indivisible. . . .

I believe that the strength which spoke in the Vedas . . . is born once more amongst us, and its name today is Nationality.

I believe that the present of India is deep-rooted in her past, and that before her shines a glorious future.

O Nationality, come thou to me as joy or sorrow, as honour or as shame! Make me thine own! (*Karmayogin*, 81)

The government closed down the *Karmayogin* within a month of this March issue, and, just over a year and a half later, Nivedita died while on pilgrimage in the Himalayas. India, or the work for India, did thus finally claim her for its own. Like Aurobindo, she had for some time entertained the strong intuition that her labour for the nation was ending: she had sacrificed as much as was in her to give.[73]

Free of British law in French Pondicherry, Aurobindo Ghose established the ashram where he developed across the forty remaining years of his life a system of Integral Yoga aimed at the unity and fulfilment of 'the whole [divine] being of man'.[74] From this distant vantage point he would survey the progress of the Indian freedom struggle through its different phases: further terrorist extremism during 1914–18; the reunification of Congress and its Home Rule

[72] Varma, *Political Philosophy*, 168–9.

[73] Foxe, *Long Journey Home*, 208–10.

[74] See Rishabhchand, *The Integral Yoga of Sri Aurobindo* (1953; Pondicherry; Sri Aurobindo Ashram, 1959), 40, 209; and Sri Aurobindo, *The Life Divine* (1939; New York: Sri Aurobindo Library, 1949), *BCL* xix and xx, which is the canonical exposition of his later spiritual thinking. Integral or *purna* yoga—a higher form of *karmayoga*—essentially aims at the wholistic combination of the more traditional yogas of the emotions, intellect, and spirit, *bhakti, jnana,* and *raja*. See also Sri Aurobindo, *The Human Cycle* (Pondicherry: Sri Aurobindo Ashram, 1949).

movement; and, after the First World War, Gandhi-inspired non-cooperation and passive resistance. For all of these developments he and Nivedita had in one or other way laid the rhetorical and ideological groundwork: through these means, they had insisted, the fulfilment of 'Nationality' might be achieved. Yet, though having apparently ceased from political work, he had in effect developed another of the dominant emphases within his philosophy. This was the idea that freedom, as well as requiring political self-determination, was in the first place a quality of soul, one that might equally be realized outside India as within it. His ideal of the ceaseless, worldwide (cross-border) expansion of harmony and strength from the basis of Hinduized India, which he had shared with Vivekananda and Nivedita, had now been translated on to a purely spiritual plane.

'TO ASSAIL AND CRUSH THE ASSAILANT': INTERTEXTUAL LINKS[75]

Following on from what we have heard, it will not be a matter for doubt that Aurobindo Ghose and Sister Nivedita were like-minded nationalist helpmeets who, even if tangentially at times, worked together for an independent India. Especially considering the intermittent nature of their cooperation, however, their most verifiable association for present-day readers remains at an *interdiscursive* or *intertextual* level. (Given that they were proficient, prolific, and well-read journalists who were both clearly aware of each other's writing, the latter term may for the moment be the more precise.) Their cross-border association, that is, manifests most prominently and persuasively for us now through the medium of the political discourse on *dharma* or religious nationalism which they shared. Based on an ideal of strenuous self-sacrifice and on an uncompromising belief in national freedom, this discourse was embodied for both in the figure of the Mother ('the realization of the Motherhood of God in the country', *Doctrine*, 83), and in the principle of martial strength and motiveless action as expressed in the *Gita*: 'the divine will [flowing] through the soldier for freedom' (*Kali*, 493).

To complete the portrait of their interrelation, this concluding section sets out to give further substance to the extremist intertextuality which, it is my claim, knits Nivedita and Aurobindo together.

[75] *Doctrine*, 67.

Drawing on their key publications and public statements, the discussion will outline the neo-Hindu nationalist ideas which they held in common, while also teasing out the (relatively few yet important) distinctions between them. Even without the evidence of what we already know of their political networking, it should quickly become apparent from this comparative reading that the two extremists must to a significant extent have developed their ideals and policies in conjunction with one another. This is confirmed in the match between specific concepts and images in their political writings.

We find for example that, as other modes of struggle were banned or became obsolete in the later years of their involvement (1909–10), Nivedita and Aurobindo both made specific recommendations advising that the chanting of slogans or political mantras like 'Bande Mataram' might work powerfully to unify a mass of people (see *Karmayogin*, 77–80). Both, too, applied Vivekananda's teaching in urging their followers to repudiate all English (or British) habits and traditions *other than* that culture's so-called manly determination. In other words, in order to wage its political battles Bengal could learn something from the bulldog spirit (*Master*, 221, 295; *Speeches*, 84). Both leaders moreover saw the self-sufficient village unit as fundamental to self-growth: this was an idea which Nivedita had borrowed from Prince Kropotkin's *Mutual Aid*, and may have broadcast by way of her Calcutta discussion groups (see *Speeches*, 51–2).

So close is their agreement on occasion, especially when speaking or writing in a public forum, that we can only surmise either that they referred to the same central political authority (but they largely *were* that authority), or that until 1910, through the medium of the press and political lectures as well as in person, they conferred closely and regularly with one another, checking their statements against each other's words. Having said this, it is worth noting that Aurobindo in arguing his case makes more cross-national references to outside models than does Nivedita, especially to Ireland and the Asiatic miracle of Japan (*Karmayogin*, 31, 39). In contrast Nivedita the comparative outsider is more concentrated on the Indian or Bengali nation in and for itself.

To adapt a term from Integral Yoga, that Vedantic system which Aurobindo as a guru was later to develop, the political beliefs to which both he and Nivedita subscribed make up what seems in several respects to be an integrated and *integral* spiritual nationalism, in which, as in Ireland during the 1890s, the retrieval of indigenous traditions and religious beliefs was deemed vital to political resist-ance.[76] Conversely put, spirituality, or a numinous concept of India's unique (and uncolonized) spiritual identity, was always to be placed at the core of nationalist politics and, hence, of the recovery of na-tional pride. As Aurobindo explained: it is when '[its] soul awakens that a nation is really alive' and so experiences *ananda*, its own par-ticular joy.

It was on the basis of this politically focused spirituality that Nivedita and Aurobindo jointly supported defensive or passive re-sistance, the reliance on inner strength, as the primary course of ac-tion for an oppressed nation. At the same time both felt that this approach could work only up to a certain point, after which a resist-ance movement should have recourse to armed struggle. For both, too, conserving a society's cultural and religious resources had im-portantly to occur *along with* the active self-development of those same resources. As Aurobindo repeatedly makes clear in *The Doc-trine of Passive Resistance*, self-defence depends on self-help. Passive resistance (including non-cooperation) could succeed only through developing the inner self, the nation's 'own independent life and civi-lization', not by fostering empty cultural forms copied from Europe (*Karmayogin*, 5). 'Become Indians,' Aurobindo enjoined, 'Recover the Aryan strength, the Aryan discipline, the Aryan character, the Aryan life' (*Karmayogin*, 9). An imitative nationalism that was 'In-dian in sentiment, yet European in practice', produced self-steriliza-tion; a nation stamped with its own peculiar individuality, however, lived. But, recalling Vivekananda's preoccupation with modernity and self-modernization, he importantly also warned that a merely nostalgic nationalism 'clinging to every detail that has been Indian' and untempered by progress, might not produce 'the [truest] expres-sion of the undying soul of the nation' (*Karmayogin*, 21, 26–7, 31–4).

From around 1905–6 Nivedita found an influential way of giving form to this 'undying soul' of the nation by becoming one of Bengal's foremost cultural champions. The nationalist art movement centred in Calcutta, in which E. B. Havell and Abanindranath Tagore were also prominent, was distinguished for its so-called naturalism, the ci-tation of recovered vernacular forms and characteristic historical and mythic motifs in juxtaposition with Western representational

---

[76] Sarmila Bose and Eilis Ward, 'India's Cause is Ireland's Cause: Elite Links and Na-tionalist Politics', in Michael Holmes and Denis Holmes (eds.), *Ireland and India* (Dublin: Folens, 1997), 54–5.

techniques. As with her other chief preoccupations, journalism became the primary channel for Nivedita's expository arguments concerning the importance of the 'common speech of art' for the
'upbuilding of the motherland'. It was through its own art movement, her keynote essay 'The Function of Art in Shaping Nationality' (1907) asserted, that a nation was able to bind itself into 'a firm
and coherent whole, self-conscious, self-directed, self-controlled'.[77]

Their joint focus on an integral cultural nationalism reminds us
that one of the major points of textual conjunction between Nivedita
and Aurobindo emerged in part (even if only in part) out of the shaping influence on both thinkers, of Irish nationalism, or at least of
their perceptions of Irish nationalism (as well as, secondarily, of the
Italian and other romantic European nationalisms which had left
their mark on both the Indian and Irish anti-colonial movements). It
was surely not coincidental that the development of campaigns
based on boycott and swadeshi (the locally made) occurred in Bengal
not long after the onset in Ireland of the Celtic Revival, and, from
1904, of the Sinn Féin political formation supporting native Irish
traditions and trades. Both Aurobindo and Nivedita, it would seem,
started out from a point of cross-cultural awareness with respect to
Ireland. Certainly, whatever the *reality* of cross-border exchange between the two national contexts, Ireland and India, the *perception* of
a constructive commonality seems to have impinged on the work of
both extremists, and they themselves moreover helped advance the
movement of influence that this perception created.

During his years in England Aurobindo, as we saw, had absorbed a
model of right action from Ireland that had lived on in his imagination after his return to India. And Nivedita, her Irish sympathies and
nationalist opinions moulded by the romantic aestheticism of *fin-de-
siècle* London, in Bengal supported indigenous design, traditional
crafts, and the nurturing of the native self, as did the artists of the
Celtic Twilight. Custom, she wrote, was the 'eternal treasure of the
nation', as was independent, self-motivated labour (*Master*, 197–8).
India therefore should reclaim these for its own self-growth. In that a
culture or religion was like a language, 'we must speak to a man in his
own language' (*Master*, 213): the 'national idea cannot be imposed
from without—it must develop from within' (*Web*, 92–3). Aurobindo agreed: 'We must take back our life into our own hands and the

[77] Nivedita, 'The Function of Art in Shaping Nationality', CW iii. 3–5; Mitter, *Art and
Nationalism*, 238–58.

change must be immediate, complete and drastic' (*Speeches*, 52). For both, therefore, a cultural nationalist impulse based on self-retrieval (partly, it could be, derived from the Irish example) was embraced to the extent that it resurfaced, though in a new form, with the rise of extremism. Otherwise put, extremism, with its continuing emphasis on the undying national soul, transformed the cultural lessons of earlier days into the theory of aggressive *and* self-reliant (or, self-remaking) boycott.

And yet, although it shared some of its key generic aspects, the expansion of cultural nationalism in Bengal should not be seen as derivatively or even necessarily linked to that of Ireland. For one, the main sources of inspiration were different. The most immediate influence on Aurobindo's and Nivedita's turn to Hindu myth or ancient religious texts, as we know, came out of their contact with or reading of indigenous religious leaders and writers like Bankim, Tilak, and Vivekananda.[78] As Aurobindo himself recognized in *The Doctrine of Passive Resistance*, Ireland also had a far longer and more consistent history of oppression by Britain than India. This had fostered in that country not only a certain political maturity (or disillusion) but also a relatively wide cultural participation in the national ideal.[79] In India, by contrast, native cultural forms, elite or otherwise, were never as severely repressed by the relatively small colonial governing class. Here, therefore, a middle-class nationalist movement based on cultural revival lacked the popular appeal it might have had in Ireland. Cultural nationalism and militancy instead ran more in tandem with one another, the different spheres of activity, as in *samiti* work, drawing upon each other's energies. Finally, if Aurobindo later distanced himself from the Irish example of self-help, and if Nivedita the 'Irishwoman' in fact made few references to Ireland in her writing on India, this was because they were, by virtue of their beliefs, primarily interested in *home-grown* obstructionism, the particular appropriateness of the Bengali version of boycott as non-violent resistance to its *own* environment.

Over and above a revised culture, however, it was always in the first instance in religion (specifically of course in Hinduism) that both

[78] Sri Aurobindo, 'The Man of the Past and the Man of the Future' (26 Dec. 1906), in Mukherjee and Mukherjee (eds.), *Sri Aurobindo and the New Thought*, 1–4.

[79] In 1890s Ireland the shift to an almost exclusively cultural nationalism (inaugurated with the formation of the Gaelic League in 1893) moreover had everything to do with the disaffected light cast on parliamentary politics following the fall of Parnell (1890–1), and the failure of the second Home Rule Bill.

Nivedita and Aurobindo located the soul of the nation. To them, unless a national revival was spiritually expressed, a people was in effect embodying the self of another people. 'Indians, it is the spirituality of India . . . that must make us free and great', Aurobindo cried (*Karmayogin*, 20–1). And again, as 'nationalism is a religion that has come from God' (*Speeches*, 6), it should be expressed as a spiritual discipline or *sadhana* demanding complete sacrifice (*yajna*) from the devotee (*Doctrine*, 69–79). Thus, while they believed, along with the Celtic Revival, that an oppressed nation might be reborn through the revitalization of its culture, they also felt that such reconstruction on its own could produce inertia or *tamas*. Ultimately the source of the nation's energy and internal harmony must lie in spiritual purification and strengthening.[80] Only through '[learning] a more sacred truth and [commanding] a diviner impulse' might nationalism rid itself of the paralysis not only of European materialism but of its own backward-looking intellectualism (*Karmayogin*, 21–2).

Religion and politics, therefore, Aurobindo and Nivedita would have agreed, were mutually imbricated in one another (and their writing about this interknitting in turn closely interrelates their work). Nationality in fact was seen as a higher form of spirituality, as is evident from their interpretation of *dharma*—literally, the right way of being—as, specifically, an all-pervading form of national 'righteousness', in support of which they cited the *Upanishads* and the *Gita*.[81] As Nivedita plainly defined it in 1902, '[n]ationality is the highest possible expression, for the time, of the spiritual life' (*CW* v. 134–5), and, therefore, conversely, 'the re-establishment of Dharma shall bring 'a great, overflowing, complex, actual, ever-strong, ever-living consciousness of the common nationality'.[82] Aurobindo was perhaps even more direct. To achieve freedom and unity, he wrote, Indians should 'devote' themselves to *dharma*, the manifestation of spirituality in politics; religion and politics were 'the two most effective and vital expressions of the nation's self'. But not only politics; social work, literature, philosophy, and science, too, were all, according to Aurobindo, involved in the 'living reality' of 'the national religion' (*Karmayogin*, 2–3, 12, 29). Just as the worship of the Mother demanded the surrender of the self within the all-demanding Self, or

---

[80] Varma, *Political Philosophy*, 194–5, 212, 245.
[81] See Srinivasa Iyengar, *Sri Aurobindo*, 161; B. B. Majumdar, 'Social and Political Ideas of Sister Nivedita', in Mazumdar (ed.), *Nivedita Commemoration Volume*, 54.
[82] Quoted in Atmaprana, *Sister Nivedita*, 153.

Divinity, of the country, so the nation should strive as a whole for an embodiment of Divine Unity and Mother Worship (*Karmayogin*, 5–7, 31).

There was in a sense no limit to this dynamic, ever-more-elevating quest for spiritual self-realization. For, if the human soul's awakening was ideally to be perfected within the manifested soul of the nation, this clearly had implications for other nations also. *Dharma*, in short, had an expansionist dimension. The Swami Vivekananda's 'universal tolerance', as he himself preached it in early 1902, was paradoxically to be achieved by India's 'conquest' of the world on the grounds of its spiritual pre-eminence: 'The sign of life is expansion.'[83]

Aurobindo and Nivedita followed Vivekananda in teaching that the achievement of harmony and unity within the Indian nation should eventually create a platform for the worldwide expansion of this same harmony and unity: bluntly expressed, for a Hindu spiritual imperialism or world 'Aryanization'. 'The wider Hinduism', wrote Aurobindo in 1909, is the goal 'to which the World Spirit moves' (*Karmayogin*, 2, 6–7, 13). Much of *The Ideal of the Karmayogin* is imbued with the sense that India's freedom will be for the sake of humanity. It was the role of nationalism, he and Nivedita agreed, to '[build] up India' to become the 'Guru' of the 'civilized world' (*Speeches*, 67). Her rebirth was essential for the world's enlightenment, to the extent that 'the whole world', Nivedita wrote, might potentially become 'India', so forming 'a unification vaster and deeper than the past has dreamt of' (*Master*, 303; CW iv. 297).

As such turns of phrase suggest, neo-Hinduist spiritual ambitions could in fact manifest as nationalist chauvinism if not as outright xenophobia, whereby all that was non-Aryan, including of course Islam, was deemed unworthy and replaceable.[84] Nivedita's second 1902 Madras lecture, again, is very clear that the awakening of India is synonymous with the re-achievement of Aryan glory and world

---

[83] Atmaprana, *Sister Nivedita*, 17, 100, 200.

[84] See Purani, *The Life of Sri Aurobindo*, 80; Sarkar, *Modern India*, 146. Although Vivekananda himself spoke of Muslims as forming part of the Indian national nexus, as did Nivedita, the terms of his expansionist nationalism have since been appropriated by Hindu fundamentalism. In Aurobindo's early 1900s writing the influence of Bankim, too, produced a marked anti-Muslim tendency. Even though he later took care to attribute splits between Hindus and Muslims to colonization, his virulent speeches against 'alien' forces based on metaphors of infection and disease, suggest a still-obsessive concern with Hindu purity. See *Speeches*, 44–7, 49, 52, 55.

superiority.[85] 'Aggressive Hinduism', she also urged in the eponymous pamphlet, should work to 'convert others' to the synthesis of religion and politics on an (eventually) worldwide scale (even if with the proviso of reciprocal infiltration, whereby India should at the same time absorb the modernity, civic ideals, and individualism of the West) (*AH* 495; *Master*, 230–1).

As also in cases of postcolonial nativism later in the twentieth century, such as negritude, early anti-colonial resistance, as here, produced what was effectively an opposite but corresponding reaction to colonial stereotyping. The denigration of Bengalis as weak, effeminate, and conquerable, evoked amongst nationalists the desire to prove themselves equally capable of conquest, or of a reverse colonization, though on a plane significantly not mastered by the colonizer, the soul, the inner self. The development of inner, and innate, strengths, more than an injunction to violent retaliation, certainly forms the central message of Nivedita's synoptic 'last will and testament', *Aggressive Hinduism* (CW iii, p. xii). The first imperative, she wrote here, with one eye on the international dimension of Vivekananda's thought, was to realize one's own nationality, to assert one's own character and particularity against, but also in relationship with, foreign influences: 'Only the tree that is firm in its own soil can offer us a perfect crown of leaf and blossom . . . cosmonationality consists in *holding the local idea in the world idea* [her emphasis]' (*AH*, 495, 499–500).[86] Or, as she wrote in the *Modern Review* in 1907, demonstrating her own assumed nativism by predicating national strength on the development of local 'dreams':

The elements abound, in our history, our literature, our traditions, and our customs, by which we can make of ourselves a strong and coherent people. It needs only that we understand our own purpose, and the method of its accomplishment. As the artist builds to a plan, so is a nation fashioned by its own dreams. (*CW* iv. 209)

Political dreamers both, Nivedita and Aurobindo were however concerned to give their nationalism a resolutely practical application,

---

[85] Bagchee, *Sister Nivedita*, 79. On the 'great web' of Aryan civilization, see also *Web*, 5, 19, 134, 208, 210. *Studies from an Eastern Home*, too, is centrally informed by ideas of how the ancient, regenerative heartland of Aryan culture was based in India.

[86] In his at the time highly influential work *Imperialism* (London: James Nisbet and Co., 1902), J. A. Hobson, like Nivedita influenced by the thought of Ruskin, discussed in particular what he called aggressive imperialism. Was Nivedita offering with this parallelism of phrases a symbolic riposte to imperial capitalism (as well as an echo of her Master's phraseology)?

to 'generalize' the idea of independence in India.[87] In this they were positively encouraged by Swadeshi action during the Bengal Resistance. To intercalate their words on the subject: even if in practice their ideals were rarely articulated beyond the confines of the *bhadralok*, both did aim in theory to appeal to 'the great areas of moral force' in the country; to 'bring in the mass of the people'; to 'nationalize and vocalize' the women and the peasants (*CW* iv. 273–4).[88] It was indeed because the people should 'awaken' to a national awareness, that in 1905 passive resistance recommended itself to Aurobindo for its potential to educate the masses politically (*Doctrine*, 26–31, 51; *Speeches*, 54). Nivedita, too, as we know, had been in search of some synthesis of religious principle with a broad-based political activism when she broke away from the Ramakrishna Mission. It was in day-to-day work, she emphasized, in the practical application of principle, that a nation might realize its character or soul—that is, its 'union of the inner and the outer', of belief and action, which Aurobindo again preached in 1909 in the *Karmayogin*, and which they both believed Vivekananda had himself taught (*AH* 492–3; *Karmayogin*, 10).[89]

Whether she was writing on caste or on women's lives, on image worship or the Calcutta dusk, Nivedita's concern was constantly to uncover where and how the elements of Indian nationality lay embedded in everyday life, or developed out of the distinctive circumstances of *place* (a term to which she gave particular emphasis) (*CW* iv. 265). As also did Aurobindo, in for example *The Brain of India* (1909/1921), Nivedita saw the subcontinent as forming an organic cultural and a sacred geographical unity—a 'living reality' again—in which each region (and caste) made its necessary and special contribution to the whole ('The Principle of Nationality', *CW* iv. 286–7). Significantly, in order in some sense to concretize this unity, and to disseminate their message as widely as possible, the two nationalists' extensive lecture tours around India (collectively taking in Bombay, Pune, Madras, Nasik, Nagpur, Baroda itself) in fact actively mapped that space to which they at the same time sought to give a national voice. It was a symbolic mapping of cohesion and integrity which any

[87] Aurobindo, *On Himself*, 26.

[88] See also Aurobindo, 'Introduction to the Speeches and Writings of Tilak', *Bankim–Tilak–Dayananda* (1918; Pondicherry: Sri Aurobindo Ashram, 1955), pp. i–iii.

[89] See also Nivedita, 'Work' and 'Realization through Work', in *Religion and Dharma*, *CW* iii. 449–51.

number of postcolonial nationalist leaders since have also performed. Both moreover, as we saw, laid hold of Kali's elements of blood and fire, literally so, in that they adopted these interconnected aspects of the goddess's avatar as rallying emblems for their cause. Nivedita designed a flag bearing Kali's thunderbolt emblem, the *vajra*, which was exhibited at Congress in 1906 (*CW* iv. 166–70, 295–7). Aurobindo insistently invoked the *Gita*'s Arjuna standing exhausted but self-justified on the blood-soaked battlefield of Kurukshetra.

Perhaps the foremost signifier of their practical commitment was this adoption of the *Kshatriya* or warrior ethic of the *Gita*, which signified for both not only the achieved synthesis of religion and politics, but also the *means* to achieve that synthesis. In his arguments for the political morality of boycott, for instance, Aurobindo forcefully propounded the selfless warrior's motto: 'Fight and overthrow thy opponents' (*Karmayogin*, 15–16). Nivedita corroborated this in *The Web of Indian Life*: 'the true seer is he who carries his vision into action, regardless of the consequences to himself, this is the doctrine of the *Gita* repeated again and again' (pp. 234–7; *AH* 494). As Aurobindo would have agreed, it was therefore essential, she enjoined her readers, for India to '*Kshatriy-ize* [emphasis in text]' itself, to dedicate itself wholly and courageously to energetic but 'motiveless' action (*CW* iv. 89, 104–5).

The emphasis on a warlike energy is of course closely tied in with Aurobindo and Nivedita's shared preoccupation, as was seen, with Indian manliness, or the lack of it. Like worldwide expansion, 'man-making', Vivekananda's synonym for nation-making, was for the Swami and his followers an overdetermined and overcompensatory response to colonization: its feminization of the oppressed, its identification of physical prowess with cultural superiority. As they saw it, the response to the hyper-masculinity of imperial ideology—with its obverse, the debilitating stereotype of the effeminate babu—must be the relentless inculcation of a countervailing muscularity at all levels of Bengali cultural life.[90]

To overturn colonial demoralization and 'blind collapse', Nivedita and Aurobindo therefore believed, a fight was necessary—a

[90] See Ashis Nandy's *The Intimate Enemy*, his influential psychoanalytic study of this phenomenon in relation to Aurobindo Ghose and others, as well as Mrinalini Sinha, *Colonial Masculinity* (Manchester: Manchester UP, 1995). For a close study of the Swami's cult of manliness, see Parama Roy, *Indian Traffic* (Berkeley and Los Angeles: University of California Press, 1998), 107–19; also Atmaprana, *Sister Nivedita*, 88–9, 200; *Doctrine*, 18–22.

fight demanding a refusal to compromise, a quest for death, and a spurning of ease; in sum, a warrior-like merging with the extremest forms of the nationalist struggle (*AH* 497, 505–7, 510). As they many times repeated, the masculinization of the nation alone could obliterate India's perceived abject weaknesses, including its very real political lethargy. In every aspect of existence Hindu males should overthrow associations of effeminacy; and Hindu women, in compensatory contrast, should become the more quintessentially submissive. The 'one thing wanting is strength', Aurobindo insisted in *Bhawani Mandir*, 'strength physical, strength mental, strength moral, but above all strength spiritual'; 'streams of energy' must replace India's inertia.[91] Nivedita bound this conviction tightly to her understanding of Kali: 'the great glory of [Bengal's] Mother-worship lies in its bestowal of *Manhood* [emphasis in text]', she wrote early on in her time in Calcutta: manhood, consequently, was the 'secret of life' ('Kali, and her Worship', *CW* ii. 419–33). Interestingly, in order thus convincingly to ventriloquize a national voice, Nivedita as before chose in effect to put on hold her own gender identity, speaking rather, if anything, with the transposed masculine authority of the white colonial.[92] In their different ways both she and Aurobindo believed that an aggressive Hindu manhood offered the highest form of homage to the Divine Mother, as well as a way of reviving the traditional martial strengths of the Aryan past.

As almost goes without saying, their aggressive nationalism related closely to the neo-Hinduist commitment to global expansion, for it was in the warlike struggle for supremacy that manhood might be conclusively proven and realized. But the success of passive resistance, too, could be measured by its level of manly strength. So it was not possible, Aurobindo wrote,

---

[91] See Gordon, *Bengal*, 112; Purani, *The Life of Sri Aurobindo*, 78, 80; Singh, *Prophet of Indian Nationalism*, 97.

[92] On Vivekananda's interpellation of Nivedita as a white woman, not as a Hindu, see Roy, *Indian Traffic*, 107 ff. Nivedita and Aurobindo's conception of the relationship of nationalist to nation evidently conformed to the time-tried template of the loyal son honouring the Motherland, as has been manifested in other, especially conflicted, national contexts also, such as that of Ireland. As this paradigm significantly lacked accommodation for the role of the warlike daughter, Nivedita evidently allowed her identity as a woman to be subsumed by her nationalism. See, for example: Elleke Boehmer, 'Stories of Women and Mothers', in Susheila Nasta (ed.), *Motherlands: Black Women's Writing* (London: Women's Press, 1991), 3–23; David Cairns and Shaun Richards, *Writing Ireland* (Manchester: Manchester UP, 1988); C. L. Innes, *Woman and Nation in Irish Literature and Society 1880–1935* (Brighton: Harvester Wheatsheaf, 1993). See also n. 37 above.

to build up a strong and great nation unless [passive resistance were] masculine, bold and ardent in its spirit and ready at any moment and at the slightest notice to supplement itself with active resistance. We do not want to develop a nation of *women* who know only how to suffer and not how to strike [emphasis added]. (*Doctrine*, 65)

In making this association of the nation with virile strength, and of manliness with resistance, he again demonstrates the interconnectedness of his political thinking with Nivedita. To both of them *dharma* equated with aggressive nationalism, which in turn equated with the *Gita* warrior's devotion to Kali and enactment of a national destiny, which once again signified *dharma*. 'Today', Nivedita cried, assuming the strident tones of the most ardent of male nationalists in an essay significantly entitled 'The Call to Nationality', '[Kali] would that we play before Her with the Sword' (*CW* iv. 294–6; also pp. 272–5).

This imperative to make oneself into a warrior, in contradistinction to the condition of colonized secondariness, produces in the prose of both nationalist writers emblems of self-assertion which have since become commonplaces in liberation theory and postcolonial criticism, even if they are now somewhat differently articulated. These emblems, which could be seen as the metonyms of resistance writing, include first and foremost the despised condition of colonial mimicry, of the wearing of borrowed rags, coupled with the idea that only a process of resistance struggle and national self-making can overturn this condition. As Nivedita has it in *Aggressive Hinduism*, 'India cannot afford to imitate foreign institutions' (*AH* 503). For several generations the condition of the Indian mind has been passive, 'walking as in a dream, without manhood'. Therefore the fight now must be the 'Indianizing of India, the organizing of our national thought, the laying out of our line of march, all this is to be done by us, not by others on our behalf'. This struggle, as later nationalists too have recognized, demands the re-creation of history 'in living terms', 'humanized, emotionalized', 're-connected with *place* [emphasis in text]'. A new literature in the vernacular must be written 'to voice the past, translate the present, forecast the future'; an authentic art must be reborn that is not 'the miserable travesty of would-be Europeanism that we at present know'. Above all, as Aurobindo, too, urged, the ancient must be clothed in new forms, suited to the new age. 'Not only to utter India to the world, but also to voice India to herself—this is the mission of art . . . Our national life is become perforce a national assault' (*AH* 501–4).

For some years around 1905, however, that national assault was in Bengal's case to be expressed in the first instance as self-help combined with self-defence, that is, as passive resistance. Aurobindo's *The Doctrine of Passive Resistance*, based on the 1907 series of articles for *Bande Mataram*, is probably his most succinct and eloquent exposition of this theory. To match the closer look at *Aggressive Hinduism* in the previous paragraph, we will briefly turn to this text with an eye once again to its exemplification of some of the symptomatic features of nationalist resistance writing. On the strength of these, indeed, the *Doctrine*'s different phases of struggle (and Aurobindo's blurring of the lines between them), bear interesting comparison not so much with Gandhian ideas of counter-modernity and non-cooperation, as with Frantz Fanon's conception of the three stages of anti-colonial protest, as outlined in 'Concerning Violence' and 'The Pitfalls of National Consciousness' in *The Wretched of the Earth* (1961).[93]

The objectives of passive resistance Aurobindo summarized in what became one of the chief mantras of his journalism: Swadeshi, Boycott, National Education, Arbitration (the four resolutions of the 1906 Calcutta Congress), and in the further motto, 'No control, no cooperation'. Practically, the policy began with self-development, its positive pole, but its most immediately powerful line of attack lay in boycott, 'the organized refusal to do anything to help' the British exploitation of the country (*Doctrine*, 35–6). These goals were therefore primary and interdependent. Self-help was the fostering of the local, in the form of national schooling, swadeshi industries, and village work (comparable with Tagore's concept of 'own force', *atmasakti*). It rested fairly and squarely, as Nivedita too emphasized, on the injunction 'Ourselves. Ourselves. Always ourselves': that is, on the development of inner strength (on which basis it very evidently bears comparison with Sinn Féin) (*CW* v. 96, 179; *CW* iv. 272–5). As in *The Web of Indian Life*: 'Only what Indian people can make Indian persons ought to use' (p. 91). The second goal, non-cooperation through mass mobilization, included administrative and social boycott, and, as a last resort, the obstruction of unjust laws. It was through these means that Swadeshi resistance was to be expanded beyond the economic sphere into an instrument of full-scale opposition to British rule.[94]

---

[93] Frantz Fanon, *The Wretched of the Earth*, trans. Constance Farrington (1961; Harmondsworth: Penguin, 1986), 27–84, 119–65. See also Gordon, *Bengal*, 120.

[94] For further corroboration of these different stages by B. C. Pal, another fellow

However, if these linked approaches failed, if the colonial state's retaliatory repression exceeded the 'limits imposed ... by the demands of self-respect and the militant spirit of true manhood', the oppressed, Aurobindo reasoned, were justified in having recourse to a third front, of active resistance or open revolt to 'vindicate their manhood': 'In a subject nationality, to win liberty for one's country is the first duty of all, by whatever means, at whatever sacrifice; and this duty must override all other considerations' (*Doctrine*, 65–7). Kali, as Nivedita too entreated, should if necessary flail the British with her sword.

And yet, though they existed in close agreement at the level of political commitment, as they did in pooling their symbols and strategies of resistance, differences in emphasis (as opposed to marked differences in conviction) did nonetheless arise between Aurobindo and Nivedita. These lay especially in the area of active politics or practical resistance. To obtain the fullest picture possible of their interdiscursivity (which here stands for intertextuality *combined with* practical policy), it is important to draw attention to these differences if only because their relative paucity underlines how close their agreement usually was.

It is probably true to say that in the years 1902–10 Nivedita was comparatively speaking less concerned with the ideologies and modes of resistance to empire than with the exegesis and the fulfilment of *dharma*, or national truth; her main focus was the spiritual and aesthetic side of nationalism, in other words. The distance set by her gender identity coupled with her ineradicable foreignness (as well as a certain strategic circumspection), meant that she remained more of an intellectual commentator on the religious and political thinking behind the national movement, in particular on the Vedanta of her guru Vivekananda, than did her co-activist. When all was said and done, she continued to be more of an outsider than he was.

Otherwise put, for Aurobindo, as his two prominent 1900s series of political reflections *The Doctrine of Passive Resistance* and *The Ideal of the Karmayogin* show, the marriage of political insurrection and religious devotion was always closer, more intimate, more intense, than it could be for Nivedita. If it is possible to draw such

nationalist, see Haridas and Uma Mukherjee, *Bipin Chandra Pal and India's Struggle for Swaraj* (Calcutta: Firma K. L. Mukhopadhyay, 1958); Bipin Chandra Pal, *Swadeshi and Swaraj* (1902–7 articles for *New India*), introd. T. Chakravarti (Calcutta: Yugayatri Prakashak Ltd., 1954).

distinctions at their high level of political commitment, where she might invoke the figure of the Kshatriya, he sought to embody it. This is encapsulated in his interpretation of *dharma* during these years, in which resistance to foreign rule is in almost every case seen as *equivalent to* the worship of the Divine. Relatedly, his other political journalism of the time is more concerned than hers with working definitions of strategy and immediate assessments of developments, all to the end of national self-realization.

If Nivedita's motto therefore could be said to be unlimited service to the nation (whether in the capacity of cultural interpreter or of social worker), his was uncompromising self-sacrifice. So it is indicative rather than paradoxical that he eventually came to interpret nationalist revivalism as leading to spiritual retreat—the pacific expansion of the non-desiring soul beyond political confinements—whereas for her devotion to the nation continued, at least until 1910, to entail practical organization, cultural critique, and quiet, disciplined networking at every available level—cultural, politico-religious, scientific, and in both local and international arenas. While he was more concerned during these later years with the ideological reconciliation of neo-Hinduism and extremist politics, Nivedita concentrated on putting her spiritualized politics into practice (including textual practice) in ways that were at once more externalized and more understated than were his. She justified herself by works; he moved steadily towards a deeper spiritual commitment, as the build-up of devotional prose across the course of both *The Doctrine of Passive Resistance* and *The Ideal of the Karmayogin* suggests.

Obedient to her guru's teachings, Nivedita even in her extremist phase moreover gave special attention to women's education, self-development, and their role in a free India. Vivekananda's ambitions for the Mother, and the calling he had devised for Nivedita, both rested on this particular point: the new manhood and future greatness of India depended on the 'raising' and 'modern education' of its women (*Master*, 359–60; CW ii. 465–7; CW v. 34–6, 221–2). Even if it was often ambivalently expressed in relation to her nationalism, this 'work for women' again distinguishes Nivedita's contribution from that of Aurobindo. His rhetoric symptomatically championed the manly warrior figure of Arjuna or Krishna and that of the fearsome Mother.

That said, however, it was a very traditional image of womanhood which Nivedita chose to uphold, as her aggressive elevation of Hindu masculinity implies. In commenting on Indian women's roles and duties, as she did extensively in *The Web of Indian Life*, *The Master as I Knew Him*, and elsewhere, she had recourse to characteristic Victorian models of an idealized womanhood, models which she had first outlined in her early London essays on women's education ('On Women's Education', *CW* v. 386–411). Her emphasis throughout was on women's service to others, in particular to the family. The success of a free India, she believed, rested on women's—usually mothers'—purity and selflessness within the sanctity of the domestic sphere, and on their ability to inspire in their sons compassion and knowledge.

In writing thus, it is worth reminding ourselves, Nivedita was as ever attempting faithfully to transmit her Bengali mentor's ideas on Indian culture, which simultaneously also meant conforming to Indian nationalist valorizations of the home.[95] The Swami as 'seen' by Nivedita, believed that Indian women should have access to the advantages of modernity in terms of scientific training and a greater individualism, but without losing their traditional spiritual and domestic attributes. Beyond this, the other important factor shaping her thinking was the interrelation of her attitudes to Indian women with her own self-image and role as a self-sacrificing (white) woman dedicated to India's cause. Clearly, in working as she did for national freedom, in subordinating her gender to her nationalism, Nivedita was locked into a never entirely settled contradiction: she was a committed and articulate activist, and a Hinduized Englishwoman, who, while demanding manly self-assertion for Hindu men, also preached self-denial for Hindu women. It was her racial identity therefore which both enabled her to live out this contradiction and made possible her objectifying perspective on Hindu society.

We saw earlier how she mediated this situation spiritually in her self-authenticating surrender to the ambivalent figure of Kali. To draw together her different motivations, another way of understanding her paradoxical position lies in seeing her ventriloquized, almost exaggerated concern with women's submission as at once a rhetorical disguise for her activism, and as its justification. That is, she alchemized her female foreignness by submitting herself wholly,

---

[95] For nationalists' compensatory constructions of the home as haven, see Partha Chatterjee, 'The Nationalist Resolution of the Woman Question', in Kumkum Sangari and Sudesh Vaid (eds.), *Recasting Women* (New Brunswick, NJ: Rutgers UP, 1990); Grewal, *Home and Harem*.

'woman'-like, to India. In the uninterrupted focus in her writing as well as her practical work on service—service in the home and service to the nation—she in a sense resolved the paradox that she herself represented. Having dedicated herself utterly to India, she came to embody two key national archetypes: she was *both* the self-denying national 'soldier in the War of Liberation' bearing 'a flaming sword', as she was commemorated by H. W. Nevinson, *and* she was Tagore's 'great-hearted' Lokmata, a Mother to the Indian people.[96] By promoting and practising selflessness at every level, she effectively rendered any charge of self-contradiction unanswerable.

Aurobindo Ghose and Sister Nivedita met one another at the crossover point between a neo-Hinduist revivalism and the adapted Western modernity which was characteristic of *bhadralok* Calcutta at the turn of the century. Each recognized in the other a 'new seed grown on the ancient soil of India',[97] that combination of local nationalism crossed with 'cosmo-nationality' which in fact constituted Bengali extremism.

If we agree with Partha Chatterjee that nationalism in the Indian subcontinent was expressed both as an imported discourse of nation-statism, and yet one that was inflected through local spiritual and cultural frameworks, then Aurobindo and Nivedita not only contributed to that reinflection, but in a very fundamental way lived it.[98] In the 1890s both carried certain theories and concepts of resistance over to India from Europe. Then, from the perspective of their own spiritualization, which they viewed as nationalization, they translated these concepts into Bengali cultural and historical terms, identifying nationalist politics with Vedantic oneness and Kali-worship. Although in Nivedita's case possibly more than in Aurobindo's, each recreated within their own political experience that fertile contact zone out of which Bengali nationalism was born.[99]

Appropriately, as admirers of Vivekananda, whose ideal it was that the global spread of Hinduism emulate as well as be facilitated

[96] Burman, in Mazumdar (ed.), *Nivedita Commemoration Volume*, 201; Rabindranath Tagore, 'Introduction' to *The Web of Indian Life* (1918 edn.), CW ii. 244–6.

[97] This was in fact Nivedita describing Aurobindo. Quoted in Reymond, *The Dedicated*, 348.

[98] Partha Chatterjee, *Nationalist Thought and the Colonial World* (London: Zed, 1986).

[99] Here it is relevant to remember that, as in 1907–8, Nivedita always retained London as a platform for her journalism and political networking.

by the new global communications system of the British Empire, Nivedita and Aurobindo in effect tapped into the potential of these worldwide networks for intellectual and political circuitry. Assisted by the interconnectedness of the Bengali intelligentsia, they networked both through and with each other in the name of their cause.[100]

Despite their predominant focus on the Hindu soul, it is a noteworthy commonality between them that perhaps the most enduring legacy of the years 1902–10 was their receptiveness to constructive influence from elsewhere, even on occasion their outward-looking cosmopolitanism. At one or other time, but especially in relationship with one other, they themselves acted as proponents of the international cooperation and harmony for which Rabindranath Tagore, too, disillusioned by Swadeshi extremism, became a prominent if controversial spokesman. Even considering Aurobindo's deepening spirituality across the 1900s, and Nivedita's self-identification as a neo-Hindu nun, what both most persuasively demonstrated was that, the forced cultural dependencies of empire aside, traditions and theories could be creatively appropriated from elsewhere (Ireland, Italy, or avant-garde London) to suit local demands for self-representation. Conversely, too, they believed, and acted upon the belief, that India had much to give the world not only in terms of spiritual awareness, but of practical example in the struggle for *swaraj* (significantly, both worked tirelessly as proselytizing journalists, and Nivedita consistently sought publication in the West).[101]

[100] The context of this activity was the post-1850s communications revolution based on the submarine cable and the Suez Canal, which had brought India significantly closer to Europe, as the imperial rail network had the different regions of the subcontinent itself. From his first days in the West Vivekananda had preached the achievement of Indian 'spiritual supremacy' through the medium of England's world dominance, apparently unaware, as were his supporters, of the irony that thus displacing one supremacy involved instating another in its place. 'The days of the steamship, railway and telegraph', opined Aurobindo, had ensured the spread of democratic systems (*Doctrine*, 20). On the national and international usefulness of the new communications networks according to Nivedita, see *Web*, 102–3, 294; *CW* iv. 260.

[101] As if in confirmation of the usefulness of 'cosmo-nationality', one of the consequences of anti-Swadeshi repression was the formation of worldwide networks of support between Bengali and other nationalist activists who had travelled abroad for training, or been forced into exile. The most prominent example of this was Har Dyal's revolutionary Ghadr party which was established in San Francisco in 1913 and had links with American Fenians, especially those surrounding the *Gaelic American*. The worldwide dispersion of Bengal's revolutionaries also helped end the religious parochialism of early extremism. Bose and Ward, 'India's Cause is Ireland's Cause', 58–61; Sarkar, *Modern India*, 124–5, 146; Visram, *Ayahs, Lascars and Princes*, 102–3.

Ultimately, for both Aurobindo and Nivedita, nationalist and cross-nationalist interaction was an art of combination and interabsorption, not a rivalry (see *CW* iv. 221). Their brief partnership itself proved how a Europe–India connection might be made not merely spiritually dynamic but politically useful, productive of policy and self-determining 'lines of march'.

4 'Able to Sing their Songs': Solomon Plaatje's Many-Tongued Nationalism[1]

> All we claim is our just dues; we ask for our political recognition as loyal British subjects.
>
> (Sol T. Plaatje, 'Equal Rights', 1902)

> the bitter blot of South Africa, this continued misrepresentation of the honest intention of the coloured subjects of his Majesty—this demon of misrepresentation and imbecility, which threatens to turn South Africa into a regular sty.
>
> (Sol T. Plaatje, 'Editorial', 1903)[2]

Across a lifetime of relentless campaigning, the South African nationalist Solomon Tshekisho Plaatje (1876–1932) ardently, and at every opportunity, advocated the principle of the equal rights of all his country's citizens before the law—and this some decades before the segregationist laws of apartheid did their worst. A pioneer black journalist, news editor, and writer, a founding member of the South African Native National Congress (SANNC) (later the African National Congress or ANC), a self-conscious prophet of modernity nonetheless fascinated by his own culture's traditions of prophecy and forespelling, Plaatje believed fundamentally in the possibility that a multicultural nation might be founded on South African soil: a nation, that is, based on syncretic relations between its different

---

[1] The words are Mhudi's, where she ends the narrative of her solitary wanderings following the massacre of her people: 'If this solitude had been prolonged for another month, I should have been able to sing [the turtle doves'] songs, and learn[ed] to converse with them'. Solomon T. Plaatje, *Mhudi*, ed. Stephen Gray, introd. Tim Couzens (1930; London: William Heinemann, 1989), 48. Page references will be incorporated in the text along with the title *Mhudi*.

[2] Sol T. Plaatje, 'Equal Rights, *Bechuana Gazette*, 13 September, 1903', and 'Editorial, *Bechuana Gazette*, 10 January 1903', in *Sol Plaatje: Selected Writings*, ed. Brian Willan (Johannesburg: Witwatersrand UP, 1996), 64 and 66 respectively. Page references to this important selection will henceforth be incorporated in the text along with the abbreviation *SW*.

racial or 'colour' groups, in which all would be free to meet and to express their opinions. At a time when emergent nationalist movements elsewhere were claiming self-determination in the interests of cultural or racial purity, as we have to an extent seen, Plaatje, though not always unambiguously, spoke compellingly of mutual harmony, integration, and cooperation between cultures. He was praised after his death for having been a patriotic channel of 'natural feelings' between black and white communities, in a manner not unrelated to 1910s commemorations of Sister Nivedita (*SW* 312).[3]

Solomon Plaatje's multicultural ideals were, significantly, voiced in several tongues, and embodied in vividly multi-generic ways. He was himself a linguist and translator of note, who worked proficiently within and between eight or nine African and European languages. Few national leaders of his time were either as versatile linguistically or used their heteroglossic eloquence across as wide a range of different media, fluently adjusting the forms of their address to match different audiences, as is demonstrated in his *Selected Writings*. Not only a campaigning journalist and nationalist politician, he was also a war diarist and a novelist (notably of *Mhudi*, 1930), a prolific letter-writer, vigorous speech-maker and pamphleteer, and a translator of Shakespeare and collector of Tswana proverbs. Besides all this he was also the author of one of the most important works of African protest to have been published before the time of political decolonization, *Native Life in South Africa* (1916).[4]

Perhaps more than any other political and literary figure discussed in this book, not excluding Nivedita, Plaatje was thus *literally*, almost *quintessentially*, interdiscursive, where, we remember, interdiscursivity refers to the interaction between literary *and* cultural

---

[3] On Plaatje as the prescient advocate of a South Africanism held in common by all the nation's citizens, see: Tim Couzens, 'The Dark Side of the World', *English Studies in Africa*, 14.2 (1971), and 'Sol T. Plaatje and the First South African Epic', *English in Africa*, 14.2 (1987), 41–65; J. M. Phelps, 'Sol Plaatje's *Mhudi* and Democratic Government', *English Studies in Africa*, 36.1 (1993), 47–53. Couzens's 'Editor's View', in Plaatje, *Mhudi* (Cape Town: Francolin Press, 1996), 188, explicitly hails Plaatje as the first author to consider 'the idea of what constitutes South Africanness'.

[4] Solomon T. Plaatje, *Native Life in South Africa*, 2nd edn., introd. Brian Willan, foreword Bessie Head (1916; Johannesburg: Ravan Press, 1995). Page references will be incorporated in the text along with the abbreviation *NLSA*. Throughout this chapter I will where appropriate follow Plaatje's precedent in referring to South African black people as 'Native'. This is in part also as a shorthand to distinguish this group from other non-white groups, such as Indians, who like Africans protested against racial discrimination in South Africa at this time.

discourses including orature and oral resources.[5] Adept in and working between oral and written traditions, Plaatje cited Tswana phrases while writing in a formal and somewhat stylized Victorian English (as in *Mhudi*), and embedded Shakespeare alongside Bunyan, Ruskin alongside the bible. In *Native Life in South Africa*, for example, he interleaves the perceptions of the African American writer W. E. B. Du Bois in *The Souls of Black Folk* (1903) with Boer prophecy, the troop song 'Tipperary', and quotations—as it were textual 'cuttings'—from English-language newspaper reports (*NLSA* 19, 20, 316–86).[6]

Native Life in South Africa, which is probably the pre-eminent testimonial of his political achievement, also most consistently showcases Plaatje's multitextured, tessellated style. Written as a record of the SANNC deputation to London in 1914 to lodge a protest with the British imperial government against discriminatory South African land legislation—offered indeed as a part of that protest—the book demonstrates its writer's protean self-interpellations as a representative of 'his' people. Within its pages Plaatje builds his argument against the discriminatory Natives' Land Act of 1913—this 'most barbarous legislation'—through an accretion of eye-witness reports of native suffering, case studies of white 'disloyalty', and official quotations placed in ironic or critical juxtaposition with one another.[7] Avoiding at almost every point openly oppositional demands or threats, the case is made instead by way of a symptomatically quiet but insistent and at times bitingly caustic reiteration addressed

[5] Ato Quayson, *Strategic Transformations in Nigerian Writing* (Oxford: James Currey, 1997), 15–17.

[6] The 'Tipperary' refrain, repeated across the over 100 pages of the book's discussion of the Boer War, is each time iconically translated 'into some of the languages which are spoken by the white and black inhabitants of South Africa' including 'Hindustani'. On Plaatje's mixed style, see, for example, Tim Couzens, introduction to *Mhudi* (1989), and his 'Sol Plaatje's *Mhudi*', *Journal of Commonwealth Literature*, 8.1 (1973). W. E. B. Du Bois, author of *The Souls of Black Folk* (London: Archibald Constable, 1905), is present in the pages of *NLSA*, as elsewhere in Plaatje, not only in the plea, both stated and implicit, that black be treated the same as white, but in his choice of phrase, of 'coloured', for instance, to signify both African and Cape Coloured. In *Mhudi* he uses 'folks' for people (p. 47). Du Bois's lifelong campaign against coloured 'double consciousness' sought 'to make it possible for a man to be both a Negro and an American' (*The Souls of Black Folk*, 4).

[7] See Sol Plaatje, 'Address to Pan-African Congress, Paris, 1921', *SW* 265. The Natives' Land Act, which was designed as a segregationist solution to the 'native problem', prohibited Africans from acquiring land anywhere other than in the areas of occupation set aside for them, less than 10% of the South African land mass. The Act transformed the majority of South African people overnight into landless squatters on 'white' land. See *Sol Plaatje: Selected Writings*, 123–6, and Brian Willan's biography, *Sol Plaatje: South African Nationalist 1876–1932* (London: Heinemann, 1984), 159–65.

at the British public, but with its own audience of 'Native South Africans' always in mind. Whereas, unlike their rival nationalists the Boers, Plaatje urges, South African blacks have consistently demonstrated imperial loyalty and political moderation, they have, again unlike the Boers, met only with bondage and injustice from Britain.

But if Plaatje's multiple, interwoven linguistic and literary resources lie prominently on the surface of his writing, his ideological determinations and political affiliations are perhaps less readily enumerated, his influences less easily prised apart. Though his beliefs were evidently broadly liberal and moderate, the main question confronted in this chapter is whether his political models and motivating contexts bear interdiscursive traces comparable to those of his writing style. Within the petit-bourgeois class of mission-educated, self-consciously 'civilized' Africans which he inhabited, Plaatje like his peers of course aimed for African self-realization, though not necessarily on a par with whites.[8] At least until the disillusionment he suffered after 1919, these aims rested on a fundamental belief in the non-racial inheritance of nineteenth-century Cape liberalism 'which knew no distinction of colour for all were free to qualify for the exercise of electoral rights' (NLSA 188). He also regarded himself as a British subject and a participant in Britain's traditions of cultural humanism, especially as these were embodied in the 'nobility' and humanity of Shakespeare (SW 210–12).[9] From the time of the First World War, his vision was expanded into an ideal of brotherhood between nations united within a framework of empire.

And yet Plaatje's writing is sometimes ambiguous as to which (other than Britain) he might have regarded as brother or sister nations. Relatedly, it is unclear whether and to what extent, despite his multicultural interests, he embraced political or cultural ideas emerging from outside the authoritative traditions of the West. As an

[8] See Tim Couzens, *The New African: A Study of the Life and Work of H. I. E. Dhlomo* (Johannesburg: Ravan Press, 1985), his detailed portrait of Dhlomo as an exemplary member of the 'aristocracy' of non-tribalist, progressive, mission-educated Africans in relation to whom Plaatje played something of the role of an elder brother. In a 1902 *Bechuana Gazette* editorial on equal rights Plaatje wrote: 'we ask for our political recognition as loyal British subjects' but 'do not hanker after social equality with whites' (SW 61–4). Given that it contradicts his ideal of intermingling, this disavowal may however have formed part of a strategy to disarm the opposition by telling it what it wanted to hear.

[9] On Plaatje's relation to Shakespeare, and the differing interpretations of that relation, see David Johnson's chapter 'The Colonial Subject and Shakespeare: 1916', in his *Shakespeare and South Africa* (Oxford: Clarendon Press, 1996), 74–110. See also Stephen Gray's influential 'Plaatje's Shakespeare', *English in Africa*, 4.1 (1977), 1–6.

always 'ambivalently positioned' colonial subject, as postcolonial critics like Benita Parry and Gayatri Spivak remind us, a subject situated at an intersection point between different ideological formations, were there not other determinants at work in Plaatje's self-construction?[10] Within his conception of world fraternity, could it be the case that some nations were seen as superior to others? Certainly America as he represents it would seem at certain points to hold an egalitarian candle to Britain, as suggested by his 'Americanist' protest both in *Native Life in South Africa* and in his journalism at African people's taxation without representation in the Union (*NLSA* 125, 216–17, 255–6, 425). As to his professed 'English' principles of universal humanism, it is interesting to observe how often these constituted not so much a credo as a rhetoric of protest. Though he professed such principles with unquestionable conviction, their citation in *Native Life*, alongside the repeated demonstration of their betrayal by Britain, develops into a strategy of oblique denunciation of the empire's abandonment of his people, a subtle deconstruction of imperialism's inconsistencies.

Plaatje not only read but travelled widely to put his case for South Africa's voteless majority (twice to Europe, and once to Canada and the United States). He therefore came into potentially formative contact with left-wing and radical figures abroad, including certain prominent South African suffragettes in London and Garveyites in New York. He was moreover respectful of and influenced by the feminism of his Cape compatriot Olive Schreiner.[11] My enquiry would therefore be as to whether or not their languages of self-determination noticeably impinged on the work of this interdiscursive stylist. Alternatively—and it is a strong alternative—could he have been as fundamentally moulded by traditions closer to home, his Rolong (in more traditional terminology, Barolong[12]) inheritance, for instance,

---

[10] Benita Parry, 'Some Problems in Current Theories of Colonial Discourse', *Oxford Literary Review*, 9 (1987), 26–58; Gayatri Spivak, *In Other Worlds* (London: Routledge, 1987), 197–221.

[11] Schreiner's *Trooper Peter of Mashonaland* (London: T. Fisher Unwin, 1897), bears interesting comparison with Plaatje's work not only for its mosaic of literary and propagandistic registers, but for its endorsement, even if oblique, of black female solidarity, and cross-national humanism. During the Anglo-Boer War Schreiner's ethical humanism, differently from that of Plaatje, drew her into taking up the Boers' cause as an oppressed people. See also Olive Schreiner, *Thoughts on South Africa* (London: T. Fisher Unwin, 1923).

[12] Unless quoting Plaatje, I follow contemporary South African naming conventions: Rolong for Barolong, Sotho for Basuto, Tswana for Bechuana.

or certain regional articulations, such as his position at the ideological faultline between mid-Victorian liberalism and its later trans-
mogrification into the 'forward' capitalist imperialism espoused by
Cecil John Rhodes? When in 1921 the—by Plaatje—much admired
W. E. B. Du Bois read Plaatje's Address to the Pan-African Congress
in Paris, which outlined South African 'black folks'' 'appalling
difficulties', did this exhibition of unity form part of a quest for a
broad pan-Africanist identification, and for an alternative Pan-
African 'League of Nations' based on deeply cherished African
loyalties? Or, my speculation continues, was Plaatje still seeking
'partnership', to quote his own word, in the late Queen Victoria's
'world empire', an equal share of the justice promised, he believed,
by British imperialism? (SW 264–74)

Plaatje wrote at a time when, as we have been seeing, small Euro-
pean-educated elites in colonized territories were living out the
difficult political paradox of claiming self-representation for constituencies from which they were themselves largely alienated. Even
if temporarily, they tended therefore to find a greater ideological or
imaginative commonality with emergent nationalist groups in other
contexts (as Bengal did in Ireland). Plaatje was a core member of one
of these elites in a country where the people he claimed to speak for
were if anything doubly colonized when compared to those in India,
both by Britain's imperial government and by the forces of white
nationalism at home. Relative to this situation, which remained
throughout his lifetime intractable, this chapter will explore the ways
in which Plaatje tapped the cross-border dialogues potentially available to his group in the process of mediating empire's contradictory
assertions. I will consider whether, and how, an interdiscursivity
might have informed not only his literary expression but his nationalist and/or pan-nationalist politics. To what extent might he have
manipulated the ideological and cultural dissonances of the imperial
narrative of European superiority in order to introduce alternative—
dissenting and decentred—nationalist perspectives?[13]

By presenting a critical portrait of his many political involvements, and of the numerous, sometimes overlapping, sometimes

---

[13] For an excellent critical reading of Plaatje's 'multilayered and radically decentred national narrative', see Laura Chrisman, *Rereading the Imperial Romance: British Imperialism and South African Resistance in Haggard, Schreiner, and Plaatje* (Oxford: Oxford UP,
2000), especially 15–19, 163–208. Chrisman draws attention to the multiple mediations of
Plaatje's nationalist script: his was not simply a 'hybrid', 'transculturated', or 'derivative'
nationalism.

widely differing, influences to which he responded, this chapter will also look at the traces of cross-nationalism, or at least of the awareness of its possibilities, that would seem from the evidence of its many-voicedness to lie in Plaatje's work. It will end by asking whether the burden of dealing with the rival (and highly exclusive) nationalism of the Boers to an extent inhibited his dialogue with nationalist groups located in cultural contexts different from his own, apart from African America. Another striking instance of local nationalism which could have suggested creative possibilities of cross-reference, yet to which he rarely openly referred, was that of the Indian movement of passive resistance elaborated by Gandhi, which made its mark on South African political life during the 1900s and 1910s (the time when Plaatje, too, was politically active). The study will explore why, from Plaatje's progressive but non-radical point of view, local Indian nationalism did not however appear to offer even the potential of an interdiscursive, cross-national bridge with India, another oppressed region of the British Empire; it will consider why, therefore, he may instead have sought nationalist siblings somewhat further from home.

A BAROLONG, A GENTLEMAN: AN EXEMPLARY CAREER

Till very recently Plaatje criticism, intent on making its case for his status as a 'Shakespearian' African, tended to overlook the complex fact of his political engagement.[14] As has already become apparent however, Sol Plaatje was throughout his career intensely political, not only as an activist and spokesman for African rights, but as a writer. As well as his lifetime's opposition to the 'ruinous' and 'dishonourable' Natives' Land Act (SW 151–2), he was energetically concerned with and discussed in print a wide range of other issues relating to the rights of African people and their equal treatment before the law: discrimination on the railways and by pass laws; the status of traditional chiefs; the position of women in both traditional and modern contexts; and, especially later in life, the retrieval of the history of his Tswana-speaking people, and the championing of their

---

[14] For their critiques of these 1970s and 1980s approaches, see David Johnson, 'Literature for the Rainbow Nation: The Case of Sol Plaatje's *Mhudi*', *Journal of Literary Studies*, 10.3/4 (1994), 345–58, and his *Shakespeare and South Africa*, especially pp. 101–4; David Schalkwyk, 'Portrait and Proxy: Representing Plaatje and Plaatje Represented', *Scrutiny2*, 4.2 (1999), 14–29.

languages and oratures. Seeking to the end of his days peaceful integration between the races of South Africa, he also negotiated between a remarkable number of different political constituencies (most notably, his own petit-bourgeois class of self-styled African 'gentlemen'; the Rolong people in general; liberal-minded Britons; and the so-called white 'Friends of the Native' in the Cape).[15]

On a public platform Plaatje epitomized the Victorian liberal. Several times he sought to ally himself (rarely with any success) with the 'large-hearted' De Beers mining authorities in Kimberley against the 'black Bolsheviks of Johannesburg' (SW 155, 237–8). Yet a spirit of recalcitrance is nonetheless detectable stirring beneath the surface even of his early writing.[16] It is sharply expressed as a mode or an approach in the dogged determination of his repeated human rights complaints, as well as in the biting sarcasm of his later journalism, its oblique unpicking of the colonial state's promises. His political articulations can therefore be said to be doubly and even multiply inflected; not only bifurcated in loyalty (to Britain and to his own people), but often openly contradictory, ambivalent, and restlessly shifting in allegiance.

Homi K. Bhabha has influentially described how the civilizing mission produced among colonially educated natives the highly disruptive and inevitably 'flawed' condition of colonial mimesis. 'Despite their intentions and invocations', the colonial mimic (the self-consciously civilized black person or 'parodist of history') 'inscribe[s] the colonial text erratically, eccentrically across a body politic that refuses to be representative, in a narrative that refuses to be representational'.[17] In his political dealings with whites, as in his reasoned arguments for the 'backward' black needing the 'scientific' white, Plaatje was on one level clearly such an ill-adjusted parodist. However he was at the same time often knowing and self-conscious in his mimicry, strategically directing it to the situation in hand. (He repeatedly, for example, lambasted the 1913 Land Act using the loaded colonial term 'barbaric'.) Although in one dimension 'assimilated', according to Frantz Fanon's definition—or 'trained to the fixed idea of English superiority' in Aurobindo Ghose's words—it is

15 Schalkwyk, 'Portrait and Proxy', 15.
16 On native recalcitrance as located outside more established narratives of protest, see David Lloyd, *Anomalous States: Irish Writing and the Post-colonial Moment* (Dublin: The Lilliput Press, 1993).
17 Homi K. Bhabha, *The Location of Culture* (London: Routledge, 1995), 86–8.

crucial to acknowledge that he was at the same time an extremely astute player of the mimic role.[18] He admired English speech, literature, dress, civil habits, liberal traditions, and commitment to the rule of law—we must take this as heartfelt—yet he also showed an increasing awareness of the extent to which this admiration, this deference, was compromising, limiting his most concerted protests to wearyingly ironic reiteration.

Plaatje therefore was caught up in all the contradictory *agon* of being 'civilized' and articulate by Western standards, but from a colonial point of view never quite adequately so because of his Africanness.[19] As in *Native Life in South Africa*, however, he cunningly used his close, seemingly imitative knowledge of the West to expose in unsettling ways its hypocrisies. He spoke to the class and cultural prejudices of his chosen audience, liberal British and Cape citizens; he appealed to an imperial tradition of universal humanism from which his own people were separated; but he remained throughout mindful of a wider audience, the Natives, whose rights and interests impelled him to speak out in the first place. In his later writings, indicatively, the much-respected 'Friends of the Native' to whom he frequently appealed (analogous to Aurobindo's much-mocked 'friends of India'), modified into 'so-called white "experts"' on native affairs.[20]

It would provide a clearer picture of Plaatje's interdiscursive complexity were we now to examine in more detail his divergent political and cultural interests as these were manifested in the course of his early life and in his career as a journalist and nationalist politician. In particular, this section would want to uncover the ways in which his 'civilized' performance departed from the 'point by point' assimilatedness of the toadying native intellectual described by Fanon, to become something far more canny, opportunistic, and willy handto-mouth. As part of this attention to his buried ambivalence and

[18] Frantz Fanon, *The Wretched of the Earth*, trans. Constance Farrington (1961; Harmondsworth: Penguin, 1986), 119–42; Aurobindo Ghose, *The Doctrine of Passive Resistance* (Calcutta: Arya Publishing House, 1948).

[19] As a striking instance of his self-contradictoriness, Plaatje the social integrationist demonstrated a noticeable ambivalence about racial mixing and its 'inauguration' of 'half-castes'. See *SW* 74, 64; 'Along the Colour Line', *SW* 163–72; 'The Mote and the Beam', *SW* 274–83; *Mhudi*, 27, 175.

[20] On 'Friends of the Native', see Stanley Trapido, ' "The Friends of the Native": Merchants, Peasants, and the Political and Ideological Structure of Liberalism in the Cape, 1854–1910', in Shula Marks and Anthony Atmore (eds.), *Economy and Society in Preindustrial South Africa* (London: Longman, 1980), 247–74.

recalcitrance, the discussion would also want to lay accent on the always judicious cross-regional and -national interconnections which shaped virtually all of his dealings—the negotiations of conflicting meanings, the solicitations, liaisings and placations, the ceaseless making of contacts and forging of ties. The portrait of Plaatje which emerges from this study should therefore begin to represent him in the light of a forerunner, a harbinger of the 'internationalism' or transnational networking which, in the critic Rob Nixon's description, has distinguished late twentieth-century South African culture in particular.[21]

Born in the north of the country he would always mockingly designate using scare quotes, the Orange 'Free' State, Plaatje characterized his family background as pastoral yet culturally mixed, almost cosmopolitan. His people, Tswana-speaking Rolong, a significant proportion of whom had been Christianized for some generations, lived in close association with not only Methodist missionaries and the German Berlin Mission Society in settlements like Philippolis, Bethanie, and Pniel, but also with the mixed-race Griqua people who governed their own independent state in the area at this time.

The hybridity of these diverse cultural influences is captured in the Dutch-seeming surname Plaatje, meaning 'the flat one'. Acquired by the family otherwise known as the Mogodis in the 1840s or 1850s, the name was reputedly first bequeathed as a nickname by a Griqua farmer-landlord. It thus aptly captured the cultural eclecticism and multilingualism, if not also the ventriloquism, the dangerous imitativeness, which was to mark the Rolong people's relationship with South African society in general, and that of their ambitious son and spokesman in particular. As his biographer Brian Willan writes, what distinguished Plaatje's upbringing from that of many of his contemporaries was the 'synthesis' of African and Christian traditions which his family had managed to achieve across a mere four generations of cultural contact with whites.[22]

As observed, Plaatje is usually regarded as a representative member of that early community of mission-educated, proto-nationalist Africans of which the somewhat older John Tengo Jabavu or Plaatje's contemporary John Dube also formed a part. It certainly is

---

[21] See Rob Nixon, *Homelands, Harlem and Hollywood* (London: Routledge, 1994).
[22] Willan, *Sol Plaatje*, 26.

true that on arriving in Kimberley in 1894 to take up his first paid job as a post-office messenger, he found among the mining town's multi-ethnic community of like-minded, similarly taught Africans a ready communality of cultural experience based on the shared values of Christian individualism, hard work, and self-improvement. Knowingly defining themselves as 'British subjects', indeed as black 'Britons' in Plaatje's phrase (*SW* 65–6), the members of this community—and Plaatje foremost amongst them—supported so-called non-racial Cape liberalism and the imperial mission of enlightened cultural upliftment. They were therefore to be distinguished, they believed, from 'raw' Natives (*SW* 155, for Plaatje's use of this derogatory term).[23]

It was in Kimberley, therefore, in the racially mixed location of Malay Camp, living amongst interpreters, teachers, clergymen, and messengers like himself, that Plaatje had his first formative encounter with class-based, cross-cultural social relations, and, in consequence, with the implications of what being broadly 'South African' rather than specifically 'Native' or African might be.[24] In 1898, as if to affirm or applaud such 'cross-border' alliances, Plaatje married in disregard of tribal differences (his wife Elizabeth M'Belle was of Mfengu or Hlubi background and the English 'language which Shakespeare wrote' was their primary vehicle of communication) (*SW* 210–12).

Yet, whilst Plaatje's ties with Kimberley's mission-educated community are to a great extent correctly attributed, it is important to remember that he was, relative to many of his peers, to a significant degree self-educated (the Pniel Berlin Mission school had simply not offered the higher standards of education available elsewhere) (*SW* 101, 270). Many of the languages in which he was fluent were therefore acquired or perfected in interaction with the different communities of Kimberley. We can also assume that much of his reading of Shakespeare, Ruskin, and the British Liberals which would make such a deep impression on his outlook and his prose, took place after he left school (*SW* 210–12).[25]

[23] In criticizing the practice of polygamy, Plaatje was also quite prepared to call his people an 'inferior race' (*SW* 97). In early articles in the *Bechuana Gazette* he even expressed a certain jingoist pride at belonging to this 'most British of towns', Mafeking (*SW* 68). To an extent, however, this vocabulary may again represent a self-consciously ingratiating imitation of colonial labels.

[24] Willan, *Sol Plaatje*, 28–39.

[25] He later translated at least four of Shakespeare's plays into Tswana including *The*

When in 1898 Plaatje was appointed as a clerk and court interpreter in the northern Cape Colony town of Mafeking, that motif of
intercultural liaising which attached to his Kimberley years—of
literally carrying messages between groups—was both confirmed
and amplified. By the following year the name of Mafeking was to be
stamped into the world map by the history of its Boer War siege (11
October 1899–17 May 1900), a collective ordeal which focused both
Plaatje's aptitude for networking, and, significantly, his British patriotism. In a way diametrically opposed to the solidarity that Irish nationalists were feeling for their fellow (white) nationalists the Boers,
the youthful Plaatje interpreted the war, and Mafeking's part in it, as
a defence of the Cape/imperial principles he held so dear.[26] His job,
in which he had ample opportunity to demonstrate his multilingual
abilities (SW 50–61), also made of him a vital intermediary in another capacity, essentially that of spy, in that he worked to transmit
military orders and intelligence between the Rolong *stadt*, the 'Native runners' who crossed the Boer lines, and the British siege authorities headed by Colonel Robert Baden-Powell.[27]

By the end of the war, as British rule was painfully established
across all four of the South African settler states, Plaatje increasingly
sought to turn his position as a double interpreter or mouthpiece
both for African rights and British interests into something more
official. The opportunity was afforded him by the establishment of
the bilingual *Koranta ea Becoana*, or *Bechuana Gazette* (1901–8,
fitfully from 1905), of which he became editor in 1902. From now on
until 1915 he would work more or less consistently as a shaper of
African opinion: as the editor from 1910 to 1912 of *Tsala ea Becoana*
(*Bechuana Friend*), and from 1912 to 1915 of *Tsala ea Batho* (*Friend
of the People*), though in an absentee capacity from 1914. From 1910
he also wrote for the *Diamond Fields Advertiser* (usually under the
emblematic title, 'Through Native Eyes'), the *Pretoria News*, and, in

Comedy of Errors or Diphosho-phosho, the only play published in his lifetime, and the
first translation of Shakespeare into any African language.

[26] See Sol. T. Plaatje, *Mafeking Diary: A Black Man's View of a White Man's War*, ed.
John Comaroff, Brian Willan, and Andrew Reed (1973: London: James Currey, 1990), especially pp. 29, 80–2, 66, 78, 82, 103, for his expressions of disgruntlement at Boer advances, and frustration at the declaration that this was to be a 'white man's war'.

[27] The Reuters representative Vere Stent later remembered him, significantly, as an in-
valuable 'liaison officer'. See Willan, *Sol Plaatje*, 83, 85. For a fictional account of Plaatje's
military intelligence work during the siege which highlights its more compromising aspects, see Andries W. Oliphant, 'The Interpreter', in Elleke Boehmer (ed.), *South African
War? 1899–1902, Kunapipi*, 21.3 (1999), 1–12.

England, for the *African World*, becoming through these various channels an important part of the short-lived heyday of the African 'spokesman'—the political leader and/or journalist. This select group, which included Jabavu and Dube, saw it as their responsibility to mould and modernize African opinion, but also to impress strenuously upon the authorities the educated African's right to self-representation. The *Koranta*, for example, was explicitly dedicated to the 'amelioration' of the Native through Labour, Sobriety, Thrift, and Education. Yet Plaatje as its editor at the same time promoted African self-representation with 'respectful' but plain-spoken editorials such as 'Equal Rights' (in which he protested at the gender bias of the Cape franchise), and 'What are Equal Rights?' (that, as the title suggests, begins to crystallize his tactic of reiterative petitioning).

The contradictions of Plaatje's 'educated' position are neatly captured in the attribution of his editorial call for 'Equal rights' (for, as he said, 'every civilized man south of the Zambezi') to the imperialist Cecil John Rhodes, towards whom he clearly felt some respect (*SW* 70–1). That overdetermined Janus ability to face in at least two if not several directions at once (that is, speaking for black rights while referencing Rhodes) is reflected in the content as well as the modes of address of his journalism. It is also present in the fact that, by using different languages even within the covers of one issue of his newspaper, he explicitly addressed different audiences and tiers within southern African society.

Like other campaigning newspapers in other nationalist contexts, as we saw in the case of the *United Irishman*, the *Bechuana Gazette* included alongside its original articles a mosaic of extracts from local and international papers deemed to be of interest to its audience.[28] Again this demonstrated the educational and cultural eclecticism of its elite nationalist audience, as well as their interest in cross-border analogies. It may have been through this pell-mell juxtaposition of different points of reference, as we will see, that one of the templates for Plaatje's later collage style was laid down, that is, the mix of vocabularies and registers in both *Mhudi* and *Native Life in South Africa*.[29] Then again, considering the imaginative fervour with which he opposed the segregation of races, it is possible to read

[28] Willan, *Sol Plaatje*, 110. See also the mélange of languages, typefaces, and snippets of news in the facsimile of the first issue of the *Koranta*, *SW* 62–3.
[29] On stylistic hybridity in Plaatje, see also Elleke Boehmer, *Colonial and Postcolonial Literature: Migrant Metaphors* (Oxford: Oxford UP, 1995), 102–3.

into the diversity of cultural and national sources from which he quotes, a dramatization-in-text of racial 'inseparability'. The journalism verbally demonstrates that mélange of Boer, Rolong, Basuto, Briton, and so on, that it itself advocates. 'Inseparability' is also to the fore, in part by default, in Plaatje's keynote, prize-winning essay of 18 January 1911, 'Segregation: Idea ridiculed' (*SW* 140–3), which argues that the white needs black labour and black taxes, and the black needs a guiding hand to help the educated rule the more traditional. Or again: 'The white race can no more do without the black, and the black without the white, than the right hand can do without the left' (*SW* 77).

With the 1910 formation of the Union of South Africa, Plaatje's public role became if anything more energetically interactive. His overriding aim was to maintain 'the open door' and 'amiable relations', as he put it, between the races of the newly formed state on the basis of their equality before the (Cape) law (*SW* 82, 86–7). But despite his hopes for the extension of Cape liberalism under the 'one umbrella' of the Union (*SW* 139), in fact a very different policy began steadily to imprint itself upon government affairs: territorial segregation 'on Free State terms' (*SW* 139, 149). This growing injustice Plaatje took it as his objective to censure at almost every opportunity.

All the same, until into the 1920s, Plaatje remained confident that the softly-softly approach of reasoned but persistent petitioning on constitutional grounds (as in a one-to-one lobbying of 'Friends'), would make an impression on white opinion, even to the extent of influencing the shape of new legislation. Holding to his belief in the effectiveness of cross-community, indeed cross-national, dialogue, he continued to talk across the emerging colour bar in defiance of the new constraints. It is especially in this area of determined non-combativeness before an uncompromising state authority that his approach bears some comparison with Gandhi's. I shall return to this parallel later in the chapter.

It was Plaatje's belief that, whereas segregation was difficult to administer equitably, integration demanded no more than that the white man give the African 'the franchise, and your confidence'. How then, he pondered, could the white with all his cultural and educational advantages ('the mastery over nature of the white man's science', the 'magical force' of Christianity) fear the black, even to the extent of seeking to segregate the population (*SW* 140–3, 409–10)? His faith in the eventual triumph of a so-called 'British' reasonableness rested on what seemed a particularly powerful claim, namely, black 'loyalty to the Throne' which had been conclusively tried and tested in the Boer War (SW 74).[30] Plaatje's strong sense was that this loyalty, especially as compared with Afrikaner 'disloyalty', deserved to win recognition from Britain. Native Life in South Africa is informed throughout by the principle of deserving loyalty, but it is also repeatedly invoked in his journalism. In 1903, for instance, he sternly condemned 'this bitter blot of South Africa', the Boer disregard for African war compensation claims despite the 'fealty' demonstrated by 'the coloured subjects of His Majesty' (SW 65–6).[31]

Ten years on, as the First World War engulfed the empire, Plaatje's protestations regarding black loyalty, especially as offset by the 'overbearing' behaviour of the Boers, had not diminished in force. Much of the polemic delivered in the second half of Native Life in South Africa is predicated on the (to him) lamentable paradox that the fraternal feelings which Africans had extended to Britain were being met with 'draconian prohibitions' (such as the law against their bearing arms), whereas the openly rebellious Boers ('who refer to the Union Jack as "the rag"') were being endlessly accommodated (NLSA 58, 124, 238, 246, 295–315, 430–5; SW 256–7).[32] Such 'colossal ingratitude' on the part of the colonial state elicited from Plaatje a potentially defiant query. As he said in his Address to the Pan-African Congress: 'we sometimes wonder whether our loyalty has not been the means of our undoing' (SW 273). Had African deference in fact invited only that aggravated repression be visited upon them?

By 1919 the contradiction represented by the continuing ill-treatment of loyal Natives brought Plaatje to the bitterest realization of all, one which he in part unknowingly shared with other oppressed peoples, like Indians and West Africans, elsewhere in the empire. Given their suffering, he felt, Natives would be justified if they concluded that 'the allies [had] lost the great war, in which they [had]

---

[30] See Christopher Saunders, 'African attitudes to Britain and the Empire', in Donal Lowry (ed.), The South African War Reappraised (Manchester: Manchester UP, 2000), 140–9.

[31] Plaatje was particularly scathing on the subject of the shoddy treatment of the Barolong by the Boers, given their long history of coming to their aid: 'If systematic dispossession of a nation's allies amounts to a reward, then, indeed, the Barolong are to be congratulated on their friendship with white men' ('The Case for the Barolongs', SW 321). The same glowering condemnation animates the historical retelling of Mhudi.

[32] He also objected to the poor treatment of Native non-combatants, in particular the South African Native Labour Contingent (SW 228).

participated in the hope that it was waged for the amelioration of the condition of oppressed people'. Very far from such amelioration, Africans now confronted the bitter disillusionment that, justice being neglected, 'a British dominion will be the first to be called to order when the League of Nations meets'.[33]

But it was not solely in relation to war conditions and Native loyalty that Plaatje's protest in these years maintained its underlying, non-conciliatory edge. In January 1912, galvanized by opposition to African exclusion from the Act of Union (and, increasingly, with the new land legislation, from South African soil itself), the SANNC had been formed with Plaatje as its General Secretary.[34] Given that the group's aims were at this stage relatively moderate, emphasizing 'mutual cooperation' with the government, it was through the channel of his journalism however that the full force of Plaatje's shocked protest and vexation at the 'Native Land Plague' emerged. Taking it as one of his chief duties as editor to monitor the Act's effects, he left his audience in no doubt as to his opposition: the new law, he wrote in a 1913 editorial, sought to 'make [Natives] roving wanderers and potential criminals' in the land of their birth, 'exile[s] and helot[s] in the land of [their] ancestors' (SW 151–4, 162, 173, 265). In fact the Act inflicted what was effectively a 'war of extermination' upon aboriginal South Africans. Here, interestingly, Plaatje adopted and repeatedly endorsed (after some initial criticism) a term first used by Dr Abdul Abdurahman, the leader of the predominantly Coloured African People's Organization (of which Plaatje was also a member) (Mhudi, 101; NLSA 81, 125, 152–71, 173, 246).[35] Six years and many editorials and speeches of protest later, he had not changed his tune, noting in his 1919 pamphlet Some of the Legal Disabilities Suffered

---

[33] The quotations are from his 1919 pamphlet, Some of the Legal Disabilities Suffered by the Native Population of South Africa, a magisterial synopsis of his case against the Land Act (SW 250–7). See also NLSA 85–6.

[34] See Francis Meli, South Africa Belongs to Us: A History of the ANC (Harare: Zimbabwe Publishing House, 1988); Peter Walshe, The Rise of African Nationalism in South Africa (Berkeley and Los Angeles: University of California Press, 1971). On the ambiguities of early black nationalist 'quiescence', see Shula Marks, The Ambiguities of Dependence in South Africa (Baltimore: Johns Hopkins UP, 1986). Prior to 1913, other segregationist laws were passed including the Native Labour Registration Act, the Mines and Works Act, and the Dutch Reformed Church Act. In contradistinction to Plaatje's imperial idealism, the Natives' Land Act in fact implemented British imperial policy formulated during the 1902–10 reconstruction period. See also Willan, Sol Plaatje, 155, 160.

[35] Again like Dr Abdurahman, Plaatje frequently made emotive reference to the (blemished) Union Jack as a symbol of Britain's tainted imperial prestige under the Land Act (NLSA 124, 131, 160, 244, 402; SW 61–4).

by the Native Population, that no single law had 'ever created so much misery and distress among the Natives as [had this one]' (*SW* 254).

In protest at this misery Congress resolved in 1914 to take a campaign directly to the imperial government and the British public. Although the Union of South Africa had become a self-governing colony within the empire (reducing to almost nothing the hope of securing an imperial repeal), Plaatje, who headed the deputation, believed that short of strike action all other avenues of appeal had been exhausted: 'what [legal] footing have we got in a country where we cannot even hire or buy a house?', as he said some years later to Lloyd George (*SW* 258–9).

So it was in May 1914, embarking on the *Norseman* in Cape Town, his typewriter and notes for *Native Life in South Africa* in hand, that Plaatje took his negotiation skills and aptitude for message-carrying on to an international stage.[36] Both now, and again in 1919–23 on his second mission to the West, he became probably the first black South African self-consciously to develop transatlantic political ties. From this time on his efforts of propaganda and petitioning, even if organized *on behalf of* South African Natives, would be intentionally carried out before an international audience, *under Western eyes*. So it is iconically appropriate that his most politically influential text, *Native Life in South Africa*, was largely written or 'compiled' on board ship. In this 'mid-ocean' region far distant from the dust of Africa, or of any place else, as he observed, he felt liberated by the racially unmarked zone that was the ship's 'floating island', encircled by unfamiliar stars. Here it was possible not only to write all day long but to sing in chorus with white stewards and enjoy the company of 'colour blind' Australians with an interesting knowledge of Polynesian languages.[37] As Nivedita, too, discovered, and as did Gandhi, his own labile cross-community balancing act was thus briefly embodied in his journeying. It was moreover significantly encouraged by the temporary freedoms which this journeying afforded. (His translations of

[36] Plaatje's description of his sea-voyage, emphasizing his lack of sea-sickness, observations of 'strange stars', and general experience of cultural difference, is recorded in 'Native Congress Mission to England', first published in the *Diamond Fields Advertiser* (14 and 17 June 1914) (*SW* 174–84).

[37] Not that it was always so. South Africa-going ships, whilst occasionally providing havens for cross-cultural networking, could also form microcosms of that segregated society, as Plaatje's second deputation to Britain was to discover on their unfortunate ejection from the *Edinburgh Castle* (*SW* 247–50).

Shakespeare, again an activity of message-bearing between cultures, were also carried out on his long sea-journeys in the decade which followed.[38])

In Britain itself Plaatje's cultural and political balancing act demanded if anything even greater caution than before, being made the more precarious first by the resistance of the Colonial Office to the Africans' campaign against the Union government, and then by the hostility which the deputation encountered from a group which might potentially have become the SANNC's greatest ally, the Anti-Slavery and Aborigines' Protection Society (ASAPS).[39] (It was to this group that Leonard Woolf, too, would appeal not long after on behalf of oppressed Sinhalese.) When, finally, after several setbacks, the outbreak of war in August conclusively sidelined the SANNC campaign, four of the five members of the delegation returned home. Plaatje however stayed on in Britain for several years, believing, as is clear from the second half of *Native Life in South Africa*, that there was yet some mileage to be gained from a solo campaign of impassioned speech-making against the Land Act. (He addressed over 300 meetings in the years 1914–17.)

In the course of this British campaign Plaatje formed, as an alternative to ASAPS cooperation, important ties with suffragettes who themselves had liberal South African connections, including Sophie Colenso, Betty Molteno, Georgiana Solomon, and Alice Werner. Inheritors of the mantle of his admired Olive Schreiner, after whom he had named his daughter, the links these feminist friends provided were important both for his emotional survival in London, and for the development of his political ideas. As *Mhudi*, the novel which he began to write during these London years suggests, these contacts contributed to his developing insight into the mutually reinforcing homologies that existed between gender and race discrimination. From this, as Laura Chrisman observes, he extrapolated a vision of the central place of African women in building a nationalist counter-narrative.[40] Certainly his heroine Mhudi's good-humoured yet sarcastic statements of self-assertion are strongly reminiscent of some

[38] Willan, *Sol Plaatje*, 331. Significantly, all of Plaatje's books were produced abroad. It is therefore telling that both *Mhudi* and *Native Life* are marked by descriptions of 'biting cold' (*Mhudi* 99, 104; *NLSA* 89–90, 403–4).

[39] John Harris, the ASAPS Secretary, gave qualified support to segregation in South Africa, believing this to be a stay against full black dispossession.

[40] Chrisman, *Rereading the Imperial Romance*, 14, 182–6.

of the later Plaatje's civil but barbed comments directed against white prejudice (*Mhudi*, 161).[41]

Almost from the beginning of his time in Britain Plaatje also established close relations with the organization that helpfully arranged many of his speaking engagements there, the interdenominational Brotherhood movement. Plaatje felt drawn to the movement because of its Christian and fraternal approach, as indicated by its name, as well as its aim of building links between peoples on the model of the empire: 'There was a great resemblance between Brotherhood and Empire', he wrote, '[both] were united in one great principle', that of justice (*NLSA* 267). It is not difficult to see that the Brotherhood movement was in this sense the inheritor of the late nineteenth-century concept of a commonwealth of British settler colonies: it allowed Plaatje to foster within its structures those inter-community ideals of social cooperation laid down in his Kimberley days, as well as his predilection for thinking imperially in spite of setbacks, for liaising in spite of, and to minimize, conflict.[42]

Yet alongside his focus on a transnational campaign, Plaatje had not forsaken his commitment to what he called in the Preface to *Mhudi* the task of interpreting ' "the back of the Native mind" '. His concern with Native tradition was kept alive in two other books he worked on and published during this time in England, *Sechuana Proverbs* (1916), a collection of 700 Sechuana sayings with their English equivalents, and a *Sechuana Reader in International Phonetic Orthography* (1916), written with the linguist Daniel Jones. Indeed each one of his texts of the 1910s, his most productive period, reveals the absolute centrality to his sense of identity of Tswana history and traditions. For the nationalist Plaatje the fundamentals of selfhood and belonging were, it seems, thrown into relief, rendered the more poignant and significant, within the international context of London. In the face not so much of the hostile Afrikaner nationalist public back home, but of his sympathetic yet still equivocal imperial audience, it was imperative to him to prove the integrity of the Tswana cultural past and the need for its preservation before the

---

[41] Phawane Mpe, ' "Naturally these stories lost nothing by their retelling": Plaatje's Mediation of Oral History in *Mhudi*', *Current Writing*, 8.1 (1996), 81–2, insightfully comments that Mhudi sets herself up as a critic of imperialism even while breaking traditional stereotypes of feminine behaviour.

[42] In the USA in the early 1920s Plaatje would work hard to raise the money required to establish the organization in South Africa.

incursions of the white 'civilization' he otherwise welcomed. As for Nivedita and Aurobindo a mere decade before this, political nationalism was effectively an empty shell without the accompaniment of cultural pride, of efforts to nurture the customs and languages which were one's own. Simultaneously, however, the work of retrieval was further justified for Plaatje by the universality of the cultural behaviour patterns thus revealed. To him far more than to Nivedita, any given nationalist movement was a particularized manifestation of, and could therefore make appeal to, an underlying common humanity.

Despite the relative success of his one-man campaign of petitioning and pamphleteering during 1914–17, Plaatje would however feel impelled to head another SANNC delegation to Britain in June 1919, a mere two years after his return to South Africa. Like Indian and other colonial nationalists in the immediate post-war period, the SANNC representatives hoped to turn to their advantage the new attention being given to the demands of small nations for constitutional rights. It was time for the protection of 'the weaker races' by the 'great Powers', as Plaatje put it (*NLSA* 298); it was time, as Leonard Woolf, too, would emphasize, for the international arbitration of imperial abuses of power.[43] Such hopes were further sharpened by the over-optimistic sense that the war effort of the empire's non-white peoples might meet with some form of political reward.

The SANNC's hard-won interview with Lloyd George in 1919, however, exposed once again the drawbacks of Plaatje's strategy of individual advocacy and appeal. For, no matter how well-disposed the British Prime Minister might be, as he indeed was, to the small party's urgent rhetoric in favour of basic justice, his hands remained tied by South Africa's self-governing status. It was in consequence of this stalemate that, after some months of lobbying in Britain, Plaatje decided to take his one-man 'agitation scheme', as the South African High Commission called it, to the USA via Canada. He hoped to expand his activity of interlinking with different interest groups (even while still working under the auspices of the Brotherhood movement), and to develop some of the connections he had already formed in London with the African and African American communities attached, for example, to the *African World* and the *African*

---

[43] Sylvia Pankhurst, *The Home Front* (London: Hutchinson and Co., 1932), 322, notes that 1916 events in Ireland were 'but the logical issue of the great war-time propaganda that the small nations should take up the sword against their oppressors'.

Times and Orient Review. In this way he might explore in reality those historical links between Africans and their 'oversea kinsmen' of which he had already written in the opening pages of *Mhudi* (p. 27).

As will be discussed in more detail, Plaatje did indeed discover much in the American context in 1920–1 to bulwark not only his sense of black identity, but his pleas for racial integration, internationalism, and brotherhood. He shared a platform (on two occasions) with Marcus Garvey, leader of the Universal Negro Improvement Association, and the Back to Africa movement,[44] and established political common ground with the more moderate Du Bois of the National Association for the Advancement of Coloured Peoples, as indicated by the latter's willingness to read his Address to the second Pan-African Congress. From now on America would become an abiding source of inspiration to Plaatje—as it would again, in the 1930s and 1950s, to other of his countrymen. Here, he idealistically believed, racial integration could coexist with a specifically black vision of cultural pride and unity; a progressive spirit of 'race-consciousness' could be tied to a bourgeois ethic of self-advancement. Yet America also came to represent considerable personal and political frustration as none of the projects he sought to set up there bore long-lasting fruit, least of all his attempt to raise support for the South African land rights campaign.

As in 1917 so even more markedly in 1923 when he finally returned home, Plaatje found that the political landscape in South Africa had polarized further along racial lines. The various structures on which his journalistic and political career had rested, had as it were crumbled where they stood. The SANNC (now the ANNC), for example, was in many areas virtually moribund, unable to respond to the new radicalism of the growing black working class. However, though still refusing any involvement with radical organizations like the Industrial and Commercial Workers' Union, Plaatje continued to make a role for himself, if necessarily a reduced one, on the side of mediation. In this, against many odds, he stayed true to his 'loyalist' kind, the ageing class of moderate, if not now conservative and marginalized, black political leaders and spokesmen (*SW* 345). His conviction remained that Native opinion must be relayed through its own

[44] Plaatje later critiqued Garvey's 'Africa for the Africans' idea due to its practical impossibility (and, implicitly, its analogy with racial segregationism in South Africa). See *SW* 355.

representatives, even if this was to be via largely ineffectual 'paper' bodies like the Government Native Conference. *Interpersonal* nego-tiation, individual intercession, speaking on behalf of: as articles of the time suggest, these remained the keynotes of his activity. He worked, for instance, to mobilize the tiny African vote on behalf of Jan Smuts's weakening South African Party in the Cape. He spread the word of the Temperance movement (itself a sign of his alienation from black urban lifestyles). Disillusioned by the Native silence in the media, he also contributed journalism putting the African point of view to a number of different newspapers, but remained to the last unable to revive his own defunct and now ironically named *Friend of the People* (*SW* 315–16, 341–3). Time and again, whilst criticizing his own people's political lethargy, he lamented the discriminatory legis-lation which was, parliamentary session by session, striking 'at the root of South African national existence' ('The Colour Bar', *SW* 343–6). It was becoming ever clearer that a 'reasonable' leader such as Plaatje had turned into something of an anachronism in an increas-ingly more racially divided South Africa.

But in spite of his growing isolation and dejection, an important social and cultural role remained to him in his work for the preserva-tion of the Tswana language and oral traditions. In this activity he was able to give concrete expression to a sense of cultural self-worth and the need to withstand the disintegration, as he saw it, of rural African life. It is telling that when he died in June 1932 he was visit-ing Johannesburg in order to see his folk tales into print. His projects in these final years embraced work on a Tswana dictionary and his continuing campaign for an orthography true to the particular lin-guistic features of the Tswana language.[45] He was also involved in collecting praise poems and folk tales, and in his important task of translating Shakespeare and seeking to have these translations pub-lished.

Paradoxically, however, given his campaigns for a united and cross-ethnic South African identity, these new projects committed him to the fairly narrow niche of Tswana self-preservation. After the many years spent developing an international forum for his petitions and polemic, he was effectively now restricting himself to foundational-ist ideas of belonging as defined by attachment to land and to

---

[45] An orthography, in other words, that did not assimilate Tswana to some theoretical Bantu mother-tongue (which white authorities indifferent to the consequent homogeniza-tion of black difference tended to favour).

language, and of both these attachments as the true basis for claims to self-determination. His international involvements, and the many frustrating campaigns dealing with political lack and loss, had eventually reinforced in him, as if by painful contrast, a parochial preoccupation with the fullness of tribal identity. It was in region and locale, he now felt, that the problems of cultural marginalization had to be worked out.

Appropriately laden with prophetic signs, Plaatje's novel *Mhudi*, a fictional account of the central South African wars (*Mfecane*) involving the Ndebele (Matabele) in the nineteenth century, was at last published in 1930 (though completed some ten years earlier). It represented an eloquent and symbolic point of closure to a difficult decade for the writer. Alongside *Native Life in South Africa*, in many ways its non-fictional companion volume, *Mhudi* has since justly become Plaatje's most celebrated work for its thematization and stylistic enactment of some of the key preoccupations of his career.[46] By way of reflecting on the main emphases of this discussion, these might be summarized as: the resistance to imperial oppression; the importance of self-representation as captured in the rewriting of inherited beliefs and traditions; the revival of Rolong oral tradition '[abounding] in allegories and proverbial sayings' (*Mhudi*, 111); and, as in *Native Life*, the centrality of history to an understanding of present political conflict. Through these different, interrelated preoccupations, as Tim Couzens has observed, *Mhudi* builds an epic of successful cultural regeneration,[47] while at the same time, as in Laura Chrisman's reading, offering a counter-history of proto-pannationalist solidarity. Produced during the decade of its author's contact with women's protest both in South Africa and Britain, the novel is moreover interestingly concerned to take account of the power and integrity of women and women's activities, as embodied in its assertive, principled, and often downright rebellious eponymous heroine. Women's political agency, Plaatje appears to insist, is central to the formulation of black nationalism.[48]

[46] Written consecutively though intermittently during the time Plaatje spent travelling to and living in London between 1914 and 1920, both works deal in their different interdiscursive ways with South Africa's bedevilled land rights issue. Couzens, 'The Dark Side of the World', 187–203, for example, reads *Mhudi* as a fictional accompaniment to the bitter indictment of *Native Life in South Africa*.

[47] Couzens, *The New African*, 150.

[48] On Plaatje's 'feminist' ideology in the novel, see Laura Chrisman, *Rereading the Imperial Romance*, 163–86, and her 'Fathering the Black Nation of South Africa: Gender and

Underlying the entire plot of *Mhudi*, both its conflicts and its emblematic 'brotherhoods', is Plaatje's characteristic faith in the universality of human nature, echoed perhaps in the shared (yet dangerously incomprehensible) language of the bees on the battleground of the Matabele's defeat (*Mhudi*, 146). An abiding hope in the possibility of cross-cultural interconnection is also expressed through the use of the English language. This, effectively humanity's language of the bees, is, as a mark of its own particular cross-national diffusions, flavoured throughout with Shakespearian, biblical, and African turns of phrase.[49] The novel does not however spare the reader in its treatment of tribal and interracial conflict, and the betrayal of the basic human harmonies which Plaatje felt potentially linked cultures. The 'tragic friendship' of the Rolong, the Sotho, and the Boers (*SW* 409), places subtle emphasis by contrast on the countervailing black national (even pan-African) loyalty which Mzilikazi the king of the defeated Ndebele implicitly but powerfully invokes. History, *Mhudi* finally points out, dramatizes the close involvement of black and white in the making of a modern South Africa, and hence the travesty represented by the systematic legal creation of a 'white South Africa' (*SW* 344).

The fissures in the novel's text suggest that Plaatje felt tightening round him in the post-war phase of his life the effects of his double marginalization: his vain efforts to secure white support had produced a growing credibility gap dividing him from numbers of his own people. All the same a great deal of his writing of the time continues to contradict that image of a deferential assimilationist which his conciliatory strategies and undramatic conservation work might otherwise support. A spirit of revolt—the indignant 'flame of black humanity' (*SW* 75) which burns in his 1900s and 1910s journalism—flares up again in the 1920s, as when he describes the bitter thanklessness of leadership (*SW* 174, 270–5). In a 1925 article 'The Colour Bar', which commends the small mercy that there remain in the country Europeans willing to 'do well' by Natives, Plaatje at the same time obliquely concedes: 'Natives who have to endure the physical and mental agony of . . . perpetual legislative pin-pricks', may '[lose] all

Generation in Sol Plaatje's *Native Life in South Africa* and *Mhudi*', *Social Dynamics*, 23.2 (Summer 1997), 57–73; also Myrtle Hooper, 'Rewriting History: The "Feminism" of *Mhudi*', *English Studies in Africa*, 35.1 (1992), 68–79.

49 See Gray, 'Plaatje's Shakespeare', 1–6. For quotations from or allusions to Shakespeare, see *NLSA* 48, 82, 110, 136, 147; and for biblical allusions, *NLSA* 84, 95–6, 282.

confidence in the integrity of the white skin' (*SW* 345–6). He can also be far more bitterly direct, as when he repeatedly and openly speaks of white South Africans' unremitting 'colossal ingratitude' to their black compatriots (for example, *SW* 371–2).

That uneasy coexistence of a cunning critical intelligence with a carefully composed 'Native' obedience, was therefore never really absent from Plaatje's work. By way of concluding this section a brief closer look at his most significant text of political testimony and most interdiscursive piece of writing, *Native Life in South Africa*, will shed more light on this coexistence. It is in this book, as we have in part already seen, that Plaatje ties the current war against an expansionist Germany to his case for African rights, on the grounds of the—to him—central principle of African loyalty. The Cape liberal understanding that Africans formed 'a partnership in a world empire in which all men would be equals' ('Address to Pan-African Congress', *SW* 273), explained to Plaatje why historically Africans had generally given the empire their allegiance. Recent developments however, which the book charts, reveal that black South Africans have in fact consistently received meagre thanks for their unswerving constancy. Even while setting himself up as a Cape patriot and imperial loyalist, therefore, Plaatje uses his account of 'Native life in South Africa' to unscroll a dismal record of the dispossession and disarming of black Africans rather than of the openly disloyal Boers. His self-construction vis-à-vis his British audience as a trustworthy Native voice, sharply offsets the chapter-by-chapter exegesis of Britain's tortuous negotiations over Native loyalty and colonial justice, and his own equally tortuous attempts to accommodate these. It is in such painstaking and conscience-paining accommodation that the deep force of Plaatje's withheld yet always palpable critique of colonial government and its values lies.

Yet his anatomization of the contradictions of colonial 'justice' can also produce more direct, swingeing criticisms, even if these are more often than not quickly passed over. For example, in the conclusion to the chapter 'The European War', in which the involvement of black soldiers in East Africa is held up as a foil to South African colour prejudice concerning enlistment, Plaatje comments:

The naughty white piccaninnies who always insult inoffensive black passersby would be taught [by African enlistment] that the native is a useful neighbour whose strong right arm may be depended upon in times of trouble, instead of being taught . . . that every man Jack of them is a black peril monster who must not only be discriminated against, but who must be in-discriminately insulted and repressed. (*NLSA* 313–14)

He then breaks off and closes with a quotation from the *Daily Chronicle* commending a charge by the King's African Rifles in East Africa, as well as the good 'behaviour' of the Jind Infantry of Indian troops. His point therefore has been made, not only with the inter-splicing of social commentary and illustrative article, but with the finely judged contrastive rhetoric of the commentary itself: the subversive adaptation embedded in the phrase 'naughty white pic-caninnies'; the play of 'discriminated' and 'indiscriminately'; the colloquial contrast of 'every man Jack' set against the stereotyped 'black peril monster'. The black South African, the reader cannot fail to realize, is treated with unconscionable hypocrisy. Elsewhere, as in Plaatje's description of his fact-finding missions to record the impact of the Land Act (chapters 4 and 5), these effects of smouldering irony coupled with rapid-fire rhetoric and telling allusion are equally strik-ing: 'if this systematic ill treatment of natives by colonists is to be the guiding principle of Europe's scramble for Africa, slavery is our only alternative' (*NLSA* 84). Or again, from the concluding lines of the book:

grapple with this dark blot on the Imperial emblem, the South African anomaly that compromises the justice of British rule and seems almost to belie the beauty, the sublimity, and the sincerity of Christianity. (*NLSA* 404)

The vertiginous oppositions of such prose ('this dark blot', 'the beauty, the sublimity'), its double-edged indictment that remains deferential, establish important correlatives for Plaatje's multiply-inflected work amongst the different ethnicities of South Africa.

A 'HAMMER MADE OF TEMPERED METAL': NATIONALISM
AND THE TRANSATLANTIC 'PEOPLE'S FRIEND'[50]

In both *Native Life in South Africa* and *Mhudi*, as we have seen, Plaatje prominently crosses and intercuts different political and aes-thetic discourses in order both to accommodate his diverse audi-ences, and to mediate his at times conflicting political agendas. It is as well to remind ourselves of this characteristic multi-strandedness as we move into this final section examining the different cultural and

[50] *Mhudi*, 113; *SW* 99–100.

political determinations exerted upon Plaatje the indignant concilia-
tionist. The reminder is important because we are in this domain of
influence (of its take-up and its anxieties) once again confronted
with a deep-seated ambivalence in the writer. Plaatje seems at the
last, in the late 1910s and 1920s, to have chosen not to go the distance
of translating his cross-national interests into the forging of *actual*
cross-border or cross-ethnic links and collaborations *within* South
Africa. As part of our enquiry into his interdiscursive political make-
up, this section will ask why, in spite of the pan-nationalist ideals of
Mhudi, and his acute awareness of Coloured and Indian rights
predicaments, he did not eventually take this step.

That said, the resonant polyphonic textures of his writing do suggest a commitment to intercultural receptiveness.[51] Indeed, by way of
beginning this exploration of his informing contexts, we might note
how Plaatje's writing instances an interesting synchronicity with
other literary experimentation of the period. The mosaic of political
quotation, literary allusion, and oral device that distinguishes both
Native Life (1916) and *Mhudi* (1920/1930) is in many ways reminiscent of the multivoiced bricolage and promiscuous citation which
also characterizes such definitive modernist texts as *The Waste Land*
(1922), *Ulysses* (1922), or *Mrs Dalloway* (1925).

It hardly needs saying of course that an apparent similitude of verbal effects can camouflage highly divergent cultural viewpoints. Yet
this particular close parallel between contemporary texts all marked
by a degree of multivoiced allusiveness is suggestive. For one, it underlines Plaatje's unembarrassed excess of cross-cultural references.
Then again, it would be extremely unlikely had his cross-border interests not been heightened by the many-cultured London of the 1910s,
that milieu which also informed Eliot and Woolf's writing. True, the
layered verbal collage that in Plaatje was the function of a mission
education combined with a powerful oral heritage, in the modernist
works stands for a far more self-conscious shoring up of the fragments of a civilization against the devastation of a war-wracked
world. The effects that in the hands of a T. S. Eliot, say, connote an
American exile's driven search for a lost cultural order in the West, in
Plaatje's case represent the attempt to reconcile a still living African
tradition with colonial modernity. His perspective is comparatively
speaking located far further out on the cultural fringe of the West.

---

[51] See Chrisman, *Rereading the Imperial Romance*, 171–3.

And yet the coincidences of time and place do tempt some plotting of deeper connections. It is compelling for instance to read symbolic significance into the serendipitous crossing of the paths of Plaatje and the Hogarth Press in Tavistock Square in the 1920s. He lived at number 43 in the latter half of 1920 (and perhaps briefly on his return from America in early 1923); in early 1924, admittedly some time later, Leonard and Virginia Woolf moved into number 52.[52] These were also the years when London was starting to witness important encounters between African and African American radicals and cultural nationalists (such as Plaatje's friend the West African lawyer F. Fredericks, or the Caribbean and Harlem Renaissance writer Claude McKay), who met within the tightly connected black expatriate world clustered around the *African Times and Orient Review*, as well as the socialist suffragette Sylvia Pankhurst's *Worker's Dreadnought*. Not long before, Theosophical and Ethical Society circles had begun to encourage contact between figures like W. B. Yeats, William Rothenstein, Arthur Symons, and Bernard Shaw, and Indian intellectuals, writers, and students living in or in transit through London. As we can tell from his membership of the predominantly Coloured or mixed-race African People's Organization (APO) back home, the multilingual Plaatje would have revelled in such an international and cosmopolitan milieu. It is even possible to imagine him delighting in the extent to which his two major works, both written in London, bore the echoes of the different cultural traditions with which he had come into contact in the course of his travels.

Yet that lack of fit as far as Plaatje and the Woolfs' respective dates in Tavistock Square are concerned, provides a salutary warning against positing causal connections between Plaatje's polyphonic style, and, for instance, the 'different voices' of *The Waste Land* (first published by the Hogarth Press). The cut-and-paste effects of *Native Life in South Africa*, or the multiple voices and narrative perspectives of *Mhudi*, do admittedly match a metropolitan world increasingly shaped by diverse colonial presences and pressures, a world in which Plaatje felt empowered to claim new cross-cultural brotherhoods. (In his last year in London, fascinatingly, he performed in a pageant as an African chief along with a 'Miss Guptu'.) But any more direct influence whether through London's little magazines, or the activist

<hr />

[52] Willan, *Sol Plaatje*, 253; Hermione Lee, *Virginia Woolf* (London: Chatto and Windus, 1996), 473.

circles he frequented, remains without further supporting evidence
highly unlikely.

All the same, as for Nivedita in the 1890s, the cosmopolitan London of the 1910s and 1920s in which elites from different colonial
contexts were able to mingle and exchange opinions in clubs, salons,
and debating halls—in effect to experience different forms of cultural and political self-representation—would inevitably have had
an impact both on Plaatje's outlook and his forms of expression. (It
certainly did on a white colonial such as Katherine Mansfield.) This
impact can be read into that shift across *Native Life in South Africa*
where verbal deference (the apparently untiring citation of authoritative texts, including the Union Hansard), gradually, by force of
accumulation, gives way to rhetorical impersonation, a calculated
and witheringly critical ventriloquism. As in his description of the
crowds flowing down Oxford Street, Plaatje, somewhat like T. S.
Eliot, was clearly both excited and enervated by the vision of the vast
'gamut of personalities and nationalities' of 'both sexes and all
colours' of the great city (*NLSA* 297–8). Imperial London, he recognized, created a climate in which cross-national relationships could
develop; in which, consequently, a self-conscious cross-cultural allusiveness might become either a disorienting noise or a mode of verbal
resistance to cultural and racial exclusivity and discrimination.
Chapter 5 will investigate further how the hubbub of empire as it
impinged on London helped shape the onset both of forms of multivoiced modernism, and, arguably, of certain modernistically inflected, cross-border nationalisms.

Apart from the solidarity he sought with fellow imperial citizens
in London, which was realized to an extent within the Brotherhood
movement, the other significant international fraternity to which
Plaatje aspired was (ironically perhaps) located outside the confines
of the British Empire, in the United States, specifically in its African
American community. It was a fraternity founded on the personal relationships with various political leaders, activists, and educationalists (W. E. B. Du Bois, Marcus Garvey, James Weldon Johnson, R. R.
Moton, amongst others), which Plaatje was able to build during his
1920–2 North American tour. As he observed, the source of his
feeling-in-common with his US 'kinsmen' lay not so much in their
African origins as such, as in a parallel history of race-based oppression—in Vereeniging and Mafeking as in Virginia and Mississippi
(*Mhudi*, 27). From the South African point of view, brotherhood

with African America was advised moreover by the inspiriting example of its history of emancipation from slavery, and, for Plaatje in particular, by the self-betterment and social freedoms which the society had since achieved.[53]

By way of sketching in the informing context to such feelings of affinity, it is worth noting that black South African connections with African America had been established as far back as the 1880s through, for example, the American Board missions, and, a rather different influence, the anti-white Ethiopianism of the American-origin Methodist Episcopal Church (from which Plaatje largely dissociated himself) (SW 93). Later interaction came in the form of bodies such as the Joint Councils (established in 1921), which encouraged interracial contact and discussion, and the Bantu Men's Social Centre (1924). There were also the important links made by prominent scholars and educationalists, such as John Dube or the West African-origin J. E. K. Aggrey.

Yet Plaatje, who was by the 1920s an established political voice, may not have experienced these as formative influences. In his case the initial cross-national contact with African America came in two striking forms: that of the 'Negro' Jubilee singers who toured the country in the 1890s, whom he twice saw perform in Kimberley, and later again in London; and, in the area of journalism, his early collaboration with the South African Spectator editor F. Z. S. Peregrino, a West African who arrived in the country via the United States, and helped him form a Native Press Association in the early 1910s. It is possible to speculate that both influences impinged on his intertextual exercises in the Bechuana Gazette, a paper which took as its pan-nationalist motto the words from the Song of Solomon, 'I am black but comely' (SW 64). As was seen, early issues of the Gazette made it a practice to juxtapose local reports with stories gleaned in particular from US papers, giving pre-eminent place, for example, to articles about Booker T. Washington.

Rob Nixon has described in Homelands, Harlem and Hollywood, his study of the Harlem effect on Sophiatown in the 1950s, how from the 1930s an 'imaginative common ground' developed out of the historical affinities shared between cultural elites in African America

[53] A strong supporter of capitalistic self-advancement, Plaatje was aware, even if marginally so, of some of the contradictions of South African capitalist development: apartheid and racial division, for example, could both help and hinder effective industrialization (see SW 155, 270).

and black South Africa.[54] Despite his early impressions of interconnection, that common ground for Plaatje however still existed chiefly as an area of potential and of wishful thinking, if compellingly so. As in his Address to the 1921 Pan-African Congress, he believed that the formation of a closer international cooperation, in effect a formal brotherhood, of African-origin peoples, might address the 'appalling' legal and political difficulties faced by South African and other Natives. This alternative (pan-African rather than white-dominated) League of Nations would make possible mutual counsel and support between Africans—support that would moreover be on their own terms (*SW* 264).[55] *Mhudi*, too, which was completed not long before the 1921 Address, presents a case for a pan-African—again racially defined—nationalist or indeed cross-nationalist solidarity. This is figured in the friendship of the two powerful women Mhudi and Umnandi: even if transitory, their togetherness represents an achievable union of different black African peoples.[56]

African America therefore came to represent to Plaatje a race-based solidarity primarily. Yet early on it had also signified a racially integrative interculturalism, that ideal of a mobile and expansive black identity which South Africa's race-tagged laws increasingly tended to disallow, yet which he regarded as having been theoretically achievable within the terms of Cape liberalism.[57] When all was said and done it was in this, the Cape tradition of a 'colour blind' franchise and equal rights, that the major formative influence on his political make-up probably lay. His initial interest in intercultural cooperation had grown, by his own admission, from the 'peaceful' and 'civilized' grounds of 'the old Cape Colony of our boyhood days' (*NLSA* 188). Indeed his justified sense that the Natives' Land Act directly threatened the Cape's property-based franchise, formed one of the main planks of his opposition to the racially marked Act.

---

[54] Nixon, *Homelands, Harlem and Hollywood*, 13.

[55] Plaatje commented bitterly in 1929 that the one lesson black Africans might learn from Boer politics was about the success that might be achieved through unanimity and 'co-operation' (*SW* 371–3).

[56] On Plaatje's pan-Africanism and the influence on him of Du Bois and Booker T. Washington, see Anthony Chennells, 'Plotting South African History: Narrative in Sol Plaatje's *Mhudi*', *English in Africa*, 24.1 (1997), 37–58; and Chrisman, *Rereading the Imperial Romance*, 187–208. Chrisman offers a finely calibrated case for the affirmation of black solidarity in *Mhudi* based on Mhudi's plea for the unity of 'kind' (*Mhudi*, 167). She interestingly does not comment however on the hysterical references to the fear of 'miscegenation' in Mzilikazi's nation-building speech (*Mhudi*, 175).

[57] Nixon, *Homelands, Harlem and Hollywood*, 4.

If we confine our attention to the surfaces of his writing, much of Plaatje's respect for imperial rule and the British constitutional system was redolent of the bare-headed colonial deference of his generation and class. On more than one occasion he spoke in positive terms of the benefits of the 'modern scramble for Africa' (medicine, the capitalist work ethic, and 'the magical force' of Christianity for forging reconciliation between warring tribes) (SW 82, 83–4, 101, 338, 409–10, 413). Yet the almost obsessive reiteration of his admiration for 'Britain's love of justice and fair play' could serve as something of a two-pronged moral weapon, as will already have become evident (SW 257). Applied with Plaatje's deadly rhetorical timing, the reiterations were turned into a strategy that disarmed at the same time as it reassured the opposition with its fair-mindedness, as is again exemplified in the text of his interview with Lloyd George (SW 257–64).

It was the case however that the Cape's colonial government *had* at one stage in fact represented an important alternative to the segregationist thinking that was gaining such a powerful hold in the new Union. Cape law, Plaatje wrote in 1908–9, fully cognizant of the urgency of his pronouncement, 'guarantees protection to the man with a black skin as much as it does to the man with a white skin': it gave some measure of political recognition to blacks, even though it denied them equal access to power (SW 53–4, 64–5). Yet, although relatively enlightened as regarded race, what the law did not do was allow women a political voice, as the liberal Plaatje was well aware (it was after all intended for 'every civilized *man* south of the Zambezi'). Although worth preserving, therefore, it also left considerable room for reform—reform which he felt inhered to the very principle of equality before the law.

Under the Union Jack every person is his neighbour's equal . . . race or colour is no bar, and we hope, in the near future, to be able to record that one's sex will no longer debar her from exercizing a privilege hitherto enjoyed by the sterner sex only. (SW 64)

That surprising insertion of the non-generic pronoun, idiosyncratic for its time, gives a clear signal of Plaatje's anachronistically far-sighted feminism.

Somewhat paradoxically founded on his critical commitment to British justice and fair play, Plaatje's belief in equal rights for women owed much to his admiration for Olive Schreiner as well as to the later friendships he formed with South Africa-linked feminists in London.[58] His criticism of the racialized sexual double standard in his country, for instance, bears comparison with British suffragist and suffragette campaigns against prostitution (SW 274–83). As in the case of Mohandas Gandhi, Plaatje's contact with the 'votes for women' movement moreover reaffirmed his commitment to determined but non-violent resistance, as well as more generally emphasizing the form-giving usefulness of cross-border political link-ups.[59] Equally important in shaping his attitudes to women's issues however were the more local examples of female outspokenness provided by some traditional African cultures, as reflected in Mhudi, and, importantly, by contemporary African women's protests, such as the Free State anti-pass campaign of 1913 (NLSA 111–13). After his 1920–2 trip, African American women, too, offered a model of progressive community action, as Plaatje recognized in an admiring letter from America to a feminist friend (SW 287–8). Multiply-determined therefore, Plaatje's feminism (broadly interpreted) forms a significant and independent constituent of his political thinking. To an extent indeed he deconstructed one of the central tenets of his liberalism—the equal rights claim—on the basis of his interlocking women-centred and nationalist (Africanist) perspectives.

By way of a retrospective comment at this point, it is possible to say that, at least until the 1920s, Plaatje's repeated recourse to the moderate discourse of the Cape amounted in almost every case (in his practical politics as in his theoretical feminism) to a strategy of conciliation. And yet, whichever way one looks at it, this conciliation can be seen as double-edged, at once genuinely appeasing yet calculated, opportunistic. A related doubleness runs through other of his allegiances, as is demonstrated by his split nationalist identification: his association, on the one hand, with the ideal of a multicultural, supra-tribal South Africa, a middle-class democracy based on co-operation between the races (ideally expanded by the addition of women's suffrage); and, on the other, with ethnic (Rolong and Tswana) self-protection, which in turn ties in with his segregationist pan-Africanism (of which Mzilikazi in Mhudi is the chief

[58] On his circumspection as regards Schreiner's views on African womanhood, see Chrisman, Rereading the Imperial Romance, 178–9.

[59] Maud Ellman suggests in The Hunger Artists (Cambridge, Mass.: Harvard UP, 1993), 11–12, that post-1916 Irish nationalist hunger strikers, too, owed much to the example of the suffragettes.

spokesman). In certain contexts he deployed the terms of democratic liberalism as a vehicle through which to promote, very specifically, the liberalism as he saw it of his own Rolong/Tswana traditions ('The case for the Barolongs', *SW* 320–3). The conservation of a 'tribal' heritage also centrally informed many of his 1920s political campaigns.[60] Emblematically, 'Barolong' substitutes in *Mhudi* for 'Native'.

At times therefore Plaatje's universalist language of free expression is used to defend a commitment to the particular and the regional. At several points, both in his journalism and pamphleteering, and in the Thaba Nchu trial scenes in *Mhudi* (pp. 104–13, 121–4), he makes it clear that 'British' justice and respect for the individual are as fully embodied in the African system of political organization as in the highly praised British constitution. Indeed, for Plaatje, the heroic stature of Rolong and Sotho chiefs like Moroka, Montsioa, and Khama, in fact highlighted by contrast the questionable claims of European civilization to ethical and political superiority.[61] Arguably, therefore, in Tswana tradition, in his own enlightened ethnocentrism, lay another important (if somewhat paradoxical) determinant both of Plaatje's liberal ideology and of his live-and-let-live multiculturalism.

As cross-national alliances with which Plaatje identified, both pan-Africanist political organizations and the British women's suffrage movement of course lay far from home. Considerably more proximate as a model for a resistance politics, as well as for cross-ethnic, -religious, and -linguistic cooperation, was South Africa's Indian Congress (formed in 1894) which, like Plaatje's Congress, appealed to principles of universal humanism and imperial citizenship. As has already become apparent from his membership of the predominantly Coloured African People's Organization, Plaatje believed that common experiences of discrimination on the part of non-white South Africans formed potentially strong bonds of 'sympathy and cooperation' which it was important to foster (*SW* 167–8). In his moving 1913 talk to the APO 'Along the colour line', he seems symptomatically to want to denote both Africans and mixed-race people with the term 'coloured'. Himself a self-conscious beneficiary of Kimberley's out-of-the-ordinary multiculturalism, Plaatje twice

---

[60] Willan, *Sol Plaatje*, ch. 14.
[61] Schalkwyk, 'Portrait and Proxy', 16. See also Plaatje's articles on Chiefs Moroka and Montsioa which he wrote for the 1931 *African Yearly Register* (*SW* 406–19).

arranged for meetings between the APO and the (S)ANNC at the critical junctures of March 1912 and 1927: the latter was a response to the introduction of the Native Administration Bill and involved 'Indian organizations' (SW 233, 358). At both meetings united action was recommended as being in the best interests of all South African peoples. At the same time, however, very tellingly, Plaatje in 1912 urged Coloured people to stick together in their organization, the APO, just as Congress members should in their own.

Even if he never overtly made the link, there is no doubt that Plaatje was aware that a politically effective non-white alliance might have extended to South Africa's diasporic Indians. In his *Selected Writings* there are at least fifteen references to India or Indians, and in *Native Life* around twelve, especially as regards the 'Asiatic' political position both in South Africa and the empire. Although many of these references point up differences between Native and Indian conditions, especially concerning their differential access to justice and opportunities for enlistment, they at the same time draw potentially constructive comparative links. Plaatje, it is clear, kept an eye on Indian cultural and political developments that related to Native interests, commenting in his journalism and letters, for example, on the high-grade selection of court interpreters in India, the exemplary 1906 election of Sir Mancherjee Bhownaggree as a British MP ('the *best* person' for the job [emphasis in text]), and the way in which 'Indian papers printed in Durban' in 1917 were monitoring local injustices (SW 60, 100, 226).

Such references suggest a tacit recognition on Plaatje's part not only of commonalities between the different non-white experiences of discrimination and protest, but also, I would suggest, of the lessons which might accrue to Africans from South African Indians' slightly antecedent struggle. Significantly, he designated as 'passive resistance' the 1913 peaceful Free State protest against new pass regulations by 600 African women (NLSA 111–13): this was subsequent to Gandhi's non-violence campaign against the 1906 'Black Act' in the Transvaal. Plaatje's friend and mentor Dr Abdurahman went further, expressing open admiration for 'British Indians' ' passive resistance in the 'war of extermination' speech that Plaatje quotes at length in *Native Life in South Africa* (p. 163).

One of the more binding of the parallels of experience between the different marginalized communities lay in the claim that Indian as well as African leaders made to an ideal of imperial citizenship built on the 'bulwark' of British 'suzerainty', and to the rights and duties such citizenship involved (*NLSA* 25). To this concept of citizens' rights was in turn linked their insistent invocation of the allegedly British political values of justice, equality, and the rule of law. As we have seen, in his numerous campaigns against 'civilized' European 'barbarism' Plaatje called upon his status and equal rights as an educated and loyal British subject. But Indians, too—both moderate Indian politicians operating from either India or Britain such as Surendranath Banerji or Dadabhai Naoroji, and South Africa-based Indians like M. K. Gandhi—saw as paramount the promise entailed by their membership of the empire, especially as enshrined in Queen Victoria's 1858 Proclamation.[62]

For both Indian and African political leaders therefore a professed belief in an idealized British rule became the basis for repeated appeals to the 'true British instincts of fair play and justice', and 'true' British government, marred but not obliterated by present aberrations. On occasion indeed Plaatje's lamentations at the disgraceful betrayal of imperial justice in South Africa (represented in the symbol of the besmirched or blotted Union Jack), sound uncannily like Naoroji's invective against 'un-British rule' before an imagined audience of 'English gentlemen', or Gandhi's complaint that anti-Indian discrimination in South Africa was contrary to British traditions of fair play.[63] In time, especially in the disillusioning aftermath of the First World War, such appeals to justice came on all sides to bear more rhetorical and emotional force than political substance. Yet the common ground in terms of moral principle, strategy, and a general experience of discrimination, remained broad. Plaatje acknowledged on several occasions for instance that Indians in South Africa

[62] The 1858 post-Mutiny Proclamation ensured—if only in theory—the freedom from racial and religious oppression of Indians empire-wide. See C. H. Philips (ed.), *The Evolution of India and Pakistan 1858 to 1947: Select Documents* (London: Oxford UP, 1962), 10–11.

[63] See Dadabhai Naoroji's Select Committee notes and House of Commons speeches collected in *Poverty and Un-British Rule in India* (London: Swan Sonnenschein and Co., 1901), especially pp. v–vi, which map neatly on to *Native Life*, 245. As in Naoroji's case, Plaatje's protests at the heavy tax load carried by non-voting non-whites rested on so-called 'British' democratic beliefs, though he may also have been influenced, as implied earlier, by the example of America's independence history. On several occasions he referred to taxation without representation as the 'black man's burden' (as he did to the sexual abuse of black women by whites, and the issue of black labour exploitation in general). See *NLSA* 17, 19, 216–17, 255–6; *SW* 172, 223, 259, 327, 339–41. For Gandhi, see the paragraphs following.

suffered 'boycotts', social ostracization, legal discrimination, and working restrictions just like Africans (*NLSA* 30; *SW* 71, 155, 167).

As well as community interests in common, suggestive parallels also arise in the area of individual leadership between, on the one hand, Plaatje, the General Secretary and leading spokesman for the SANNC, and, on the other, Mohandas Gandhi, later the champion of satyagraha in India. Gandhi, who was resident in South Africa between 1893 and 1914, served as Secretary to the Natal Indian Congress, which he helped establish, and developed the central tenets to his political philosophy of non-violence while in the country.[64] Indeed, as will be seen, the number of comparative links between the two historically contemporaneous, South Africa-based leaders is so remarkable as almost to tempt one into plotting some form of virtual relationship between the two men which, though it went unrecorded, yet shaped their attitudes and policy. The surprise is only that neither made explicit acknowledgement of the example nor the presence of the other, nor of the other's political movement.

Moderate representatives of their people in the years 1905–20, but outspoken in the face of racial oppression, both Plaatje and Gandhi were deeply involved in and fascinated by the law, a foremost area of potential exchange between them. Gandhi as a barrister and political activist, Plaatje as court reporter, editor, and political spokesperson, both concerned themselves intimately with the fine processes of negotiation, mediation, legal interpretation, and the representation of grievances. True to the nature of such involvements, both men objected publicly to racial discrimination on the South African railway network—that potentially democratizing agent of modernity newly linking the country's major centres. In the nearly twenty years he spent in South Africa Gandhi also launched a series of determined protests at legislation curbing or restricting entirely Indian franchise, immigration, and freedom to trade: most notably, the 1897 Licensing Act in Natal; the 1906 'Black Act' insisting on the registration of all

---

[64] On Gandhi's formative South African period, see Judith M. Brown, *Gandhi: Prisoner of Hope* (New Haven: Yale UP, 1989), 30–94; Judith M. Brown and Martin Prozesky (eds.), *Gandhi and South Africa: Principles and Politics* (Pietermaritzburg: University of Natal Press, 1996); Maureen Swan, *Gandhi: The South African Experience* (Johannesburg: Ravan Press, 1985). See also Bhikhu Parekh, *Gandhi's Political Philosophy* (Basingstoke: Macmillan, 1989). For Gandhi's own teacherly account of his political experiences in South Africa, see his *An Autobiography; or The Story of my Experiments with Truth*, trans. Mahadev Desai (1927; Ahmedabad: Navajivan Publishing House, 1958), and *Satyagraha in South Africa* (Ahmedabad: Navajivan Press, 1928).

Indian residents in the Transvaal; the 1913 immigration law; and the restriction on 'non-Christian' marriages in the same year (to which Plaatje, too, objected).

As for Plaatje, Gandhi's appeal was consistently to a 'British' discourse of rights, and his methods were constitutional, relying on public meetings, petitioning, and one-on-one argument. At the same time—again the approach strikes a chord—Gandhi fundamentally questioned the so-called constitutionalism and justice of colonial legislation and the methods of its enforcement, and therefore, in both 1899 and 1914, interrogated what his loyalty as a British subject entailed as regarded the war effort, '[doing] duty for [one's] Sovereign on the battlefield'.[65] He, too, formed part of two deputations to London, in 1906 and 1909, to protest directly to the imperial government. Just like Plaatje's, his campaigns therefore were tiered, aimed at different authorities (liberal opinion in England, white 'friends' in South Africa) and spanned several continents. Gandhi was also instrumental, again like Plaatje, in setting up an interest group in London to promote his (Transvaal Indian) campaign in his absence.

At the level of self-perception and political ethics the similarities continue. Both leaders, who were proficient in several languages, viewed themselves as interpreters, mediators between communities. Strongly influenced by Christian belief, as by their reading of John Ruskin, if in differing proportions, both also tended to see social improvement as conjoined with moral transformation, and therefore as an antidote to the damaging effects of industrial modernity, which neither positively welcomed.[66] As part of this commitment to regenerative change, they exerted themselves where possible to forge wide democratic representation and cross-community links. Gandhi, for instance, insisted on a Muslim member forming part of his 1906 deputation to London, and, in his Phoenix Settlement and Tolstoy Farm experiments, sought cooperation across caste and gender barriers. During his campaigns in London he made sure to consult both with moderates and with revolutionaries like Shyamaji Krishnavarma.

[65] See Gandhi, An Autobiography, 156–7, and his Satyagraha in South Africa, 68–79. See also Judith Brown, 'The Anglo-Boer War: An Indian Perspective', in Boehmer (ed.), South African War? 1899–1902, Kunapipi, 21.3 (1999), 26. For Plaatje's awareness of Indian involvement in the First World War, see NLSA 305, 308, 323, 326.

[66] Patrick Brantlinger, 'A Postindustrial Prelude to Postcolonialism: John Ruskin, Morris and Gandhism', Critical Inquiry, 22 (1996), 466–85, looks at Unto this Last's energizing effect on Gandhi. See also Francis O'Gorman, Late Ruskin, New Contexts (Aldershot: Ashgate, 2000).

His concept of *ahimsa*, universal love linked to non-violence, he derived from the *Gita*'s ideal of selfless action, though clearly via a different line of ethical argument than Aurobindo Ghose's.[67] For Gandhi, too, national identity, specifically Indian national identity, should be fully encompassing, bridging ethnic and religious divides, and should include women on an equal footing with men. Iconically, as in the case of Plaatje's *Native Life in South Africa*, Gandhi wrote *Hind Swaraj*, his most developed political treatise, on board the *Kildonan Castle* en route from London to South Africa between 13 and 22 November 1909.[68] Some years earlier he had set up in Durban his own paper *Indian Opinion* to publicize issues of importance to Indians: the paper was bilingual, as were Plaatje's newspapers.

And yet, despite this interesting web of comparative links embracing the two leaders, and the commitment of both to cross-communal ties, history records no direct connection or openly acknowledged understanding between them. If anything, we can surmise, the South African Indian model of protest was to the slightly epigonal Plaatje more of a source of frustration and resentment than an inspiration. In 1919, during a debate on Native rights in the British Parliament, Plaatje seated in the Speaker's Gallery heard Gandhi's successful persistence on behalf of Transvaal Indians praised by Leo Amery.[69] However, revealingly for a man who attached significance to individual role models, Plaatje made no reference in his published work to Gandhi at this or at any other time. What were the reasons for this in many ways puzzling silence? The short answer to the question is in all likelihood captured in the names of the two South African Congresses led and authored by Plaatje and Gandhi: respectively, the South African Native National Congress, and the Natal Indian Congress. Although both were dedicated to non-white people's freedom, the organizations retained racial labels—'Native' and 'Indian'—and to this extent subscribed to the mentalities of the segregationist state.

Plaatje's own at times exclusionist language also unambiguously situated the Indians as a people apart. To him they remained predominantly expatriates and 'sojourners': 'the few thousand Hindus

---

[67] Brown, *Gandhi: Prisoner of Hope*, 84–5.

[68] M. K. Gandhi, *Hind Swaraj and Other Writings*, ed. Anthony J. Parel (Cambridge: Cambridge UP, 1997). Originally written in Gujarati for publication in *Indian Opinion*, the book was published in English translation in 1910 under the title *Indian Home Rule*.

[69] Willan, *Sol Plaatje*, 235–6.

resident in South Africa' (SW 271–2). Effectively aliens in the land of his birth, they were in other words what the Natives' Land Act was scandalously threatening to make of his own properly indigenous people. Dr Abdurahman of the APO, too, denoted the community as nationally distinct, as 'British Indians'. For both Cape leaders the background to this shared sense of Indian difference was probably that the number of 'Asiatics' in their 'liberal' colony was relatively low by comparison with the Transvaal and Natal where Gandhi's campaigns were focused.

Grounded in demographic formations, therefore, the Indians' difference of status was further highlighted for Plaatje by, as he saw it, their more favourable treatment under imperial law. In *Native Life in South Africa* as in his journalism he makes sufficient reference to this fact as to suggest that 'British Indians'' officially recognized position as subjects of the Crown (*pace* the 1858 'Magna Carta') was for him a source of considerable annoyance. There is in operation he perceives a rank order of injustices, a grade scale of political advancement and favouritism which is coded for race. This explains why, when Indians in South Africa experience hardship, as they did in 1913, 'Westminster and Bombay' step in to effect reform (*NLSA* 149–50, 215–16, 233, 235):

The Indians are more fortunate because their protests are always backed and powerfully reinforced by the Viceroy of India and the united pleas of over three hundred million swarthy British subjects of the Indian empire in the far east. But we Natives may commend our interest to the loving care of our heavenly father. (*SW* 358)

Plaatje's views concerning Indian advantage were evidently exaggerated, or Gandhi would not have had to campaign as concertedly as he did. Yet for the African leader the inequality with respect to the treatment of his people and of South African Indians was clearly exacerbated by the Africans' paradoxical condition of being addressed as aliens in their native land. Unlike Indians, whose place of origin lay elsewhere, oppressed Natives had in their state of abandonment 'no other place to go' (*SW* 262). He was by no means incorrect in making this charge. The Indian government *was* keenly interested in the problem of Indians in South Africa: the Viceroy Lord Hardinge had for instance intervened on their behalf with the London government in 1912 (*SW* 262).[70] They did therefore have recourse to powerful external authorities concerned for their welfare.

[70] Brown, *Gandhi: Prisoner of Hope*, 32.

However, the racial coding of their treatment under the law which so preoccupied Plaatje to an extent corresponded with his own view of Indians as 'aliens', so alienating them the more from his political agendas, and distorting his picture of South Africa's rank order of injustices. In short, that Indians were politically less oppressed was the greater outrage not only because they *were* to Plaatje alien (by racial origin if not by birth, as the law itself repeatedly sought to enforce), but also because they *acted* as aliens. Indians, as Plaatje remarked, lived in South Africa in exclusivist ways: they remitted their profits to their homeland; their trading practices could be discriminatory; their produce was overpriced (*SW* 146, 165, 168–9). The colonial stereotype of Easterners as economic parasites does not lie far beneath the surface of these perceptions.[71] At moments Plaatje could go so far as to imply that South Africa was the domain of white and African only, and it was for these two groups primarily to find their mutual accommodations within it.[72]

There is a definite sense therefore in which nationalist and nativist leaders in colonial South Africa such as Plaatje, repeated and so contributed to the overdetermined distinctions which the system of discriminatory legislation was putting in place. Gandhi, too, was by no means innocent of a racially informed political chauvinism. Despite the fact that South Africa fostered his theories of resistance and cross-communal cooperation, he was while resident in the country always primarily concerned with issues specifically of *Indian* identity and rights. India remained 'home': his political vision had this nation's freedom as its goal and his African struggle therefore was ultimately for India's self-realization.[73] To this extent therefore Plaatje's charges of exclusivity did stick.

[71] Gandhi, *Satyagraha in South Africa*, 71, is painfully aware of this stereotype and the need to counteract it. See Chrisman, *Rereading the Imperial Romance*, 181–2, for a discussion of Plaatje's Orientalist images of Mzilikazi's 'harem' in *Mhudi*. Given this, there is irony in the fact that, as Plaatje notes, it was 'a man of Indian origin' who sponsored the first printing of his translation of Shakespeare (*SW* 384).

[72] In a 1912 article Plaatje emotively referred to Natives as 'aboriginal Afrikanders' (*SW* 150). The mutual suspicion and charges of chauvinism between African and Indian groups in South Africa as well as in the rest of the continent continued across the twentieth century. In 1949, for example, these tensions came to a head in the Cato Ridge clashes in Durban between Indians and Zulus. Couzens, *The New African*, 276, points out that the writer H. I. E. Dhlomo spoke of passive resistance in India and in South Africa with admiration, yet his attitude to the Indian community itself was ambiguous. See also Elleke Boehmer, 'Without the West: Southern African and Indian Women Writers in the 1990s', *African Studies*, 58.2 (2000), 157–70.

[73] Brown, *Gandhi: Prisoner of Hope*, 69. See also Karen L. Harris, 'Gandhi, the

It was briefly noted earlier that, in the aftermath of 1914–18, both Plaatje and Gandhi increasingly lost their belief in the legitimacy of imperial rule, certainly as this rule was constitutionally and practically expressed in the Union of South Africa. In its stead Gandhi, back in India, developed his theory of moral opposition to an immoral state, articulated as civil disobedience, whereas Plaatje, still banking on a deep-seated faith in the sheer symbolic staying power of being native, gave increasing emphasis to ethnic and racial self-strengthening and the preservation of 'kind' (*Mhudi*, 167).[74] It is significant that he was, as was seen, uneasy about cultural mixing in the sense of miscegenation or racial hybridizing.[75] Despite his symbolic inclusion of the 'Tipperary Chorus' in 'Hindustani' as well as in other South African languages in *Native Life in South Africa* (p. 323), despite the Shylockean chapter epigraph taken from Edwin Arnold in the same volume—'there is no caste in blood' (p. 199)—he saw the preservation of the solidarity of race, as advocated in Mzilikazi's important final speech in *Mhudi*, as a crucial defence against 'unnatural' and potentially disempowering partnership. It was also the reassuring, self-affirming commonality of race which after 1918 encouraged and reinforced his interest in forging pan-nationalist ties with African America.[76]

And yet, even as we observe the racial underpinning to his cross-nationalist loyalties, it is important to take note of one final factor which will have been important in shaping Plaatje's interdiscursive thinking. Although committed to promoting African rights, he clearly had strong reason to be wary of certain nationalist formations, in particular that of Afrikaner nationalism, especially where

Chinese and Passive Resistance', in Brown and Prozesky (eds.), *Gandhi and South Africa*, 69, on Gandhi's 'failure to ally with any other "ethnic grouping" '; J. D. Hunt, 'Gandhi and the Black People in South Africa', *Gandhi Marq* (Apr.–June 1989), 7–8; Les Switzer, 'Gandhi in South Africa: The Ambiguities of Satyagraha', *Journal of Ethnic Studies*, 14.1 (1986).

[74] However, as on his 1931 trip to Elizabethville in the Congo, Plaatje retained an interest in finding comparative links between different cultures and legal systems. See Willan, *Sol Plaatje*, 376–7.

[75] On the contradictory ideologies of racial mixing, see Robert J. C. Young, *Colonial Desire: Hybridity in Theory, Race and Culture* (London: Routledge, 1995).

[76] By the 1950s, following the achievement of Indian national independence, the ANC became prepared openly to make its accommodations with the policies of the Indian National Congress and the South African Indian Congress. The first public display of this new commitment to both multiculturalism and Gandhian passive resistance came with the 1952 Defiance Campaign.

such formations asserted territorial claims which conflicted with his own. *Mhudi* paints a bleak picture of the consequences for Plaatje's own people, the Rolong, or the Tswana more generally, of collaborating with another marginalized people, the Boers, against a common enemy. The Irish nationalist logic of 'my enemy's enemy is my friend', which had applied in the Irish volunteers' relationship with the Afrikaners in 1899–1900, could not hold for Plaatje. Had formal cooperation with Indian nationalists in South Africa ever suggested itself to him on the basis of their common oppression, he would in all probability finally have rejected the possibility, citing his own people's historical experience in his defence. His fear would no doubt have been that the Indian Congress use its more favourable legal position vis-à-vis the imperial authority in a way eventually harmful to its African colleagues, by analogy with Boer behaviour in the latter half of the nineteenth century (*NLSA* 121–35).

As Plaatje wrote in a 1924 article 'Nationalists and Natives' lamenting new restrictions on African representation, 'nationalists'' interests could in many South African contexts be inimical to those of 'natives' (*SW* 323). Boer national traditions, he also bluntly observed, were 'to enslave the dark races' (*NLSA* 76, 149). At the same time however it does not need re-emphasizing that Plaatje was himself explicitly nationalist in orientation: he devoted himself to African people's self-representation; their achievement of legal and political subjecthood was his constant aim. Despite his cultural cosmopolitanism, he was concomitantly also hostile to 'internationalists', by which he meant the apparently rootless, non-loyal immigrants of the Transvaal (that is, as he said, republican Americans, Italian socialists, East Europeans, 'Belgian Jews', but not 'British Indians') (*SW* 71, 99). It was outrageous to him that those whose rights were not grounded in physical belonging, could claim a political advantage over Natives.

Due to his ambivalences regarding nationalism, and his awareness of the contradictory claims of sovereign rights, Plaatje's signifieds of the nation continually shift, becoming now the Rolong people, now a pan-African alliance, now a South Africa built out of social, cultural, and interracial cooperation. Yet despite his concerns about racial hybridity, it was probably within the terms of a protean or multiply-constituted nationalism, that he found perhaps his most compelling reason for invoking pan-African loyalties that bridged the Atlantic. In his Christian Brotherhood and humanist vision of a pan-nationalist fraternity linking 'man and man ... nation and nation, race and race' (embracing but also extending beyond the 'Black Atlantic'), the different valencies of his nationalism could be, at least on an imaginary level, contained (*NLSA* 264).

5   'Immeasurable Strangeness' between Empire and Modernism: W. B. Yeats and Rabindranath Tagore, and Leonard Woolf

I would have Ireland re-create the ancient arts, the arts as they were understood in Judaea, in India, in Scandinavia, in Greece and Rome, in every ancient land; as they were understood when they moved a whole people.

(W. B. Yeats, 'Ireland and the Arts', 1901)[1]

The scene has changed here too & one changes inside too. After all I am today & to be impinged on by innumerable todays, the change is inevitable. I have no connection with yesterday: I do not recognize it or myself in it. I am of & in today moulded & marked by innumerable things which have never touched you.

(Leonard Woolf, letter to Lytton Strachey, 1908)[2]

a country which has no national institutions must show its young men images for the affections.

(W. B. Yeats, 'J. M. Synge and the Ireland of His Time', 1910)

TOWARDS A THEORY OF MODERNISM IN THE IMPERIAL WORLD

The modernist art forms which emerged in the West in the period that straddles the First World War, register in ways at once oblique yet significant the manifestations of empire. These manifestations are, in Edward Said's adaptation of J. R. Seeley's theory of imperialism, 'the contending native' as well as the threat and unease

---

[1] The two Yeats epigraphs are taken from, W. B Yeats, *Essays and Introductions* (1961; Basingstoke: Macmillan, 1989), 206 and 312–13, respectively. Hereafter *EI*.
[2] Leonard Woolf, Letter to Lytton Strachey (2 Oct. 1908), in *Letters of Leonard Woolf*, ed. Frederic Spotts (London: Bloomsbury, 1990), 137.

occasioned by European imperial rivalries.[3] The saturation of metropolitan culture with artifacts from the imperial abroad, as well as with different kinds of knowledge (even if these were universalizing), willy-nilly imported into Europe foreign cultural texts, the testimonials of other social, aesthetic, and spiritual experiences.[4] Despite empire's prevailing assumptions of unassailable sovereignty, the cross-border networks of survey, command, and communication which were utilized by Britain and other imperial powers at their height, brought the metropolis into contact with at least the signs of other subjectivities, both recalcitrant and subjugated, which were emerging out of—or out from under—colonial contact with other cultures.

So far this study has looked at certain cross-national ties and correspondences between (proto-)nationalist movements and revivalist thinking in different regions of the British Empire in its heyday. Attention has also been paid to the diversity and interlinking of different discourses of self-representation, reflected in the mixes of generic media and of cultural and political influence which mark the work of the early intellectuals and thinkers associated with such emergent groups. These mixes, the products of cross-border interaction, we have also had occasion to notice, resemble in certain respects the layered and multivoiced style of some of modernism's key canonical works.

In this final chapter the focus on the interface between different cultures brought into contact both by empire and by anti-imperial forces will be extended into the dimension of metropolitan modernism, specifically into the work of two important writers associated with this cultural moment, Leonard Woolf and W. B. Yeats. I will consider whether the cosmopolitan connections and cross-border intersubjectivity promoted within dissident and avant-garde circles in imperial capitals like London, and encouraged by nationalist elites at home, impinged on their metropolitan cultural practices in any recognizable way. Moreover, if such cross-national or cross-cultural impacts can be delineated with respect to Woolf and Yeats's writing, are these comparable in effect with the more widely documented transformative influence on modernism of the so-called

---

[3] Edward W. Said, *Culture and Imperialism* (London: Cape, 1993), 225–9.

[4] On imperial control as organized via knowledge-producing systems, see Thomas Richards, *The Imperial Archive: Knowledge and the Fantasy of Empire* (London: Verso, 1993).

primitive arts,[5] or of the alternative forms of understanding introduced by the new spiritual experiments of Theosophy, mesmerism, and so on?

In a controversial 1988 essay 'Modernism and Imperialism' the Marxist critic Fredric Jameson established a schema which separated the culture of the conventional modernist metropolis from the colony, based on their mutually exclusive categories of cognitive and political experience.[6] The spatial and economic disjunctions of the colonial (specifically the imperial) system, he wrote, occluded the colonized from metropolitan perception, yet at the same time (all too typically) allowed the metropolitan a greater degree of self-perception than the oppressed colonized.[7] This separation was further reinforced by his characterization of the sphere of the colonized in the imperial period as essentially one of brute existential resistance.

In contradistinction to Jameson's argument, this book has suggested that the boundaries between metropolis and colony were porous and shifting, and that, as Laura Chrisman also emphasizes *contra* Jameson, colonized resistances *were* visible within European horizons.[8] Extending this point the contention here is *also* that the cultural and political *exchanges* between the conventional colonial centre and periphery, as well as between subjects of the different peripheries, impinged in different ways on the cultures of the centre,

[5] Marianna Torgovnik, *Gone Primitive: Savage Intellects, Modern Lives* (Chicago: University of Chicago Press, 1990), offers a detailed study of the cultural complexity of the primitive figured as both other and familiar, whereas Michael North, *The Dialect of Modernism: Race, Language and Twentieth Century Literature* (Oxford: Oxford UP, 1994), considers dialect impersonations in modernism as a particular form of stylistic and indeed primitivistic 'truancy'. For David Richards, *Masks of Difference* (Cambridge: Cambridge UP, 1995), the primitive is the modernist 'fundamental' through which to assault the modern world (as the Classics were to the Renaissance). Neither North nor Richards however investigates the relationship of primitivism to the hierarchical political and social cultures of modernism.

[6] Fredric Jameson, 'Modernism and Imperialism', Field Day Pamphlet 14 (Derry: Field Day Theatre Co., 1988), 11, 17, 19–20. For critiques of Jameson's totalizing and 'ahistorical' position, see Howard Booth and Nigel Rigby, 'Introduction' to their edited *Modernism and Empire* (Manchester: Manchester UP, 2000), 5–7, as well as the contributions by Patrick Williams and Rod Edmond in the same collection; Laura Chrisman, *Rereading the Imperial Romance* (Oxford: Oxford UP, 2000), 9–12.

[7] The tendency to see the metropolis as the cultural heartland of modernism is widespread. Despite his commitment to escaping the terms through which we habitually interpret metropolitan culture, it also circumscribes Raymond Williams's analyses in *The Politics of Modernism: Against the New Conformists*, ed. Tony Pinkney (London: Verso, 1989).

[8] Chrisman, *Rereading the Imperial Romance*, 8–10.

to form a complicated and interconnected web. Globalized empire at the turn of the twentieth century, in other words, had for the first time in history made of the world an intermeshed, criss-cross network of communication link-ups, and cross-national political and cultural relationships. Within this web Britain formed *one* nodal point, even if an influential one, amongst others.

Despite constructions of modernism as but tenuously related to dominant pre-1950s colonialist involvements, it is now quite widely accepted that prominent features of modernist culture bear signs of 'the external pressures . . . of the *imperium*', in Edward Said's words.[9] 'The material and psychic circulation of empire within the imperial homeland', which had also shaped nineteenth-century so- cial forms and cultures, as Patrick Brantlinger, Benita Parry, and Gauri Viswanathan amongst others have noted, was expressed in modernist writing in characteristic images and structures denoting perceptual uncertainty or hesitancy.[10] The geopolitical reach of cap- italism which marked the time of high empire, or of empire at its height, was thus symptomatically, and paradoxically, accompanied in metropolitan culture by expressions of cognitive failure—the fail- ure to see fully, to know completely. Such failure is signified in the cat- alogue of misrecognitions that is Conrad's now iconic *Heart of Darkness* (1899), or in his eponymous *Lord Jim*'s failure to know himself (1900); or, more broadly, in the aesthetic of disintegration and the fragment that dominates modernist representation, as in Cubist painting, or T. S. Eliot's *The Waste Land*.[11]

In Said's understanding, the inevitable retreat from empire's as- sumptions of 'irreversible presence' and inexhaustible knowledge was registered in modernism by an ironic attempt at imposing a new inclusiveness and synthesis at the level of the aesthetic—not globally therefore, but structurally, as in the reformulations of inherited

[9] Said, *Culture and Imperialism*, 227.

[10] See Benita Parry, 'The Circulation of Empire in Metropolitan Writing', unpublished seminar paper, University of Leeds (3 Nov. 1999), 2, 15, and her *Delusions and Discoveries: Studies on India in the British Imagination* (London: Verso, 1998). See also Patrick Brantlinger, *Rule of Darkness: British Literature and Imperialism, 1830–1914* (Ithaca, NY: Cornell UP, 1988); Gauri Viswanathan, *Masks of Conquest: Literary Study and British Rule in India* (New York: Columbia UP, 1989), and her *Outside the Fold: Conversion, Modernity and Belief* (Princeton: Princeton UP, 1998), both of which present powerful, nu- anced arguments as to how religious and social realignments in Britain were affected by colonial reforms and policy changes from before the accession of Victoria.

[11] Linda Nochlin, *The Body in Pieces: The Fragment as a Metaphor of Modernity* (London: Thames and Hudson, 1992).

cultural systems in *Ulysses, The Waste Land*, or Ezra Pound's *Cantos*. By contrast, in Simon Gikandi's analysis of modernism's relation to its imperial context—which however owes much to Said's thesis—a more direct connection is plotted: modernist art forms in fact 'derive their energy from their diagnosis of the failure of the imperial enterprise'.[12] This is a failure which is precipitated and in part signified by the entry of challenging native voices, artifacts, and other presences—as found in primitivism—within the space of the *imperium*. Gikandi and others cite as further evidence of the interrelation of the modernist and the imperial, the pervasive fascination with narratives of degeneration, decline, and extinction, as well as widespread admissions of cultural loss and outbreaks of nervous energy.[13]

Turn-of-the-century preoccupations with failure and loss may however be worked into a rather less pessimistic reading of imperial culture. Instead, European modernist self-questioning can be seen as motivated by a strong and not invariably corrosive sense of cultural relativity, as much as by a *fin du globe* conviction. To this sense of cultural relativity can be attributed the modernist search through the symbolic systems of other cultures to find alternative aesthetic potential (such as in T. S. Eliot's poetry of this time, or in the 'savage pilgrimage' recorded in D. H. Lawrence's novels *Kangaroo* (1923) and *The Plumed Serpent* (1926)). As the global context, or the imperial abroad, impinged on early twentieth-century culture in the shape of the new and the strange introduced by, for instance, ethnography and the study of myth, and explorations in psychology, as well as by mysticism and spirituality, numbers of writers, artists, and intellectuals were forced into a reconsideration of inherited values. Struggling with the difficulty of interpreting a modern world that seemed to be at once expanding and collapsing cataclysmically (again in part as a consequence of empire), modernists creatively challenged the limits of their own beliefs against symbolic systems imported from other, so-called primitive, intuitive (and usually politically subordinate) contexts.[14] It is in respect of these differing approaches to cultural

---

[12] Simon Gikandi, *Maps of Englishness: Writing Identity in the Culture of Colonialism* (New York: Columbia UP, 1996), 161–4.

[13] See Rod Edmond, 'Degeneration in Imperial and Modernist Discourse', in Booth and Rigby (eds.), *Modernism and Empire*, 39–63; Daniel Pick, *Faces of Degeneration* (Cambridge: Cambridge UP, 1989).

[14] For a further reading of modernism situated in an expanded global context, see Elleke Boehmer, *Colonial and Postcolonial Literature* (Oxford: Oxford UP, 1995), 123–33.

relativity that, as Patrick Williams citing Ernst Bloch suggests, the phenomena of modernism and modernity can be seen as 'combined and uneven' developments; as only partially overlapping axes ('simultaneous uncontemporaneities') along which, as here, the literally disturbing signs of the other may be now accepted, now disavowed.[15]

True, such regenerative invocations of and even negotiations with otherness were usually transposed into the epistemological frames of the West. Writers and artists rarely moved beyond a superficial, self-consciously cosmopolitan level of citation or questioned the continuing existence of colonial hierarchies (where the dominating West as ever imposed its always 'superior' forms of knowledge). Either the signs of difference represented essentially a grafting or a pasting on, and were thus transformed into the insignia of Anglo-American spiritual or cultural dilemmas; or, at a more substantive level, they became, as in *The Waste Land*, an appropriation to the end of shoring up a European cultural and spiritual landscape still perceived to be of central importance, even if disintegrating.[16]

All the same, if modernism is indeed conceptualized as a nexus of *uneven* developments, it is as well to ask what this means for its representations and apparent appropriations of the other. A rethinking of metropolitan modernism as invariably appropriative becomes particularly suggestive if we expand our understanding of the phenomenon into the global context that contributed to shaping it; that is, if the modernist self-questioning which makes contact with cultural difference, is more consistently read as situated and conducted in the perspective of empire. Within this expanded framework it becomes possible to see the interface between modernist cultural forms and the other as far more reticulated and diffuse than previously. No longer specifically confined to Europe or America, the modernist–other interface or contact zone is spread across an inevitably interactive imperial and cross-border terrain, in which Mary Kingsley's appreciation of fetishes on her West African travels, or Bronislaw Malinowski's journals, for example, may be read as proto-modernist, or as reproducing a 'modernist' involvement with and citation of colonized and indigenous cultures.

[15] Patrick Williams, 'Theorizing Modernism and Empire', in Booth and Rigby (eds.), *Modernism and Empire*, 27–35.
[16] See David Trotter, 'Modernism and Empire: Reading *The Waste Land*', *Critical Quarterly*, 28.1/2 (1986), 143–53, which suggests that the poem's 'modernist apocalypse' was 'formulated within hearing distance of . . . militant imperialism'.

The expanded picture of a globalized and constellated modernism encompasses that way in which nationalist movements in the empire's outer regions were inflected through modernist prisms (in other words, how cultural nationalist texts at different historical moments across the twentieth century deployed modernist techniques). This is manifested in instances as geographically far apart as the eclecticism of the 1900s Bengal art movement pioneered by E. B. Havell, Abanindranath Tagore, and Sister Nivedita; the Jamaican Claude McKay's 1910s self-articulations both in Caribbean patois and standard English; the atmospheric 1920s poetry of the Australian Ken Slessor or the Fauvist paintings of his compatriot Margaret Preston; and the Eliot-influenced progressivist Hindi poetry of Ajneya and Gajanan Madhav Muktibodh in the 1940s and 1950s.[17] Conversely, nationalist movements of self-assertion out in the empire—the emergence of new Indian, Caribbean, and Pacific voices, for instance—can be seen in this reticulated context to have had repercussions, even if tangentially so, for existential questions in the metropolis or for its preoccupations with the stylistic or psychic reconstitution of the self.

The globalized interface of modernism also adds resonance to Said's reading of modernism's stabilizing imperative: that way in which many cosmopolitans attempted to reconcile the disturbance represented by the empire's newly emerging subjectivities, of which they were increasingly and uneasily aware, in the hermetic realm of the aesthetic rather than that of politics. Attempted aesthetic resolutions are dramatized for example in the multivoicedness that characterizes much writing of this time, or in the rapid shuttling between different consciousnesses in the narratives of Virginia Woolf or the New Zealand-born Katherine Mansfield.[18] For Mansfield, indeed, writing from a double-angled modernist-and-colonial perspective, narrative strategies of incompletion, as in *Prelude* (1917, first published by the Hogarth Press), may have provided ways of encoding her own geographic and psychic displacement. Her personal Pacific

---

[17] On T. S. Eliot's influence on Hindi poetry, see Harish Trivedi, *Colonial Transactions: English Literature and India* (Manchester: Manchester UP, 1995), ch. 4 'T. S. Eliot in Hindi: Modes of Reception', 69–79.

[18] See Kathy J. Phillips, *Virginia Woolf against the Empire* (Knoxville: University of Tennessee Press, 1994); Angela Smith, *Katherine Mansfield and Virginia Woolf: A Public of Two* (Oxford: Clarendon Press, 1999). Consider also T. E. Hulme's influential advocacy of a dry, 'non-human', geometric classicism (and its saving abstraction of form) in *Speculations: Essays on Humanism and the Philosophy of Art*, introd. Herbert Read (London: Kegan Paul, Trench, Trubner and Co., 1924).

history overdetermined the formal disjunctions and concern with collapsed and uncertain identity which are typically read as characteristic of her modernist writing.[19]

The expanded perspective on modernism seen in the context of, and in interaction with, alternative forms of cosmopolitan and nationalistically inspired self-expression in the empire draws important attention to that underlying link between the emergence of anti-imperial nationalism and of aesthetic modernism which is modernity itself. That is to say, modernism is, like the nationalisms which emerged in response to empire, an outgrowth and an expression of modernity (its levelling technologies, its accelerated communications, its atomized subjectivities).[20] As with many articulations of modernity, nationalism typically oscillates between a self-conscious sense of newness, and backward-looking claims to lineage and deep history—which are also among the defining characteristics of modernist art. As in modernity, too, nationalism is concerned with progress defined as self-individuation and situated in relation to an othered or objectified world.[21]

It was suggested at the beginning of this book that, across the empire, the many occurrences of cultural nationalism or claims to self-expression through culture, created the potential for reciprocity, for moments of interaction between different elite nationalisms (if not also between their self-consciously modern, and modernist, forms of self-articulation). The emergence in various regions of the colonized world of articulate yet isolated modern subjectivities which shared a political language of rights and self-improvement, set up the basis for an interrelation that noticeably differed from the relation of colonial self and objectified other. Although such nationalisms remained unavoidably self-centred in intention, they allowed for the possibility of ideals in common, or of making a common cause. There was that in them which approaches (although does not match) what Emmanuel Levinas describes as the unconditional recognition of the alterity of

---

[19] Katherine Mansfield, 'Prelude', The Collected Short Stories (Harmondsworth: Penguin, 1982), and The Aloe, ed. Vincent O'Sullivan (London: Virago, 1982).

[20] The 'belated' emergence of modern black nationalisms, as Bhabha and Fanon remind us, is oppositionally located in relation to the violent ontology of white modernity. See, for example, Homi Bhabha, ch. 12 'Conclusion: "Race", Time and the Revision of Modernity', The Location of Culture (London: Routledge, 1995), 236–56.

[21] For his still evocative study of the imaginary dimensions of modern nationalism, see Benedict Anderson, Imagined Communities: Reflections on the Origin and Spread of Nationalism, rev. edn. (London: Verso, 1991).

the other (of being-for-the-other).[22] Where, for Levinas, the other is defined by its absolute right to exist, for which the self bears responsibility, it follows that 'political self-affirmation should mean from the outset a responsibility for all'.[23] We have seen, *to a degree*, such a focus on alterity (the declaration of a generalized being-in-common), emerging out of certain early cross-nationalist relationships (as in Sol Plaatje's support for pan-Africanist bonds with African America).

In the context of interaction between early anti-imperial yet often cosmopolitan nationalisms, the question arises of whether modernism, too, might not have gained from or responded to such interrelations. Might a respect for alterity not have been stimulated in the metropolitan self through its relationship with the native or the foreign, whether on the basis of shared dilemmas of self-making, or, more tangentially, under the influence of a world situation in which such interaccommodations were increasingly being taken into account? Could the dialogic agitations in the air, as it were, have prompted an interest and a response that went deeper than did the more conventional cross-culturalism of cosmopolitan contacts? These questions will come to have a particular relevance in the discussion of Leonard Woolf's fictional evocations of community in Ceylon (Sri Lanka) which, as he writes, were shaped by his deep absorption in the colony's 'slow-pulsing life'.[24] By contrast, W. B. Yeats's brief collaboration with the Bengali poet Rabindranath Tagore demonstrates more directly the interrelation of cultural nationalisms with aims in common.

In Levinas's view alterity manifests in the realm of saying rather than that of consciousness, that is, it occurs between speaking beings. The idea bears some comparison with the theory of signification *in dialogue* which is central to the work of the Russian philosopher Mikhail Bakhtin, who was influenced, like Levinas, by Husserl. Bakhtin's theory, which concentrates on the interaction of different conceptual systems or discourses, 'languages', within a given (often initially 'imperial' or monologic) context, becomes

---

[22] See Emmanuel Levinas, *Alterity and Transcendence*, trans. Michael B. Smith (London: Athlone Press, 1999); his *Ethics and Infinity*, trans. R. A. Cohen (Pittsburgh: Duquesne UP, 1985); and *Otherwise than Being or Beyond Essence*, trans. Alphonse Lingis (The Hague: Martinus Nijhoff, 1981), from which the important chapter 'Substitution' is extracted in Seán Hand (ed.), *The Levinas Reader* (Oxford: Blackwell, 1999).

[23] Seán Hand, 'Introduction', *The Levinas Reader*, 7.

[24] Leonard Woolf, *Growing: An Autobiography of the Years 1904–1911* (London: Hogarth Press, 1961), 32.

particularly pertinent when we approach the problem of how to understand the articulation of the alien, or of alterity, in early twentieth-century modernist writing. Several linked questions emerge from this. What is it that happens when Bakhtin's discourses or 'languages' intersect across the power differentials imposed within *colonial* hierarchies? How are such interrelations encoded? Does that at once ideological *and* verbal decentring take place which according to Bakhtin occurs when a self-enclosed unitary language is exposed to others? What is the impact on literary expression of the vertiginous disorientation, the profound psychic agitation which, as we will see, proximity to the other produces in the white writer?[25]

Bakhtin's situation of ideological or discursive decentring is again comparable to, though not equivalent with, the state of being in which (an always primary) alterity may be acknowledged in Levinas. Yet his analysis of 'dialogical agitation' is particularly helpful here in that it offers a theoretical model through which to conceive of how the colonial voice begins to open out to other voices and to inter-rogate itself *in language.*[26] Specifically, Bakhtin's concept of inten-tional, directed hybrid formations (as opposed to the 'organic' or unconscious mixtures of world-views we find in any language) use-fully concentrates on the linguistic and fictional *processes* through which decentring is expressed.[27] This focus also allows us to ask whether and how ideological decentring eventually transforms into a constructive attempt at interdiscursivity. The question can be ap-plied, for example, to Leonard Woolf's attempt in *The Village in the Jungle* (1913) to record alterity from within, as when the already syn-cretic Katagarama/Beragama pilgrimage, which he himself wit-nessed and supervised, is focalized through the perspective of its central players, the Sinhalese people themselves.[28]

[25] Bakhtin discusses ideological decentring as part of his theory of heteroglot multi-plicity in the novel. Heteroglot instability will here be taken as a metaphor through which to conceptualize modernist efforts to take account of the 'native' and the 'foreign' in the imperial world. See Mikhail Bakhtin, 'Discourse in the Novel', *The Dialogic Imagination*, trans. Caryl Emerson and Michael Holquist (Austin: University of Texas Press, 1981), 257–422. [26] Ibid. 276.
[27] On intentional hybridity or 'double-languagedness' in novelistic discourse, that is utterance which is intentionally hybrid because it both takes into account and is *directed towards* a listener, see ibid. 355–62.
[28] As Woolf, *The Village in the Jungle* (1913; London: Hogarth, 1961), 88, writes: '[The Beragama deviyo] is a Tamil god, so they say; but Sinhalese kapuralas serve him in the tem-ple'. Page references to the novel will henceforth appear in the text along with the abbrevi-ation *Village.*

The monologic utterance in Bakhtin, like Said's 'irreversible' and 'consolidated' colonial view, is aware of other utterances, if at all, only as 'objects' exterior to its primary commitments and concerns.[29] However, where this closed and self-sufficient 'voice' is confronted by another world of meaning, in such a way that the other world cannot be ignored—as for example, in the colonial context, with the colonial officer or agent's unsettling involvement in trials and hangings, or proximity to native crowds and chain-gangs[30]— what results can be described as that Bakhtinian disturbance which comes about when an utterance *addresses itself to* others. As in Woolf's Ceylonese letters about fisheries, fatigue, and hangings, the colonizer develops a qualified relationship with his own voice; the authoritative language regards itself, often with disruptive effect, as if refracted through another language, hears itself as if being spoken from another place.[31]

A related condition of colonial self-awareness and consequent ambivalence is described by Homi Bhabha, though for him the emphasis is on how colonial perception is split from the outset, constantly oscillating through aversion and attraction.[32] As Robert Young observes in his discussion of hybridity in both Bakhtin and Bhabha, Bhabha's crucial intervention is to demonstrate how, in any colonial context, a discursive hybridity is dramatized and laid bare in the presence of indigenous cultures.[33] In the present discussion the focus is, somewhat differently, on the *intentioned emergence* of colonial dissonance in writing; on the symbolic dynamics of the decentring experienced by those whose encounter with the alien colonial world, or with colonized self-expression, becomes self-consciously transformative. As suggested, despite its apparently unshakeable

---

[29] Bakhtin, *The Dialogic Imagination*, 285–6.

[30] See George Orwell's baldly reported take on Woolf's thesis of the disaffected *yet still* complicit colonial officer in 'A Hanging' (1931) and 'Shooting an Elephant' (1939), *Collected Essays* (London: Secker and Warburg, 1975). Woolf, too, supervised hangings, as recorded in letters of 10 Mar. and 29 Sept. 1907, in *Letters*, 125–6, 132–3. See also Douglas Kerr, 'Colonial Habitats: Orwell and Woolf in the Jungle', *English Studies*, 78.2 (1997), for a comparative study of the two writers' representations of foreignness, in which Woolf is seen to deliver a far more closely experienced 'theatre of alterity' (p. 149).

[31] See, for example, Bakhtin, *The Dialogic Imagination*, 298–300.

[32] Homi Bhabha, *The Location of Culture*, ch. 6, 'Signs Taken for Wonders: Questions of Ambivalence and Authority', 102–22, and his 'Foreword: Remembering Fanon', to Frantz Fanon, *Black Skin, White Masks*, trans. Charles L. Markmann (London: Pluto, 1986), pp. vii–xxvi.

[33] Robert Young, *Colonial Desire* (London: Routledge, 1995), 20–6.

confidence, it was the very confrontation of an expansive, turn-of-the-century colonialism with myriad different social, cultural, and political 'worlds' across the globe that undercut the possibility and plausibility of its unifying languages of power. What we are interested in therefore are the modes through which that undercutting and decentring were recognized and registered in colonial modernist writing.

In the Bakhtinian model, the self-aware colonial voice (such as that of the young Leonard Woolf or, to an extent, Joseph Conrad), when confronted by cultural difference, and its own seeming superfluity in the colonial context, moves from the unconscious ambivalence described by Bhabha, towards a self-conscious double-voicedness. A studied awareness develops of other subjectivities, of local resistances, and of the possibility of discursive interchange with—and between—them. It is a development that occurs in spite of, and in opposition to, the reassuring separations imposed by the colonial situation in which that voice is enclosed. In the face of this perceptual noise—or, to take an image from Woolf's letters, leakiness—in the foreign environment, a sense of relativity emerges through which the European voice admits of its own ill-adjustedness and illegitimacy. It begins to objectify, displace, deform, and even ironize itself as only *one* within a tangle of 'shared thoughts, points of view, alien value judgements and accents', to quote Bakhtin again.[34] As a variation on this theme, an energizing awareness of dialogic interaction may also emerge through nationalist and cross-national engagements in the heart of the metropolis, as we will see happen in the case of Yeats.

If in different ways, both W. B. Yeats and Leonard Woolf exposed their words and world-views to 'alien', 'dialogically agitated' environments at that crucial informing moment for modernism, the years just before the outbreak of the First World War. This was also of course a time of political emergence for figures like Margaret Noble, Aurobindo Ghose, and Sol Plaatje. Though obviously located at very different points in the colonial hierarchy—Woolf as a Cadet and later an Assistant Government Agent in the Crown Colony of Ceylon (1904–11), Yeats as a member of the lower ranks of the Anglo-Irish gentry—both writers drew on a form of colonial experience in their attempts to conceptualize alterity. No doubt as a result of this contact, both, too, came relatively quickly to underwrite political and

---

[34] Bakhtin, *The Dialogic Imagination*, 276. See also pp. 298–300.

cultural formations other than those of the dominant West, and, partly through historical accident, primarily invoked the East in order to do so. At the same time both also played their different roles within metropolitan modernism. Therefore their writing—in particular that work which stages a confrontation with the colonial other—provides a sharply focusing lens through which to observe, as the following sections will do, not merely the impact of empire on early twentieth-century modernism, but how modernist self-questioning (and self-remaking) was expressed through the medium of cross-cultural encounter.

Leonard Woolf played an influential role in post-First World War modernism not least through his involvement with the Hogarth Press. The aim of the Press, which Leonard established and in its early years ran with his wife Virginia Woolf, was to publish 'difficult', avant-garde writing, alongside, a little later, anti-imperial work.[35] His colonial experience having transformed him into an anti-imperialist, as his autobiography records, Woolf spent the rest of his career as a publisher, journalist, and political adviser translating his opposition to imperialism both into committee action on decolonization, and into unprecedentedly far-sighted political analyses of imperialism-as-violence and the benefits of international government.

'An indisputably national poet', in the words of Edward Said, W. B. Yeats played a central part in the formation of a modern Irish cultural tradition.[36] He is also widely recognized as one of modernism's defining voices, who, especially from the time of *Responsibilities* (1914), came to stand at the very centre of experimentation with 'objective' personae and reinvented custom. In the early 1910s Yeats's brief engagement with the Bengali poet Rabindranath Tagore, whose national status in a colonized country was both like yet unlike his own, acted as an important catalyst in this process of self-transformation, as will be seen. Yeats's reading of Tagore arguably contributed to shaping his theories concerning the formation of identity (including nationality) through struggle and difference, passion and abstraction.

[35] Hermione Lee, *Virginia Woolf* (London: Chatto and Windus, 1996), 371–2; J. H. Willis, *Leonard and Virginia Woolf as Publishers: The Hogarth Press, 1917–1941* (Charlottesville: University Press of Virginia, 1992).

[36] Edward Said, 'Yeats and Decolonization', Field Day Pamphlet 15 (Derry: Field Day Theatre Co., 1988), 5, 8. A reworked version of the essay appears in *Culture and Imperialism*, 265–88.

The rest of this chapter places these two questing and self-questioning writers, the anti-imperial socialist economist and internationalist Woolf and the Irish nationalist and traditionalist Yeats, alongside each other, yet the clear differences between them should also be underlined. While deeply identified with the freethinking, intellectual world of Bloomsbury, Leonard Woolf even as an assimilated Jew was confronted with the anti-Semitism endemic to the liberal bourgeois individualism of that chosen social milieu (amongst others). His wife Virginia Woolf herself confessed to 'hating' his Jewishness.[37] Though 'always conscious of being primarily British', and of being accepted as such, he retained throughout his life a profound if ambivalent awareness of his Jewish identity.[38] This sense of his own difference, 'his dark Eastern blood',[39] which must have impinged on how he experienced difference in the empire, can help account for Woolf's change of political conviction between 1911 and 1918—his shift from a largely unthinking imperialism to an open and far-reaching interrogation of imperialism's central tenets.

Woolf went out to Ceylon 'having given little or no thought to the problems of imperialism'; he returned with a nascent belief in the Ceylonese right to self-government.[40] During the course of the First World War, through his work with the Women's Cooperative Guild, the Fabian Society, and the International Labour Party, he developed a radical moral, cultural, and economic critique of empire as driven by 'capitalistic imperialism', and necessarily based on racial conflict, destructive fetishism, and the breakdown of the 'internal cement of societies'.[41] *Empire and Commerce in Africa* (1920), *Economic Imperialism* (1920), and *Imperialism and Civilization* (1928), as well as the later two-volume *After the Deluge* (1931, 1939), projected J. A. Hobson's thesis concerning jingo-imperialism as the non-rational expansion of capitalist monopolies, especially in Africa, into a critical economic analysis of an entire system of global inequality. To

---

[37] Lee, *Virginia Woolf*, 313–15.　　　　　[38] Woolf, *Letters*, 566.

[39] Leonard Woolf Papers I N (University of Sussex Library Manuscripts Collection). Hereafter LWP.

[40] 'Ceylon Fifty Years After', draft, LWP I L5. This was published as the Preface to *Diaries in Ceylon 1908–1911: Records of a Colonial Administrator, and Stories from the East, Ceylon Historical Journal*, 9. 1–4, ed. S. Saparamadu (July 1959–Apr. 1960), pp. lxxv–lxxx.

[41] Leonard Woolf, *Imperialism and Civilization* (London: Hogarth Press, 1928), 117, 120. See also his *Empire and Commerce in Africa: A Study in Economic Imperialism*, introd. Peter Cain (London: Routledge/Thoemmes Press, 1998), and the distillation of this study in *Economic Imperialism* (London: Swarthmore Press, 1920).

this analysis Woolf added a theory of socialist and international government (as in *International Government* (1916)), which, in part developed out of the theories of the Cooperative Movement, was probably more radical than the politics of any other member of Bloomsbury.[42] As in his work from 1918 for the Advisory Committee to the Labour Party on International Questions, Woolf defined international government as a cooperative 'synthesis' of civilizations which would supervise imperial withdrawal and allow each nation to stand up for itself. This, he believed, was the most effective if not the only remaining modern 'cure' for the inequities of empire.[43]

For his part, W. B. Yeats the Anglo-Irish patriot had worked since the early 1890s in support of Ireland's 'war' to '[affirm] her own individuality' and to oppose English materialism.[44] On the basis especially of his 1930s eugenicist 'race philosophy', Yeats is sometimes regarded as an elitist modernist contemptuous of democratic nationalism.[45] Yet his preoccupation across his lifetime with Irish nationality—its character and symbolic make-up, the nature of its community—and his efforts to revivify Irish cultural traditions and build a new national literature, have more recently been rightly placed in a broadly postcolonial context of resistance to imperial hegemony. From the time of his work for the Irish National Theatre, the way in which the Irish might overcome the debilitating effects of their colonization, Yeats believed, was to 'awaken . . . the national idea' through culture: it is an awakening for which any number

[42] See Duncan Wilson, *Leonard Woolf: A Political Biography* (London; Hogarth Press, 1978). Patrick Brantlinger, '"The Bloomsbury Fraction" Versus War and Empire', in Carola M. Kaplan and Anne B. Simpson (eds.), *Seeing Double: Revisioning Edwardian and Modernist Literature* (Basingstoke: Macmillan, 1996), 149–67, makes a case for a highly politicized Bloomsbury (in the persons most notably of Keynes, Forster, and the Woolfs) which began in liberal cosmopolitanism, yet evolved into a sustained anti-imperialism and internationalism. Its key critical text was Virginia Woolf's *Three Guineas* (1938). The role of Leonard Woolf's colonial experience in this politicization however is not discussed.

[43] Woolf, *Imperialism and Civilization*, 135. See also the 1960s letter to W. T. Stace (LWP I A3b), in which he writes that no civilization can be imposed on another without 'force': the colonial project was thus flawed from the outset.

[44] Letter to T. P. Gill (13 Nov. 1898), in *The Collected Letters of W. B. Yeats*, vol. ii, ed. John S. Kelly, Warwick Gould, and Deirdre Toomey (Oxford: Oxford UP, 1997), 302.

[45] Prominent voices for and against this view are, respectively, Conor Cruise O'Brien, 'Passion and Cunning: An Essay on the Politics of W. B. Yeats', in *In Excited Reverie: A Centenary Tribute to W. B. Yeats 1865–1939*, ed. A. Norman Jeffares (New York: St Martin's Press, 1965), and Elizabeth Cullingford, *Yeats, Ireland and Fascism* (Basingstoke: Macmillan, 1981). For a nuanced discussion of Yeats's 'kindred politics', see Marjorie Howes, *Yeats's Nations: Gender, Class and Irishness* (Cambridge: Cambridge UP, 1996), 160–85.

of chronologically postcolonial novelists and poets since have struggled.[46]

Yet while both writers, though so differently, set themselves in opposition to the dominant imperial culture, they also, as will be seen, remained to an extent complicit with its values and perceptions, especially with regard to racial thinking. Even while the challenge of cultural otherness preoccupied them and the possibility of alternative cultural knowledge held their attention, others (for Woolf, natives in Ceylon, or 'non-adult' Africans in his later economic work; for Yeats, Indians as well as Irish peasants) continued by and large to be described *en masse* or as representatives of generic groups usually situated at a lower point of development relative to the time-line of Western progress. Although the later Woolf, for example, explicitly rejected any belief 'in inherent superiorities and inferiorities in peoples',[47] his descriptive writing about Ceylon routinely draws on stereotypes of the savage, slavish, and somnambulant East, in particular as associated with women.[48] European-constructed difference in this respect continued in both cases to obstruct a more grounded view of the particular social and material worlds which colonized people inhabited.

LEONARD WOOLF: RELUCTANT IMPERIALISM

Leonard Woolf's letters home from Ceylon, where he worked as a colonial officer between 1904 and 1911, along with his official *Diaries*, provide a point of entry to the unsettled contact zone between metropolitan British culture at the start of the last century, and the empire.[49] The letters significantly form the first textual

[46] See the letter to Alice Milligan (23 Sept. 1894), in *The Collected Letters of W. B. Yeats*, vol. i, ed. John S. Kelly and Eric Domville (Oxford: Oxford UP, 1986), 399. Declan Kiberd, *Inventing Ireland* (London: Cape, 1995), offers a spirited and encyclopedic study of modern Irish literature including Yeats as postcolonial.

[47] Woolf, *Imperialism and Civilization*, 119.

[48] Jane Marcus, 'Britannia Rules the Waves', in Karen R. Lawrence (ed.), *Decolonizing Tradition: New Views of Twentieth-Century 'British' Literary Canons* (Urbana: University of Illinois Press, 1992), 151; Phillips, *Virginia Woolf against the Empire*, p. xxxiv; Woolf, *Letters*, 117, 120. In *Empire and Commerce in Africa*, Woolf writes that imperialism has in recent decades been particularly concentrated in Africa as opposed to Asia as here 'there was no old or intricate civilization to resist' the policy of grab. He does allow however that the Africans' present 'non-adult' state is largely due to their gross exploitation by Europe (pp. 54, 229, 354, 357, 364).

[49] Woolf, *Letters*, 55–151; Woolf, *Diaries in Ceylon 1908–1911* (London: Hogarth Press, 1961), and LWP I A1ci.

interrogation of colonization in the new century to take Joseph Conrad's own ambiguous and self-questioning *Heart of Darkness* as an informing (indeed already paradigmatic) text through which to understand empire's paradoxes.[50] The formal echoes of Conrad in Woolf are strong enough to suggest that the younger writer was increasingly relying on Conrad's epistemological questions rather than Rudyard Kipling's influential yet to him ultimately superficial colonial caricatures in order to represent his own personal and political anxieties as an imperialist.[51]

As will be elaborated in the later discussion of his anti-imperial fiction, Conrad's imprint on Woolf's writing continues into the short story 'Pearls and Swine' (1921; composed *c*.1912/13), arguably his most achieved short fiction, which is in part based on material in the letters.[52] It is not noticeably present in the contemporaneous *The Village in the Jungle*, his only colonial novel, which however is once again informed by the close knowledge of local cultures Woolf had acquired during his work as an Assistant Government Agent in Hambantota (1908–11).[53] Radically for their time, both fictions are, even if only at certain moments, centred in native customs and lifeways.[54] In the novel in particular Sinhalese village existence under colonialism is sympathetically—though also highly ambivalently—represented as nasty, brutish, and short.

---

[50] Joseph Conrad, *Heart of Darkness* (1900; Harmondsworth: Penguin, 1973). Any number of anti-imperial (or uncertainly imperial) reworkings of Conrad would follow Woolf's, including those of André Gide, Graham Greene, Wilson Harris, V. S. Naipaul, and Chinua Achebe.

[51] On the presence of Kipling in the story, see Shirley Chew, 'Leonard Woolf's Exemplary Tale "Pearls and Swine"', *Journal of Commonwealth Literature*, 13.1 (Aug. 1978), 44–9.

[52] First published in Leonard Woolf, *Stories from the East* (London: Hogarth Press, 1921); repr. in Saros Cowasjee (ed.), *Stories from the Raj: From Kipling to Independence* (London: Bodley Head, 1982). The original story is reprinted in Elleke Boehmer (ed.), *Empire Writing* (Oxford: Oxford UP, 1998), to which page references in the text will refer together with the abbreviation 'PS'. For the story's earlier time of composition, see Woolf, *Letters*, p. xxx; Willis, *Leonard and Virginia Woolf as Publishers*, 57. The resonances with Conrad emerge primarily in the stress on the redeeming reality of work, and in the absurd farce of the white man's presence among watchful and inscrutable natives.

[53] Basil Mendis, 'The Official Diaries of Leonard Woolf', *Ceylon Daily News* (21 June 1950); Woolf, *Letters*, 61–2.

[54] Woolf based his other short prose fictions from this period on his Ceylonese experience. In addition to 'Pearls and Swine' the two 'stories from the east' (1921) are: the cynical colonial romance 'A Tale Told by Moonlight' in which the narrative techniques and ironies are again informed by Conrad, and the fabulistic 'The Two Brahmans'.

What is immediately striking about Woolf's letters is how markedly they contrast with the efficient and scrupulously factual administrative records which he was keeping in his official *Diaries* at the time. Especially in the often anguished expostulations addressed to his close friend Lytton Strachey, Woolf responds to his experience of governing Tamils (in Jaffna) and then Sinhalese (in Hambantota) as a Marlow who, moving into the unknown of another culture, though cushioned by white colonial structures, is unnerved and shaken. On almost every level, he observes, the accepted colonial premisses of entrenched superiority come into conflict with those of humanist but paternalistic overlordship. Woolf however finds—unlike Marlow—no secret sharer, no Kurtz through whom to recuperate his illusions about the civilizing mission or the value of his labours. Paradoxically (again in a manner akin to Marlow), the structure supplied by the formalities and fact-collecting of his colonial work alone functions as a survival mechanism, a guard against mental and emotional instability: 'one has no time to think at all about anything but work & food & facts ... if it weren't for that, one would probably go mad'.[55]

Read chronologically, we see in the letters a growing awareness of British colonial culture as caught in a contradictory and unreal, indeed even absurd, position. Confused about the purpose of their rule, people at the club in Woolf's view act out a Kiplingesque fantasy which lacks any connection with local life.[56] Woolf experienced this displacement as an increasing 'political schizophrenia'. On the one hand the hardworking colonial officer was attempting to follow the best principles of disinterested yet efficient colonial administra-

---

[55] Letter to G. E. Moore (4 Jan. 1909), in Woolf, *Letters*, 143–4. The *Diaries*, his administrative report on his own activities, record not only tank or water reservoir check-ups, improvements in salt collection, and cases of cattle sickness, but also the number of miles ridden and rupees spent in any one month. Woolf would maintain this discipline of meticulous record-keeping throughout his career as a political commentator and publisher. In this respect the early Hogarth Press accounts showing *inter alia* lists of subscribers to publications, are comparable to the Hambantota tank register. See LWP I A1f, which includes a register of tanks; LWP I Q1a, the Hogarth accounts; and LWP I A1a, his 1906–12 account books. A 'modernist' attention to structuring form, one might say, initially came to Woolf from his colonial experience. 'These artists do not seek to imitate form, but to create form', Roger Fry's manifesto for the second Post-Impressionist Exhibition in 1912–23 memorably proclaimed. See Lee, *Virginia Woolf*, 324.

[56] As Woolf wrote in *Growing*, 17: 'White society in India and Ceylon, as you can see in Kipling's stories, was always suburban. ... the social structure and relations between Europeans, rested on the same kind of snobbery, pretentiousness and false pretensions as they did in Putney or Peckham'. See also p. 46.

tion; on the other, while becoming gradually more involved in local Sinhalese life, he was growing increasingly resentful about acting the colonial charade, playing at being 'a ruler of the ruled'. (The response was no doubt exacerbated by his efforts as an 'internal' cultural outsider, a Jew, to conform as a 'good fellow' and a 'gentleman'.[57])

In retrospect it was this estranging self-awareness that, back in England, changed Woolf into an anti-imperialist. In the conflict at the centre of the story 'Pearls and Swine', as well as in *The Village in the Jungle*, the process and the consequences of his cultural shock and self-alienation are starkly dramatized: the fictions can in effect be arranged along a continuum of ideological transformation, as will be demonstrated. In both works, importantly, the motive power behind this process is the contact with and concern for cultural alterity, what Woolf calls his engrossing 'obsession' with 'those strange jungle villages'. The novel, which effectively represents an entire culture in trauma, Woolf later called 'the symbol of the anti-imperialism which had been growing upon me more and more in my last years in Ceylon'. His attempt 'vicariously to live [the] lives' of the inhabitants of a Sinhalese jungle village became, as he himself said, a 'catalyst' in his decision to leave the colonial service: 'The more I wrote [the novel], the more distasteful became the prospect of success in Colombo.'[58]

An iconic case in point of Woolf's early disorientation or ideological decentring occurs in a letter to Strachey of 21 May 1905, written within the first year of his arriving in Ceylon (in October 1904).[59] From the start the (conscious and unconscious) Conradian notes from *Heart of Darkness*, as well as 'Youth' (1898), are unmistakable: the pervasive sense of disgust at the white man's self-involved and pointless rule in the tropics; the devotion to work as giving a hold on things despite their tedium; the inevitable stereotyping of natives, here of their fatalism. The predominant mood however is created out

---

[57] Woolf, *Growing*, 158, 36, 40, 64, 70, and his *Beginning Again: An Autobiography of the Years 1911–1918* (London: Hogarth Press, 1964), 100.

[58] Woolf, *Beginning Again*, 47, 52; *Growing*, 224–5.

[59] Woolf, Letter to Lytton Strachey (21 May 1905), in Woolf, *Letters*, 89–91. This is one of the five or so letters that Woolf later quoted in *Growing* as evoking 'very vividly the atmosphere and savour of those early days in Jaffna' (p. 58). This group includes the immediately following letter to Strachey (4 June 1905), in *Letters*, 92–3, in which he describes the alienating work of being a police magistrate, as well as, probably, the letters of 9 Apr. and 21 May 1905.

of the cognitive slippages and Conradian misrecognitions concerning what colonial reality really involves. There is a profound sense of the fragility of the perceptual world such as it was previously understood—a sense which, interestingly, at this point intersects to an extent with the response of the natives. Not so much despite but *because of* participating fully in the day-to-day rituals of colonial life—riding, flirting, hunting, and tennis—'this curious mixture of intense reality and unreality', even of 'theatrical unreality', as Woolf describes it, is a perception that grows inexorably upon him.[60]

The perception is one that he returns to again and again in his letters, as he does in *Growing* (1961), his autobiography about the years in Ceylon. There is 'the strange sense of a complete break with the past', and of 'no connection with yesterday'. '[O]ne feels as if one were acting in a play or living in a dream', in relation to which, significantly, not only Ceylonese life but existence back in London and Cambridge seems unreal.[61] '[A]ll Anglo-Indians and imperialists who were colonial government servants' resemble '"displaced persons"': 'in a foreign country, [we] had therefore become unreal, artificial, temporary, and alien'.[62] Right across his time in Ceylon, Woolf speaks of a deepening depression at this general 'futility' of existence, which was for him exacerbated by the central undermining contradiction of imperialism: how liberal humanitarianism disguised, yet was upheld by, authoritarianism (it was the same contradiction which Plaatje so profoundly experienced). 'Theoretically everyone is told that he is equal with everyone else, while practically we try to be paternal, despotic.'[63]

In the May 1905 letter, Woolf's sense of the general uncertainty of things in the foreign colonial context is given dramatic point by his description of a great hole (due to subsidence) that appears to be opening in the Jaffna Peninsula, threatening to tumble the whole province over which he as Cadet has authority, into the sea. Beginning with the observation, 'A cataclysm is hourly expected here', he goes on:

[60] Woolf, *Growing*, 21, 24. Letters written to Woolf during the early years in Ceylon (LWP I A1bi), record his many social activities.

[61] Woolf, *Growing*, 26–7; Letter to Strachey (8 Apr. 1908), in *Letters*, 137; *Growing*, 21, 23.

[62] Woolf, *Growing*, 23, 46, 47. See also the letters of, for example, 20 Dec. 1904, 5 Jan. 1905, 4 June 1905, and 17 Nov. 1907, in *Letters*, 68–9, 70–1, 92, 134.

[63] Letter to Strachey (3 Mar. 1907), in *Letters*, 124–5. See also the letter to Strachey of 25 Sept. 1905, pp. 101–2.

a hole had suddenly appeared in the midst of a field about 5 miles from Jaffna, that . . . had gradually in a few hours increased from about 3 to 90 square feet & . . . was still increasing . . . It is like a big pond with the water about a foot from the top, there is a curious heaving in the water. . . . Hundreds of natives stand round, looking on with their usual appearance of complete indifference, & every time another foot of the ground disappears, a long 'aiyo, aiyo' goes up. The water is obviously from the sea . . . and I expect that it means that Jaffna Peninsula is going to return to the seabed from which it came.

Even if we let alone the self-conscious melodrama of the language, Woolf can be read as using the incident and the feeling of incipient disaster it evokes as a signifier of his state of mind, the profound unsettling of his world: not only a part of the geographical colony, the peninsula, but of the colonial structure, the province as administrative unit, is crumbling away. The description ends abruptly with one of the refrains concerning his mental inertia which are recurrent in the letters to Strachey: 'I neither read nor think nor—in the old way—feel.' The curiosities of local life are 'the only realities'; there is nothing else of importance, other than, intriguingly, in the account of an inspection of a leaky (and again Conradian) ship which follows, further suggestions of imminent danger and flooding, and of holes and cracks in the stability of things.[64] And yet, significantly, it is not the colonizer's reality alone which is unstable and shifting; the threat is to the natives' also. The faultlines in the colonial edifice are seemingly tearing the island open from within; in this respect native and colonial worlds are coterminous.

The implicit, perhaps even unconscious, connections that Woolf makes in the May 1905 letter between his feelings of alienation and displacement, and scenes involving a leaky earth and leaky vessels, once again bear echoes of Marlow's narrative in *Heart of Darkness*. At this point the parallel with Conrad highlights yet also counterpoints the emptying out of Woolf's preconceptions that occurs in response to the foreign unreality that is also the 'only reality'. Like Woolf, Marlow registers a perceptual shock at the seeming inscrutability of the native environment *and*, at the same time, at the grotesque, 'objectless' farce of empire.[65] And, like Woolf, he too comes to compare his experience to dreaming:

[64] It is noteworthy that the same letter opens with a further reference to uncertainty and anxiety, indeed to literal displacement, where Woolf speaks of having been forced to move house and the fear of catching a colleague's consumption.

[65] At the Outer Station, while attempting to avoid following the 'deathlike' spectacle of

It seems to me I am trying to tell you a dream . . . that commingling of absurdity, surprise, and bewilderment in a tremor of struggling revolt, that notion of being captured by the incredible which is of the very essence of dreams.[66]

Unlike Marlow, however, and arguably unlike Conrad, Woolf, the social constructionist and economic analyst of empire, attempted both in his fictions and in his more theoretical writings eventually to dismantle this colonial 'dream' rather than to recuperate it. In particular in his only colonial novel, the isolated and intractably other 'village in the jungle' of the title, as well as being a symbol of cultural dissolution, can be read as a correlative for Woolf's own alienation as a colonial officer. Two socially distinct worlds, the European and the Sinhalese, are brought into proximity in the novel in order to make a point about how imposed imperial structures distort and destroy rather than in any sense improve the natives' existence.

In Woolf's case therefore the encounter with another world of meaning in the empire eventually acted with displacing and eventually disintegrating force both on his imperial beliefs, and on his sense of self as an imperial European. In later letters home from Ceylon (which significantly decreased in frequency) he speaks of being 'done for' with regard to England, of his alienation not so much in relation to local life, into which he increasingly feels he might sink, but to home: 'The scene has changed here . . . & one changes inside too.'[67] The proximate presence of the indigenous culture, and his perception of its integrity, of the coherence of its internal relations, worked to cast doubt on the system of authority (and on the justifications of that system) which he as a colonial officer represented: 'We are all doomed, I imagine,' he wrote, 'we treat them as inferiors & tell them

---

the chain-gang, Marlow tells us, he sidesteps a vast hole dug for no apparent purpose, and then nearly falls into a ravine dumped full of imported and broken drainage pipes before finally stumbling into the hellish grove of trees where slaves disabled by their work lie dying. Later, at the Central Station, where he is occupied in mending the steamer which has had the bottom torn out of it, there is a fire which one of the white men attempts to put out with a leaky bucket. Withheld from working by an absence of rivets, Marlow is overwhelmed by a deep sense of unreality: the brickmaker, a hollow 'papier-mâché Mephistopheles', has nothing to make his bricks with; there is a pervasive 'air of plotting about [the] station, but nothing came of it, of course'. See Conrad, *Heart of Darkness*, 22, 40–1, 35.

[66] Ibid. 39.

[67] Letter to Lytton Strachey (2 Oct. 1908), in *Letters*, 137. See also the Woolf epigraph above.

that they are their own equals'; 'They don't understand and they don't believe in our methods.'[68]

THE CULTURAL NATIONALIST AS MODERNIST:
W. B. YEATS

The cultural nationalist channels along which W. B. Yeats drew close to the Eastern aesthetic integrity, as he saw it, of the Bengali poet Rabindranath Tagore in some sense predisposed their crossing of paths long before their actual meeting at the London home of William Rothenstein on 27 June 1912. Once they had met, their mutual sense of their affinity encouraged each poet for a time to see in the other an artist in his own mould, one who aspired to a union of sensuous and spiritual beauties yet, at the same time, struggled to restore his country's 'faith in herself'.[69]

Across his long career as an Irish man of letters, Yeats's conception of nationality constantly shifted in line with his changing ideas about Irish community, class, and femininity, and of the relationship of these with English culture.[70] In this he closely approached the nationalist vicissitudes and ambivalences of Tagore, who, across a similarly long career, moved from an early identification with the nationalist project of cultural self-realization in 1905–7 Calcutta, to a condemnation of what he saw as the chauvinistic violence and selfish fanaticism of such a politics around the time of the First World War. In one of his most explicit expostulations against nationalism, *The Home and the World* (1916), a work which Yeats admired for its conviction, Tagore wrote: 'man's history has to be built by the united effort of all the races in the world, and therefore . . . this making a fetish of one's country, won't do'.[71]

So, although the lines of connection which forged the brief 'imperfect encounter' between Yeats and Tagore, were broadly founded

---

[68] Letters to Lytton Strachey of 3 Mar. and 28 Apr. 1907, in *Letters*, 125, 128.

[69] Tagore quoted in R. F. Foster, *W. B. Yeats: A Life*, vol. i (Oxford: Oxford UP, 1997), 470.

[70] See Howes, *Yeats's Nations*, 13, on the 'multiple possibilities and fluid constructions that characterize [not only Yeats's nationalism but] the discourses of nationality in any period'.

[71] Rabindranath Tagore, *The Home and the World (Ghare Baire)*, trans. Surendranath Tagore, rev. R. Tagore (1916/1919; Madras: Macmillan India, 1992), 224–5; Ketaki Kushari Dyson, 'Introduction' to Rabindranath Tagore, *I Won't Let You Go: Selected Poems*, ed. and trans. Ketaki Kushari Dyson (Newcastle: Bloodaxe, 1991), 26–7; Krishna Dutta and Andrew Robinson, *Rabindranath Tagore: The Myriad-Minded Man* (London: Bloomsbury, 1995), 225.

upon their shared concern with aesthetic unity—the unity of a culture, the spiritual integrity of the poet's calling, the intersubjective metaphysics of 'soul'—yet these lines probably converge most closely in the area of their often critical cultural nationalism.[72] Both poets became in their respective contexts architects of a national culture; both believed in fostering the essential elements of such a culture, its language and its legends; yet both could vigorously repudiate nationalist commitment as being artistically limiting and culturally stifling. For Tagore, the nationalist passion for selfhood, an intensely modern impulse, a 'fierce self-idolatry', could work upon a society with 'tyrannical' and regressive effect, distorting value systems, converting political life into endless 'wranglings' over the national good.[73] Yeats, too, was scathing about how nationalist orthodoxies dressed up as aesthetic value-judgements ('my country right or wrong'), polarized a people and imprisoned its intellect, making of national existence a ceaseless argument choked with 'hatred'.[74] A truly national literature, Yeats opined in a 1893 lecture, was born not

[72] Mary Lago (ed.), *Imperfect Encounter: Letters of William Rothenstein and Rabindranath Tagore* (Cambridge, Mass.: Harvard UP, 1972). As recent biographies of both poets point out, the understanding between the two was transitory, even though it always exceeded (in Yeats's case) an Eastern fad or (in Tagore's) a fascination with the Irish poet's authority and glamour. On both sides however the collaboration all too quickly became the victim of the vicissitudes of modernist fashion, of a general impatience with the other's untranslatable difference, and, in Tagore's case, apprehension as to the part Yeats had played in creating the phenomenon of *Gitanjali*, the translations on which his reputation in the West, and the award of the 1913 Nobel Prize, were founded. See Dutta and Robinson, *Rabindranath Tagore*, 3–4, 225; Foster, *W. B. Yeats*, 439–73; Mair Pitt, *The Maha-Yogi and the Mask* (Salzburg: University of Salzburg Studies in English Literature, 1997), 39–41. By 1917 Yeats was suggesting that Tagore had debased his spiritual verse through oversentimentality, while Pound, a fellow admirer, wrote as early as 1913 that Tagore in translation equated to 'mere theosophy'. See Pound's letter to Harriet Monroe (22 Apr. 1913), in *Selected Letters of Ezra Pound 1907–1941*, ed. D. D. Paige (London: Faber and Faber, 1950), 19. In a letter to Rothenstein (7 May 1935), in *The Letters of W. B. Yeats*, ed. Allen Wade (London: Rupert Hart-Davis, 1954), 834–5, Yeats ultimately attributed Tagore's failure to his writing in English: 'Nobody can write with music and style in a language not learned in childhood and ever since the language of his thought.' It was a deficiency of which Tagore himself was well-aware. See Pitt, *The Maha-Yogi and the Mask*, 38.

[73] Tagore, *The Home and the World*, 74–5; *My Reminiscences* (London: Macmillan, 1917), 128; and *Nationalism* (London: Macmillan, 1917); Dutta and Robinson, *Rabindranath Tagore*, 193–4, 239; Ashis Nandy, *The Illegitimacy of Nationalism: Rabindranath Tagore and the Politics of Self* (New Delhi: Oxford UP, 1994). See also the several references to the wearisome struggle that is the (political) world, and the countervailing 'freedom' of 'ever-widening thought and action', in *Gitanjali* itself. Rabindranath Tagore, *Collected Poems and Plays* (London: Macmillan, 1938), 3–48.

[74] W. B. Yeats, 'J. M. Synge and the Ireland of His Time', *EI* 318–24, and his 'Prayer for my Daughter', *The Collected Poems*, ed. Richard Finneran (London: Macmillan, 1993), 188–90.

merely from within, autochthonously, but out of a cosmopolitan mix of influences, in relationship with the writing of other cultures.[75]

These are words which Tagore would have applauded, yet which Yeats himself, on other occasions, gainsaid, as when he wrote that the true essence of an oppressed culture was embodied in its own surviving myths and stories, 'its ancient arts' and passionate rituals. Therefore, 'a country which has no institutions must show its young men images for the affections';[76] a nation's coming-into-being had to be self-generated. To resist the corrupting effects whether of modernity or of materialist imperialism, nationality for Yeats, as once again for Tagore, had to find its foundation in its own spiritual resources, out of which defining forms might be forged. If there is a contradiction here, Yeats resolved it in the realm of cosmology, in the image of the Great Mind or Anima Mundi which he saw as comprising many minds, an interconnection of souls and, hence, as demonstrating a distinct intersubjectivity, whether between individuals or between social groups and nations.[77] This World Mind compares once again to the concept of universal affinity and understanding on which Tagore believed international relations might be built.[78]

Yeats and Tagore were therefore, one might say, acting on a shared, intersubjective awareness when, in 1912, they formed the partnership on which *Gitanjali* (*Song Offerings*), Tagore's first publication in English in the West, was built. In many ways they could not have chosen a more fitting instrument with which to substantialize their cross-cultural relationship. The 1912 *Gitanjali*, a collection of prose poems in English translated from his own subtly rhymed Bengali poetry by Tagore, and arranged and introduced by Yeats, was itself a 'hybrid'; a selection from three of Tagore's earlier Bengali collections, *Kheya*, *Naivedya*, and his 1910 Bengali *Gitanjali*.[79]

Not inappropriately for one who believed the earth's 'ancient ways' to be filled with dreams,[80] Yeats in his promotional Introduction to *Gitanjali* used the language of dream perception when speaking of the early effect on him of Tagore's work. The Bengali's lyrics

[75] W. B. Yeats, 'Nationality and Literature', in *Uncollected Prose*, vol. i, ed. John Frayne (London: Macmillan, 1970), 266–75. But see also *EI* 208.

[76] Yeats, *EI* 203–6, 312–13.

[77] On Yeats's occult notions of 'intersubjectivity', see Howes, *Yeats's Nations*, 66–101.

[78] Pitt, *The Maha-Yogi and the Mask*, 41.

[79] Dutta and Robinson, *Rabindranath Tagore*, 164–5, 184; Foster, *W. B. Yeats*, 470–1.

[80] See the early poems 'The Song of the Happy Shepherd', and 'The Rose upon the Rood of Time', *The Collected Poems*, 7–8, 31.

or *Song Offerings*, he wrote, displayed a world that he '[had] dreamed of all [his] life long'.[81] In effect the imagery did not differ from that of either Woolf or Conrad in describing their first contact with cultural otherness. Differently from Woolf, however, in Yeats's case the dream-metaphor is clearly intended to suggest a profound sense of sympathy and fellow-feeling with the East, one which dates back to his early attraction to Theosophy and interest in Indian myth and epic (notably, Kalidasa's play *Sakuntala*, whose lyricism may have moulded his responsiveness to Tagore's own lyrical Vaishnava approach). In some of his first published poems, collected in the significantly entitled *Crossways* (1889), Yeats inflects mystical yearnings through an Indian symbolism (for instance, 'The Indian upon God', or 'Anashuya and Vijaya').[82] Even so, as it were in the same breath, the language of the Introduction betrays, we cannot fail to notice, an unmistakable Orientalism, the notion of an East suspended at an earlier, simpler, and more intuitive stage of civilization.

As we saw, Yeats's position as an Anglo-Irishman and Irish cultural nationalist relative to British colonialism was obviously different from that of Leonard Woolf, even though neither writer found

---

[81] W. B. Yeats, 'Introduction', to Rabindranath Tagore, *Gitanjali (Song Offerings)* (London: Macmillan, 1913), p. xiii (pp. vii–xxii). The book was first issued along with Yeats's Introduction in a limited 1912 edition by the London Indian Society. Page references will henceforth be included parenthetically in the text.

[82] Yeats, *The Collected Poems*, 10–14. From about 1885 Yeats had begun to seek in the 'maze of eastern thought', as he said in his opening address to the Dublin Hermetic Society (later the Dublin Theosophical Society), answers to his questions concerning the nature of the soul, the poet's identity, and the mystical underpinnings of the nation. Following his first collection, *Crossways* (1889), with its clear symbolic resonances from Indian myth, the next, *The Rose* (1893), continued his meditation on ideal forms and dreamlike states in which, as he said, 'only body's laid asleep' ('To Ireland in the Coming Times', *The Collected Poems*, 50–1). Though his chief mystical authorities were Western—Blake, Boehme, and Swedenborg—Theosophy was for Yeats a philosophy that 'confirmed my vague speculations and seemed at once logical and boundless'. His contact in Dublin in 1886 with the Indian Theosophist Mohini Chatterji, led in 1888 to a two-year membership of the Esoteric Section of Madame Blavatsky's Theosophical Society in London. Put off by the leadership cult surrounding Blavatsky, he joined MacGregor Mathers's Hermetic Order of the Golden Dawn in 1891. As essays such as 'Magic' or 'The Symbolism of Poetry' suggest (*EI* 28–52, 153–64), Eastern mysticism and the occult supplied Yeats with a supporting framework for his own theory of an evocative symbolism connected with 'certain disembodied powers'. Till late on in his career, the East, especially India, would continue to represent for Yeats a 'spontaneity of the soul', and, in general, a more integrated and complete culture than his own nation could offer. See Richard Ellman, *Yeats: The Man and the Masks* (Harmondsworth: Penguin, 1979), 44, 68; Foster, *W. B. Yeats*, 45–52, 101–7; Howes, *Yeats's Nations*, 83–101. See also *EI* 208, 342, and the 1932 essay on Shri Purohit Swami, 'An Indian Monk', *EI* 426–37.

himself close to the core of the British establishment. Yet it is note-worthy that in his promotional Introduction the Irish poet, once a seeker after Indian wisdom, initially takes up the position of writing self-consciously as a Westerner.[83] He does this moreover even while searching for terms that will at once evoke *and* effect the 'stirring' en-counter with a distant Eastern culture that Tagore's poetry seems to him to invite (p. vii). The Introduction, as this might suggest, forms a vehicle through which to express at one and the same time his long-standing involvement with the East, *and* his Europe-centred perspec-tive. Within its triptych structure the Western poet attempts carefully to explicate the Bengali's mystical appeal in a way with which his English-speaking audience will be able to identify (an effort reflected also in Yeats's emendations of Tagore's literal translations). Yet, even as he does so, he is concerned to accentuate the Bengali poet's self-contained spiritual remoteness as a powerful cultural resource: 'the birds and the leaves seem as near to him as they are near to children' (p. xx). At this level, as will be demonstrated, the essay offers a coded nationalist statement of Yeats's continuing ambitions for an inte-grated Irish culture: Tagore's Bengal is constructed as a channel for his own political ideals. Thus unfolding its several different layers of meaning, the Introduction becomes probably the core expression of Yeats's cultural and poetic contact with India.[84]

The first contextual or biographical section of the Introduction develops as a straightforward hearsay narrative (pp. vii–xiii): al-though it is impressionistic, Yeats wrote that he was here 'anxious' to get the facts about Tagore's background right.[85] It is in the second section or 'little chapter' as he called it, that he moves on to chart the *process* of the poetry's effect on its Western reader. Passing rapidly from his initial impressions of the poet's baffling foreignness, he at-tempts within a few sentences to identify on some level with the work's 'immeasurable strangeness' (p. xvii), its passionate intercon-nection of the love of nature with the love of the spirit. He does this even as he reflects on the lack of integration which marks public life

[83] The Introduction to *Gitanjali* was written and published, we might observe, not long after Woolf's return from Ceylon, when he was beginning work on *his* account of the East.

[84] Read strictly as a promotional text, the Introduction can moreover be seen as a reflec-tion of the considerable influence Yeats was by this time able to wield in the London liter-ary world.

[85] Letter to William Rothenstein (7 Sept. 1912), in *The Letters of W. B. Yeats*, 569–70. See also William Rothenstein, *Men and Memories: Recollections 1872–1938*, introd. Mary Lago (London: Chatto and Windus, 1978), 267.

in Europe, and more specifically in Ireland, relative to the 'complete-ness' of Tagore's poetic world in Bengal. No doubt springing out of his preoccupation with Eastern mysticism, there is for Yeats some-thing deeply revelatory, if not confirmatory, in this poetic connection with a distant, 'ancient' culture, the 'unbroken . . . common mind' which *Gitanjali* represents. Similar to Woolf, an intentioned turn to-wards the foreign begins to generate in Yeats, in spite of cultural pre-conceptions, an objectification of the familiar and the proximate, a tentative expansion or reticulation of accepted modes of thought. Europe's mind, in effect, allows itself to feel the influence of the greater 'common mind'.

Setting aside his early bafflement, therefore, Yeats establishes in the second section of the Introduction an affinity with Bengal. How-ever erroneously given its different history and its self-conscious sense of difference, however correctly given the existing term 'the Bengal Renaissance', he has already called the literary movement from which Tagore has sprung a 'new Renaissance' (p. ii). Impressed by the Bengali poet's status as the voice of his people, by the way in which his multigeneric appeal is based on a noble lineage yet is im-mediate in its impact, Yeats in effect tries to read into Tagore's repu-tation a more achieved parallel for what he himself has tried to forge in his own country with the Irish National Theatre. He then goes on to compare this civilization of which Tagore is the consummate voice, to the (to him) integrated world of medieval Europe, in which meditation and politics, love and philosophy, were expressed in and through each other. On very similar lines, Yeats's new acolyte and fel-low Tagore promoter Ezra Pound, in his own adulatory 1912 write-ups for the *Fortnightly Review* and Harriet Monroe's *Poetry*, compared Tagore's poems to the 'troubadours songs [which] were sung through Europe'.[86] (For Pound, too, the keynote in 'discovering' Tagore was the cultural contact and fellowship his work appeared to represent. Europe's 'more intimate intercourse with Bengal' in the form of Tagore's 'deeply calm' work resembled 'the restoration of Greek to Europe in Petrarch's time'; the poetry was an important cor-rective for an overmechanical age.)

For both Pound and Yeats, therefore, a reading of Tagore triggered a characteristic modernist nostalgia for a fuller, vibrant, and more

---

[86] Ezra Pound, 'Tagore's Poems', *Poetry*, 1.3 (Dec. 1912), 84–6, and 'Rabindranath Tagore', *Fortnightly Review*, 99 (1913), 571–9. See also Helen Carr, 'Imagism and Empire', in Booth and Rigby (eds.), *Modernism and Empire*, 81–2.

unselfconscious life, marked by a reciprocity between the elite and the 'unlearned' (p. xiv), a unification of the spiritual and sensual aspects of being (p. xv). Within a shared context of colonization, Yeats develops the contrast between the Calcutta Renaissance and the 'warfare' that is aesthetic and political life in modern Ireland, to project his own image of an integrated East upon Tagore and upon Bengal. This romantic idealization again carries clear Orientalist overtones, especially in the way in which he in effect homogenizes 'a whole people'.[87] Indeed Yeats chooses entirely to ignore, if he ever knew about, Bengal's own internecine nationalist quarrels, in which Tagore had been widely castigated by Aurobindo Ghose amongst others for his criticism of the nationalist movement and his seeming abandonment of the anti-imperialist cause.

However, the yearning towards a closer connection with India that moves through the writing also qualifies such crude homogenizing. Differently put, Yeats's romanticization of Tagore serves as a pathway along which the self-modernizing *and yet* patriotic Irish writer can embrace and underwrite what he believes Tagore the national poet represents in the Bengali context. After all, what for Yeats differentiates Ireland from India ultimately lies not in the terrain of ideals—of cultural cohesiveness or unity—but of practical politics, the mundanities of factionalism or the Irish 'culture wars' in which he himself was still embroiled. So, even whilst sketching the differences that separate Europe from Tagore, Yeats prepares for the turning point two-thirds of the way through the essay, when he says that despite its effects of estrangement, the Indian poet's work makes its strongest impression because we find within that strangeness 'our own image', we have 'heard, perhaps for the first time in literature, our voice as in a dream' (p. xvii). He is invoking, in effect, a double 'we', that of Europe *and* of Ireland: what else would so deeply 'stir' his blood (p. i)? Here, in Tagore's work, Yeats finds at last, fully realized, Ireland's dream self. Affinity with Bengal is based on a cultural wholeness which Yeats feels has long been latent in his own country.

---

[87] At moments in the essay, too, Yeats can be seen as patronizing and stereotyping 'my Indians' (p. xiii). Pound, relatedly, homogenizes much of *Gitanjali* in the *Poetry* review. There was, it must be recognized, much hype in the promotion of the Bengali by Yeats and Pound. It was, as Pound put it, 'a piece of wise imperialism'—'in honouring him we honour India'. If for no other reason, such a welcome was bound to implode due to its own overextravagance. See James Longenbach, *Stone Cottage: Pound, Yeats and Modernism* (Oxford: Oxford UP, 1988), 17.

Selective European self-representation in the terms of the other is admittedly once again a commonplace mode in conventional colonialist writing. Yet what is significant about Yeats's language in the Introduction is that the perceived cultural difference is not only recognized as reflecting a division within the self, but that the difference, the other, is seen as paradoxically closer to the self, more real, more passionate and human, than are aspects of Europe's religious culture. As do anti-imperialist aversions in Leonard Woolf, nationalist and indeed cross-national yearnings thus bring the other and the other's values into the very heart of Yeats's anti-materialist and modernist framework. Like Woolf, too, Yeats uses suggestions of unreality, and of a splitting of the self, to evoke the impact of a strangeness that yet accommodates, an unhomeliness that can be welcomed home. In Woolf's *The Village in the Jungle* the sorrows of Punchi Menika appear far more immediate than the machinations of colonial justice. Relatedly, as Yeats admits towards the end of section two, there is a deeper responsiveness in Tagore than we find in Western mysticism, a greater fullness of spiritual experience. As a means of resolution and healing, Tagore's poetry thus offers a more effective comfort for the alienated society of contemporary Europe, and especially Ireland, than does European ascetic literature. As if to dramatize this closeness within his own writing, Yeats devotes the final section of the Introduction to long quotations from *Gitanjali* which, to him, illustrate the Bengali lyricist's spontaneous intensity and unity of being (pp. xx–xxii).[88] He, so to speak, takes Tagore into the body of his own work.

Paradoxically, it was around the time he was thus praising the Indian poet, that Yeats, in an attempt to cultivate 'a less dream-burdened will', was turning to a greater precision of form and an objectifying impersonality in his own work. It may be however that the simultaneous identification-and-contrast that Tagore represented, enacted for Yeats that conflict out of which he believed all creativity was born. We can speculate, in other words, that the contradictory encounter with the Bengali poet that Yeats describes—this encounter with an opposite that was also in part himself—served as one of the catalysts of the changed, pared-down poetry Yeats was beginning to write. Tagore's devotional poetry in the Vaishnava tradition of

---

[88] The concluding quotation in the Introduction is from the poem 'On the Seashore', in *The Crescent Moon* (1913), Tagore's second collection in English. See Tagore, *Collected Poems and Plays*, 51–2.

intensely personal spiritual longing,[89] exemplified the type of work Yeats could identify with but was seeking to divest himself of. Conversely, however, the achievement that Tagore represented as the national voice of Bengal (although this was a deeply conflicted position for Tagore himself), may have suggested to Yeats a model for a disciplined aesthetic that yet retained powerful cultural and political resonances. Some critics in fact go so far as to claim that Tagore's simplified or generic spiritual imagery offered Yeats a model, as Synge's prose had earlier on, on which to base his own resistance to poetic ornamentation.[90]

At one level, therefore, Yeats comes across in the Introduction as a Western poet encountering work of suggestive cultural remoteness. Yet this response can be further broken down if it is read against the backdrop of Ireland's own colonized position in relation to Britain, and Yeats's particular nationalist interests as expressed in the Celtic Revival and in his labours for the Irish National Theatre. Like artists of the decolonizing world since his time, as we have seen, Yeats confronted the question of how to give structure to a national culture emerging out of a history of dispossession. In the absence of rallying symbols of identity in the political or religious arenas, he realized, an artist had to attempt to forge these out of the detritus of the colonial past, and the surviving myths and stories of the downtrodden. The cross-cultural contact with the Bengali poet became in this sense, therefore, very specifically recuperative and, again, confirmatory. Yeats felt attracted to the cultural idealism of a writer like Tagore because of the latter's evident concern with local traditions and rural scenes. He could relate to the compulsion to retrieve or preserve an image of the homeland untouched by the colonial presence (for Tagore this comprised the pastoral; for Yeats the folk or peasantry of Ireland). In short, Yeats saw in Tagore an exemplar of a lyrical and spiritual nationalism which harmonized with his own: hence perhaps his over-idealization of features of the other oppressed culture. In this context his later resistance to Tagore's working in English can be read as a backhanded acknowledgement of the Bengali's own efforts to champion his native tongue. To take liberty with the watchword of the Bengal Resistance (which itself owed something to the Irish example of Sinn Féin), both writers espoused a kind of

[89] On the Vaishnava mode in Tagore's poetry, see Mary Lago, *Rabindranath Tagore* (Boston: Twayne Publishers, 1976).
[90] See Pitt, *The Maha-Yogi and the Mask*, 54.

spiritual self-help or swadeshi, a reliance on the nation's own cultural strength.

Impelled by his ambitions for Ireland, Yeats's quintessentially Western yet also nationalist approach to Tagore's achievement demonstrates how Bakhtin's 'foreign' or 'alien' might also *at the same time* be the familiar, the already uttered, this intersection taking place not only in the unconscious world of dreams and symbols, but in a political, anti-imperial sphere. In this case a modernist concern with cultural relativism and self-invention, in so far as it was shaped by a colonial background, subtly reversed the accepted connotations of the Eastern and the exotic. Strangeness in the Introduction in effect becomes 'measurable', captured in the forms of Yeats's own immediate experience. To put it another way, where modernist and colonial realities conjoin, as in Yeats's world, where received tradition is an expression of imperial authority, the modernist drive to 'make it new', to unsettle a received tradition, might be that much more vitally interpreted. Breaking inherited moulds becomes the radical recapture of native myth and an uncolonized spirituality.[91]

Declan Kiberd has suggested that Tagore may have found models for his own work in Yeats's attempts through stylistic innovation to project new forms into the cultural void of the nation.[92] However, taking into account not only the relative ages of the two writers, but also that from the 1880s onwards Tagore formed part of the powerful cultural nationalist movement in Bengal, it is clear on the contrary that, if there was a transmission of influence, it would have operated as or even more powerfully in the other direction, from Tagore to Yeats. As part of that effort which we find in his poetry and short stories to project visions of an unspoilt pastoral Bengal, Tagore helped partially to reveal and certainly to confirm for Yeats what it was in the nation that might be resistant to the materialist imperial centre (as well as what it was in the poet that might remain separate from the fanaticism and 'baseness' of nationalism).[93] His nationalist identification with Ireland, in sum, brought Yeats to an

[91] The anti-colonial condition thus adds another political dimension to Walter Benjamin's well-known dictum from 'Theses on the Philosophy of History', in *Illuminations: Essays and Reflections*, ed. Hannah Arendt, trans. Harry Zohn (New York: Schocken, 1969), 255: 'In every era the attempt must be made anew to wrest tradition away from a conformism that is about to overpower it.'

[92] Kiberd, *Inventing Ireland*, 4–7, 117–18.

[93] See Rabindranath Tagore, *Selected Short Stories*, trans. William Radice (Harmondsworth: Penguin, 1991).

acknowledgement of an intersubjectivity with Bengal. The foreign came to the Irish poet in the form of another colonial's mystical lyricism and revealed to him his own image. Reading Tagore he rediscovered the whispers of that 'common mind' which he believed interconnected all nationalities and peoples.

CONCLUSION: A NARRATIVE CLAIM UPON THE JUNGLE

In Yeats's Introduction to *Gitanjali* the Western writer's objectification of a native culture is unsettled and complicated by that writer's own culturally subordinate position relative to the metropolis. In Leonard Woolf's case however such a cultural and political identification could not be immediately forthcoming. Yeats explored those pathways of mysticism and cultural nationalism along which certain forms of modernism approached alternative sources of meaning even while remaining embedded in empire's social and political hierarchies. For the British colonial officer Leonard Woolf, the assimilated Jewish Apostle bent on trying to conform, these pathways were not similarly available.

For him, by contrast, a gradual decentring of accepted views emerged rather out of the alienating juxtaposition, and later the clash, between opposing perspectives on his own colonial rule, and the seemingly more viable world-views of native cultures. As suggested by Simon Gikandi's analysis of modernism's stochastic narrative of empire's decline, Woolf viewed the imperial space as an unstable zone in which a colonial British identity could no longer be defended or indeed made good.[94] Instead he became increasingly more 'absorbed' in lives remote from his own: the more extreme the remoteness, the greater his 'enjoyment'.[95] In due course, on his return to England, this absorption prompted him to a vicarious narrativization of alterity or extreme otherness—a 'living their lives' in story, as his own description in *Beginning Again*, quoted above, suggested. It was a fictional experiment which, significantly, accompanied his political radicalization, his growing commitment to 'social revolution', native self-determination, and his work to develop a worldwide system of international cooperation.[96]

[94] Gikandi, *Maps of Englishness*, 165–6.
[95] As he wrote in *Growing*, 27, 180, 224–5, his 'passion' was 'to understand the people and the way they lived in the villages'.
[96] Woolf, *Beginning Again*, 100; Wilson, *Leonard Woolf*, 82–91.

It is important to note however that in Woolf's case sympathy for the native probably stopped short of political or ethical identification. His ultimate concern was rather to demonstrate the irrelevance to colonized lives of the mechanisms of colonial rule. Even if it was not necessarily completely comprehended, cultural otherness, he felt, should be respected; concomitantly, his understanding of international law was that it should in no way infringe on the 'independence of nations'. The beginnings of this process of ideological adjustment—of a growing regard for (but not embrace of) the other—are refracted in the careful narrative patterning of his short story 'Pearls and Swine'. The story's Conradian double framing has the advantage of allowing both a moment of recognition between the first and second narrators, who are both returned colonial officers, and at the same time a distancing objectification of the second—liverish, aggrieved, acclimatized to 'the meaningless march of life under blazing suns' ('PS' 417). Dramatizing the absurd, even criminal incongruities of colonial rule, 'Pearls and Swine' sets the stage for the close study of difference that is *The Village in the Jungle*. In the novel, unusually for its time, the interiorization of white colonial consciousness is abandoned almost completely.

In Woolf's colonial fiction therefore a Bakhtinian dialogic agitation can be seen to move through two distinct phases. First there is colonial self-doubt expressed in the short story predominantly as anxiety and pointless in-group interrogation. This is then followed by the attempt which we find in *The Village in the Jungle* to read cultural difference from within even while preserving narrative distance. As we see, there is not however, unlike in Yeats, an acknowledgement of satisfactory cross-cultural interaction or of the existence of a common mind. The proximity of the colonial and the native does not produce an approximation of the one to the other, though it may lead to what was earlier called an interaccommodation within the narrative of different subjectivities.

The story-within-a-story of 'Pearls and Swine' is set in the smoking room of a Torquay hotel where the two returned and disillusioned Indian civil servants, the narrators, encounter three others: a retired colonel of solid establishment views, a self-opinionated Liberal clergyman, and a pro-imperialist 'stock jobber', none of whom have travelled into 'the heart of the East' ('PS' 416). Although the second narrator with his experience of governing a Tamil district 'about as big as England', stands closer to Woolf, there is in fact little to distinguish him from the first: both narrators are unnamed, and both notice and speak in similar terms of the solid, too-comfortable smell of horsehair and varnish which to them characterizes 'civilized' 'reality' in England ('PS' 415–16, 425). Their participation in a conversation with the three other men about the Durbar of 1911 and attendant 'unrest',[97] goads the 'fierce' 'Anglo-Indian', whom the first narrator does not directly address, into telling his story. He offers this tale, a thinly fictionalized account of Woolf's own experience of nerve-deadening toil superintending a pearl fishery on the west coast of Ceylon, by way of setting the (once again distinctively Conradian) 'facts' straight concerning what rule really involves in the Indian subcontinent ('PS' 419).[98]

The climax of his tale, which is also the end of the frame-narrative, occurs on the night that an unscrupulous European dealer in pearls called White, who has gatecrashed the fishery, dies of a horrifying bout of delirium tremens in the company of the (second) narrator and his young European assistant, Robson. As in the opening scene to the first narrative, the build-up involves drawing out different European opinions with respect to empire: Robson's progressive 'scientific' humanitarianism; White's grossly exploitative and hypocritical despotism; and the narrator's own jaded indifference despite his pragmatic commitment to keep working at his job. All of these are shown to be of little or no consequence in the context of the fishery, both its long, multicultural history and its day-to-day drudgery and chaos.

Reminiscent of the disjointed and dislocating images of the letters, Woolf's subversive method in the short story is to create a bricolage of voices, highlighted by the double frame and echoed in the many 'different tongues' of Asia and Africa spoken by the oyster fishers ('PS' 428). From between the gaps and cracks of these voices, the untenability if not the impossibility of 'the strong hand' and the white man's presence is allowed to filter ('PS' 417, 423). It is as if a permanent discrediting of European ideas and values cannot yet at this stage, or in this story, be spoken in so many words, being implied rather through the juxtaposition and interanimation of the now opposing, now overlapping, points of view. This is most strikingly

---

[97] Presumably in connection not only with the scanty Morley-Minto reforms of 1909, but with the ongoing nationalist resistance in regions like Bengal and Maharashtra.

[98] As described to Lytton Strachey in two letters of March 1906. See Woolf, *Letters*, 113–16; *Growing*, 86–92.

dramatized at the end of the second narrator's story with the almost simultaneous deaths of White and an 'Arab'.

During the night of White's terminal agony, as a crowd gathers round to observe 'unastonished' and 'dignified' the white man's writhing, the stark contrast between the two deaths is subtly prepared. On the one hand there is White's 'civilized, corrupted cruelty', and the gross imposition which he represents, a Kurtz without mystique; on the other, there are the 'Arabs, Negroes, Tamils', their steadiness, their adaptation to one another and to their work despite their fierce internal conflicts ('PS' 427–8).[99] Whereas the strong hand of the East has 'got hold' of White, the Easterners unambiguously have a hold of *their* lives: (more so than Conrad's Africans) they have an ethical purchase on where they live, how they work. Like Yeats, Woolf might admittedly be criticized at this point for surrendering to embedded stereotypes of an ageless, imperturbable East—an East which possesses greater reserves of impassivity and patience than Europe. Yet, within this reproduction of the already known, Woolf is also making a more significant point about native dignity, which is to say, the dignity of belonging, of literally being in place, which will be developed in *The Village in the Jungle*.

Within moments of White's obviously symbolic ceasing, the narrator is called to check on another death. An Arab who has expired while diving for pearls, is quietly and unostentatiously carried in to the shore by his brother and work companions. The impromptu oration which is spoken over his body on the beach outlines an ordinary, respectable life of work, fatherhood, and communality. The 'sheik', the leader of his boat, invokes resignation, acceptance, in effect, a dignified being-in-place. In comparison White's brutalizing existence exhibits no redeeming virtues: he is at the last hastily buried, without ceremony. As an encapsulation of Woolf's growing attention to layered and qualified cultural awareness, the story ends with a quoted Tamil proverb which is applied to the white man's view of (and fate in) governing India: ' "When the cat puts his head into a pot, he thinks all is darkness" ' ('PS' 430).

Similar to Yeats's Introduction, 'Pearls and Swine' tests the boundedness of colonial perception in a staged encounter with other subjectivities. Building on this, what was earlier called the second phase of dialogical agitation—that is, the effort to accommodate (though

---

[99] The contrast emerges out of Woolf's fictional development of the incident: in his letters he records the death of the Arab but not of a white man.

not assimilate) native cultures which follows from the initial admission of colonial incompleteness (and of the dysfunction of the imperial idea)—Woolf captures in the narrative proximities and empathies of *The Village in the Jungle*.[100] His attempt at accommodation is anticipated however in the subtle repetition of the word 'unastonished' in 'Pearls and Swine', first used to describe not the natives, but the expression in the disillusioned Anglo-Indian's eyes ('PS' 417). It is as though, acclimatized to the East, the second narrator has also somehow internalized his district's dominant approach to whatever fate brings: his is the writer's principle, reiterated in the later letters from Ceylon, of 'nothing matters'—nothing perhaps but a stoical endurance. In Woolf's case, as in part suggested, a life 'buried' in Ceylon held strong attractions: a life, that is, not of promotion through the Crown Colony ranks, but of social service, of work dedicated to the welfare of the Ceylonese people themselves.[101]

Of 'being an imperialist', Woolf later reflected: 'by ruling others, I had become convinced that the people of Ceylon ought to be allowed to govern themselves'.[102] Written while Woolf was in fact deciding on his colonial future, *The Village in the Jungle* represents this conviction-in-formation. Contrary to the colonial fantasy of imposing a useful regulation and control upon subject peoples, the novel pictures a world in which order relentlessly descends into entropy despite the 'Government''s presiding authority. Native society is caught in the grip of a malaise, both from the impact of a modernizing colonialism, and from its own internal crises of corruption and fatalism against which the authorities are powerless. Across the course of the narrative the number of huts in the village symbolically decreases from ten, to eight, six, five: then, at the last, there are none at all (*Village*, 44, 136, 286–8). Eventually the jungle, itself a significantly contradictory presence ('a world of bare and brutal facts, of superstition, of grotesque imagination', p. 22), overwhelms the last lingering signs of human habitation.

Seen from one angle therefore the crumbling village of Beddegama (meaning literally 'the village in the jungle') occupies one of

---

[100] Like 'Pearls and Swine', germs of *The Village in the Jungle* lay in observations recorded 'on the ground' in Ceylon, in particular in the *Diaries*, See for instance the reports on chena cultivation (17 Nov. 1909), the irresponsibility of village headmen (28 Mar. 1910), and Woolf's supervision of the Kataragama pilgrimage (7–22 July 1910). On the Katagarama pilgrimage, see also *Growing*, 225–32.

[101] Letter to Lytton Strachey (8 Apr. 1908), in Woolf, *Letters*, 136–7 and also p. 155. See also *Beginning Again*, 52.   [102] Woolf, 'Ceylon Fifty Years After', LWP I L5.

modernism's typically disjointed and fragmented geographies. At the same time, however, it is autonomously constituted, possessed of its own inassimilable life force. Although incorporated into a Western narrative of imperial and cultural decline in which centres do not hold, the community is simultaneously located as external to Western narratives of justice and the rule of law entirely. While the central characters are at home in—though paradoxically imperfectly adapted to—the hostile zone of the jungle, they are remote from, and inassimilable to, both the legal apparatus of the colonial state represented by the white magistrate (Woolf's surrogate), *and* to the 'cunning' self-made 'native' modernity of an acculturated 'town man' like Fernando, the moneylending agent of the village's demise, or of the judgemental Ratemahatmaya, the 'Sinhalese gentleman' headman (*Village*, 145, 246).[103]

The four fateful encounters of the hunter Silindu's family with different, ascending tiers of local and government authority, which constitute the novel's action, are consistently marked by manipulation, incomprehension, and misjudgement, and end in death (*Village*, 178–82; 185–211; 275–81): 'Silindu understood nothing of what was going on; he did not know and could not be made to understand the law . . . he wanted only to be left in peace' (p. 276). Witness boxes, forts, and courthouses all float emblematically far above the heads of the people, and at a distance from the 'interminable' jungle itself (p. 189).[104] It is not surprising therefore that it is eventually the always 'overhanging' jungle—either too wet or too dry, sterile yet burgeoning with growth, inflicting fear yet itself imbued with fear—that becomes the most powerful if not the triumphant presence in the novel (304–7): it quintessentially represents the resistant, anomalous zone of the subaltern, to adapt from David Lloyd's discussion of recalcitrant forces in Ireland.[105]

Structurally the novel's irreconcilable oppositions are reflected in its (residually) dual narrative perspective: the collective point of view of Silindu's family dominates, but the organizing frame is that of a European witness, implicitly the white magistrate or 'Agent

---

[103] On rural and other resistances which are inassimilable to the narratives of state legality, see David Lloyd, *Anomalous States* (Dublin: The Lilliput Press, 1993).

[104] See Woolf, *Growing*, 50; *Letters*, 92–3.

[105] Lloyd, *Anomalous States*, for example, pp. 7–8, 125–8. Woolf's representation of the jungle compares with the characterization of Egdon Heath by his much admired Hardy in *The Return of the Native*, itself an elegiac chronicle of disappearing forms of rural life. See Woolf, *Growing*, 53–5.

Hamadoru'. Due to the marginal if not sketchy European presence however the duality is more deeply buried than in 'Pearls and Swine'. The 'I' narrator who sets the opening jungle scene (and whose perception later briefly resurfaces at the point where the magistrate confesses to Silindu to 'knowing' the jungle as a hunter (*Village*, 2, 244)), rapidly gives way to a third-person narration focalized through the travails of Silindu's family, in particular his twin daughters Punchi Menika and Hinnihami. Brought up as boys, the girls live with their father and foster-mother close to the edge of the village, in the 'twilight' area between human habitation and the wild. From this liminal perspective much of the narrative is conveyed. (Underlining their liminal state, the family members, especially Silindu, are seen by the other villagers as 'yakkos' or devilish madmen, touched by the jungle; and Hinnihami suckles both her own baby and a wild fawn, whom she is said to love more dearly than the child.)

By incorporating oral forms and modes of address, including what Sri Lankan critics have identified as a transliteration of local Sinhalese idiom, the third-person narrative gives a strong impression of a view from within, of subjectivities which are in place in this environment.[106] Courthouse conversations 'in English' are said to be 'unintelligible' and are significantly left mostly unrepresented (*Village*, 189), whereas indigenous beliefs are refracted via the local people themselves. The tradition behind the Beragama pilgrimage, for example, is transmitted as a legend exchanged around evening fires and in the courtyard of the temple of pilgrimage itself (p. 104). The Buddhist ethic of peaceful endurance on 'the path' (which corresponds to an extent with Woolf's own stoical principles), is expounded by an aged beggar in painstaking dialogue with Silindu on the way to his trial. And Silindu communicates his understanding of the jungle's ethos of just desserts via his incantatory, often repeated tale of the wounded buffalo. Even those states of mind which would conventionally be seen by a Western reader as foreign and untranslatable, such as Hinnihami's ecstasy before the Beragama god (p. 109), or her delight in suckling the fawn, are plausibly relayed as part of her family's passionate involvement with the wild. (Indeed it is

---

[106] Yasmine Gooneratne, 'Leonard Woolf's Waste Land: *The Village in the Jungle*', *Journal of Commonwealth Literature*, 7.1 (1972), 33, and 'A Novelist at Work: The Manuscript of Leonard Woolf's *The Village in the Jungle*', *Journal of Commonwealth Literature*, 18.1 (1983), 101–2, 106; Mervyn de Silva, 'Introduction II', to *Diaries in Ceylon, Ceylon Historical Journal*, 9.1–4 (1959–60), lvii–lviii.

worth noting in passing that the unrestrained zone that is the jungle allows Woolf a significant degree of licence for the period in representing sexual desire. This could be seen as another potential area of symbolic interaccommodation in the novel.[107])

Yet Western readers are not left unreminded of the governing interpretative frame which is as it were channelling the story to them. Superimposed upon the view from within are the near-scholarly footnotes which are scattered through the text to explain local words and practices. Even while centred within native subjectivities, therefore, the narrative also objectifies these: the white magistrate significantly both senses that his judgement of Babun is inadequate, yet makes it anyway (*Village*, 209–10). Also significant is the fact that the opening paragraph of the novel, which was in the original manuscript written in the historical present (like the descriptions of the jungle), Woolf later changed to the past tense.[108] The othering effect that this objectifying view creates is inevitably intensified in the course of the narrative by the repeated representation of the village people as savage and animal-like, as quickly reduced to a mere bodily existence (pp. 284–5), as well as by the overdetermining characterization of the jungle which they identify as a disembodied evil. Village residents, the third-person narrative voice typically comments, 'are very near to the animals; in fact, in [their violent desires] they are more uncontrolled than the brutes' (*Village*, 69).[109] In spite of the ongoing attempt to interiorize, the accumulated impact of such imagery is conventionally reductive, though it *is* qualified by the white magistrate's clear view that all judgements of savagery are relative (p. 247).[110] Assimilated or 'modern' Sinhalese in the novel notably

---

[107] See, for example, *Village*, 48–9. Gooneratne, 'A Novelist at Work', 95–9, comments that the major excisions from Woolf's manuscript of the novel all lie in the area of sexual reference. Throughout male desire is seen as violent and socially disruptive.

[108] See Gooneratne, 'A Novelist at Work', 91–5.

[109] In 'A Tale Told by Moonlight' the prostitute Celestinahami is similarly described as a simple-minded pet animal filled with a doglike devotion for her white lover and master. See also *Growing*, 212, where Woolf observes that, while writing *The Village in the Jungle*, the jungle as a 'personified hostile and dangerous force' 'obsessed [his] memory and imagination'. It is however important to acknowledge that Woolf wrote eloquently about the 'cosmic strangeness' of animals and would not necessarily have regarded such comparisons as demeaning (*Growing*, 100–1).

[110] This can be compared with the relativizing view of the following, from the description of the Katagarama pilgrimage in *Growing*, 231: 'at least there was something fundamentally genuine, primitively real there in the jungle. The people believed what they believed simply and purely. The beliefs were deplorable, no doubt, but the purity, simplicity . . . I respected.'

behave more cruelly or 'savagely' towards their neighbours than does Silindu.

It reveals much about the deep-seated contradictoriness of *The Village in the Jungle* that its stereotyping coexists with, rather than being counteracted by, its internalized 'native' perspectives. Woolf creates a sense of his own self-confessed obsession with Sinhalese life by continually shifting his readers along a scale of relative values: he gives us the jungle village as seen from within, as well as from its boundaries, and from the perspective of the town and the gaol. However, he cannot transmit this view without also translating it into a white discourse of prejudicial judgement, a discourse which, we observe, eventually contributes to the total obliteration of the community. European authority and knowledge, Woolf seems to say, cannot approach what is native without damaging it also. This point he later elaborates in his studies of economic imperialism. Ostensible identification with the other, in political terms 'trusteeship', which Woolf's distancing frameworks in the novel both mimic and transcend, inevitably leads to a destructive assimilation.

Despite the novel's largely conventional language and structure, it is this simultaneous recognition of alterity and yet disavowal of any conclusive attempt fully to contain it in representation, which makes of *The Village in the Jungle* a decidedly innovative and indeed modernist work, an unprecedented 'symbolic decolonization'.[111] Its self-reflexive comment upon its own impossibility is perhaps encapsulated at that curious point in the narrative where the illiterate Buddhist traveller uses an old piece of 'English newspaper' as a kind of magic script through which to 'read' or scry not only his immediate environment but 'the white Mahatmaya's country' to which he has never been (*Village*, 261–2). In the 'glass' of this paper he 'sees things [in] themselves'; much like the third-person narrator he is able to look both at Europe and into the life of 'a little hut up there in the jungle'. At the same time however we know that he is mad, and that the succour he offers Silindu is transitory.

In the cases of W. B. Yeats and Leonard Woolf, the impact of cross-cultural, cross-national interactions on modernism is perhaps most

---

[111] See Kerr, 'Colonial Habitats', 159. Yasmine Gooneratne, 'Leonard Woolf's Waste Land', 32–3, remarks that Eliot's images of desiccated barrenness in *The Waste Land* may have been an unconscious borrowing from his publisher Woolf's descriptions of the counter-intuitively dry and 'modern' jungle in *The Village in the Jungle*.

conclusively demonstrated in the Irish poet's restless nationalist and aesthetic quest for defining images that might move 'a whole people'. Trying out different conceptions of nationality as idealized woman, spiritual brotherhood, kindred community, Yeats committed himself from the 1890s to a remarkable degree of formal and cultural experimentation. In 1912 this quest came to a brief point of resolution in the shape of the spiritual intersubjectivity which he was able to discover in the translated poetry of the Bengali Rabindranath Tagore.

In Woolf, by contrast, after the unprecedented degree of native interiorization which characterizes *The Village in the Jungle*, the impact of cultural alterity on the modern is relatively speaking more mediated and difficult to trace. On the one hand this impact is, after 1913, transferred into a different mode of writing completely: Woolf's overtly anti-imperial political journalism and economic analyses. On the other, as Kathy Phillips has convincingly suggested, the impact is transmuted into another writer's work, that is, into the criticism of the British social system that is embedded in his wife Virginia Woolf's modernist fiction of the 1920s and 1930s.[112] The displacement which Leonard Woolf saw as an inevitable consequence of empire was in his case therefore as it were doubly performed, in the medium of both his and his wife's prose.

I will consider this second, more etiolated impact first. In recent years it has increasingly been recognized that, far from being the apolitical artist which the overprotective Leonard once described her as, Virginia Woolf centrally condemned imperialist values, both as manifested at home, and as they were exported abroad. Not only Leonard Woolf's knowledge, but his political understanding of imperialism as an interconnected system, contributed to her critical association of empire-making, warmongering, and oppressive gender relations (which culminated in the social and political analysis of *Three Guineas* (1938)[113]). In *Growing*, for example, Leonard Woolf remarked how, within the perverse scene of the colonial relationship, even an 'innocent' gesture on the part of the colonialist (such as accidentally 'touching' the face of a local lawyer with a riding whip), might rightly be construed as offensive by the colonized underling. The officer was willy-nilly perceived by the native as a tool and a sym-

---

[112] Phillips, *Virginia Woolf against the Empire*, pp. vii–viii, observes that Virginia Woolf's 'detailed knowledge of colonialism' was derived in particular from her reading of Leonard Woolf's analyses of imperialism.

[113] Virginia Woolf, *Three Guineas* (London: Hogarth Press, 1986).

bol of autocracy.[114] Correspondingly, in Virginia Woolf, empire, which is invariably associated with self-delusion, purblindness, and a destructive unreality, habitually distorts characters' gestures and attitudes. At Clarissa Dalloway's party in *Mrs Dalloway* (1925) the guest Miss Helena Parry with her one glass and one memory-clouded eye becomes an icon of such distortion, lost at once in the past and within a dream 'at the mention of India, or even Ceylon'.[115]

As we noted, the years of self-criticism and 'beginning again' following his return to England from Ceylon, also produced in Leonard Woolf an increasingly more radical political commitment. From 1915 onwards, in his Fabian Society and Labour Party committee papers and memoranda, as in his political journalism for, *inter alia*, the *New Statesman* and the *International Review*, he would raise ever more searching political and economic questions directed at the foundation of the imperial and international status quo itself. In this context it is curious that *The Village in the Jungle* and *Stories from the East*, both of which he began soon after his return, constituted his first and last critical word on empire *in fiction*. That medium through which he was able immediately and critically to reflect on his self-disgust and moral displacement as an imperialist, was one which, after the 1910s, he did not again take up.[116] He chose instead to bracket off the unusually intimate understanding represented by his Eastern experience.[117] Henceforth, in *Economic Imperialism, Empire and Commerce in Africa, Imperialism and Civilization*, he would continue to write voluminously on imperialism, in particular

[114] For Woolf's description of this controversial incident, see *Growing*, 111–14. See also his letter to the *Ceylon Observer* (20 Jan. 1962), LWP I A3e(i) and f, in which he refutes the libellous charges of a former headman; and 'Ceylon Fifty Years after', LWP I L5. Related to this is his *Three Guineas*-like observation in *Growing* that 'nastiness and brutishness pervade the whole legal system, in Britain as elsewhere' (p. 79).

[115] Also in *Mrs Dalloway* (Harmondsworth: Penguin, 1982), 195–6, Peter Walsh, recently returned from India, consistently acts as a disruptive and predatory presence. See Jenny Sharpe, *Allegories of Empire* (Minneapolis: University of Minnesota Press, 1993). Differently again, in Virginia Woolf's first novel *The Voyage Out* (1915; Oxford: Oxford UP, 1992), 29, 246, 350, in which the pro-imperial Richard and Clarissa Dalloway are first introduced as characters, the English travellers in an imaginary South America (Guyana?) appear at once cumbrous and insubstantial without the supportive backing of their routine-based life back home. Mark Wollaeger, 'Woolf, Postcards, and the Elision of Race: Colonizing Women in *The Voyage Out*', *Modernism/Modernity*, 8.1 (Jan. 2001), 43–75, remarks that the novel is unique in Virginia Woolf's oeuvre for its insightful transcription of gender identity via racial otherness.

[116] His second and last novel *The Wise Virgins* (London: Edward Arnold, 1914) was a grim autobiographical study of his suburban upbringing.

[117] Letter to Lord Fisher (12 Mar. 1967), in *Letters*, 553.

its 'economic motive power', yet these writings would be overtly analytical and informative, non-fictional. He would think in terms of broad trends and global structures to the end of finding alternatives to the 'profit-making capitalistic system' and so eventually dismantling empire.[118]

Seemingly as a consequence of this radicalizing process, the world of Ceylon with its local detail and doom-laden atmosphere, to which he had so intensively responded as a colonial officer, disappeared from Woolf's work until his autobiographies of the 1960s. It was as if he could take that engrossed yet also qualified embrace of native alterity which *The Village in the Jungle* had afforded him, no further— no further, that is, without also making a full commitment to Ceylon and, almost impossibly, 'immersing' himself for good in its cultural life-worlds (as he had indeed once fantasized doing).[119] In summary, therefore, for Woolf himself the political and literary implications of his disorientation as an imperial officer effectively represented two discursive alternatives: continuing political critique, as outlined, and after a relatively short outburst, fictional silence. The former pathway of critique seems to have been encouraged by the distanced, rationalizing perspective that he had already demonstrated in his fiction and that the metropolitan vantage point of England reinforced in him. It would additionally be expressed through the agenda of the Hogarth Press, which especially in the 1920s and early 1930s published anti-imperial works alongside aesthetically avant-garde writing.[120] By contrast, fiction, as we have seen, demanded of Woolf a process of ever closer identification, made difficult by the already

[118] Woolf, *Beginning Again*, 99–100, 111.

[119] In *Beginning Again*, 52, Woolf remarks: 'I did not want to go back to Ceylon and succeed in the Civil Service and end as a Governor. I had a vague notion that I might return and immerse myself for ever in the administration of a remote, backward district like Hambantota, but at the back of my mind I must have known that this was a mere fantasy.' Relatedly, again using the metaphor of immersion yet recognizing its impossibility, he writes in *Growing*, 247: 'But if I could go back and immerse myself in a District like Hambantota . . . I might welcome it as a final withdrawal, a final solitude, in which, married to a Sinhalese, I would make my District or Province the most efficient . . . in Asia.' Immersion for Woolf interestingly meant native marriage, a total cultural and bodily commitment. As well as the other factors influencing his shift in focus, it is clear that marriage to Virginia, his recognition of her exceptional talent, and his preoccupation with her mental illness, forced fundamental changes in Leonard Woolf's life. See Willis, *Leonard and Virginia Woolf as Publishers*, 56. In *Beginning Again* he represents his decision to 'stop writing novels' as probably more pragmatic and decisive than in the event it could have been.

[120] Willis, *Leonard and Virginia Woolf as Publishers*, 231–2, observes that in these years the Press published on Marxism and Soviet culture and produced books critical of imperialism and racism in Africa.

yawning gulf of alienation between the colonial European and the native, as both *The Village in the Jungle* and 'Pearls and Swine' had recognized.

From the time of the First World War, therefore, and the global political vistas it insisted upon, Woolf put Ceylon on hold, so to speak. Yet even so, though covertly, Ceylon continued to underpin his political and cultural views as well as his working practices. In Hambantota he had attempted much like a prototypical Kiplingesque officer to master a whole terrain through exhaustive documentation (and in this way to elide his growing internal conflicts as an imperialist). Later he pursued these methods of carpet-recording and meticulous accountancy in all his business, political, and domestic dealings, including the notes in Tamil and Sinhalese he kept on his wife's mental illness.[121] As though apprehensive of outbreaks of disorder on these fronts as on others, he in this way managed his non- and anti-imperial as he did his imperial activities. The guards or stays against disorientation he had evolved in the empire, he discovered, could be relocated and adapted to suit more familiar yet potentially disruptive contexts.[122] A 'modernist' attention to structuring form and aesthetic detachment, such as he might have found in Mansfield's *Prelude* or T. S. Eliot's *The Waste Land*, early Hogarth Press publications, therefore was practically recommended to him by his Eastern experience.[123]

In the domestic context of the imperial metropolis Woolf did not however lose sight of Ceylon as itself a political and anti-imperial space, even if he did not publicly discuss its emerging demands for self-determination. Between 1915 and 1918, the years running up to his own Labour Party work on international government,[124] he was involved in a correspondence with two Sinhalese activists, Edward Perera and D. B. J. Jayatilaka, concerning the British government's miscarriage of justice in response to the so-called Ceylon riots of 1915.[125] Feeling 'very strongly about these riots', Woolf gave the

---

[121] Lee, *Virginia Woolf*, 178.

[122] On the relativizing perspective introduced by imperial experience, see Woolf's late letter to William Plomer (12 Aug. 1968), in *Letters*, 568.

[123] See n. 55; also Willis, *Leonard and Virginia Woolf as Publishers*, 15, 401.

[124] As noted by Wilson, *Leonard Woolf*, 89, this work contributed to the formation of the League of Nations. Woolf was however critical of the League of Nations as it developed after 1919, seeing it as a front for the economic imperialism of European nations which had been victorious in the First World War.

[125] See LWP I A2a, b, c, e(ii). On 24 May 1915 a conflict had arisen in the Kandy district

activists' campaign his full support, going to the length of paying a visit to the Colonial Secretary, and, in December 1917, writing to Sir Travers Buxton of the Anti-Slavery and Aborigines Protection Society (with which Sol Plaatje too had dealings) requesting a full inquiry into the alleged injustices. Ceylon had undoubtedly convinced him, he wrote fifty years later, that colonized people 'ought to be allowed to govern themselves'.[126] His conviction became the motive force behind his shift from Ceylon-specific concerns to an internationalism unprecedented for its time.

As for Nivedita, Plaatje, and also Yeats, therefore, Woolf's recognition of the claims of native self-representation, which *The Village in the Jungle* insistently registers, had ultimatelly to be resolved at a more all-inclusive and pragmatic level than literature alone permitted. He turned to the development of an innovative theory of international government, under the aegis of which, he believed, imperial conflict and colonized demands for self-determination might be worked out on a basis of equality rather than paternalism. Whereas Nivedita and Plaatje confronted political setbacks by continuing to explore issues of cross-border representation and surrogacy in their writing, for Woolf, finally, cross-national involvements deflected yet also creatively transmuted his early writerly 'modernism'. Speaking always as a westerner, he converted the innovative accommodations of the native perspective in his novel into a political remaking of the modern, post-imperial world.

of Ceylon between a Sinhalese Buddhist procession and a group of Muslim bystanders, to which the colonial government reacted with 'extreme methods', including the imposition of martial law. That Woolf saw the campaign against this miscarriage of justice and his own involvement in it as significant is indicated by his later gift of the correspondence to the Ceylon Government Archive.

[126] Woolf, 'Ceylon Fifty Years After', LWP I L5.

Bibliography

PRINTED TEXTS

AHMAD, AIJAZ, *In Theory: Classes, Nations, Literatures* (London: Verso, 1992).

AMIRATHANAYAGAM, GUY (ed.), *Writers in East–West Encounter* (London: Macmillan, 1982).

ANDERSON, BENEDICT, *Imagined Communities: Reflections on the Origin and Spread of Nationalism*, rev. edn. (London: Verso, 1991).

—— *The Spectre of Comparisons: Nationalism, Southeast Asia and the World* (London: Verso, 1998).

APPIAH, KWAME A., 'Is the Post- in Postmodernism the Post- in Post-colonial?', *Critical Inquiry*, 17 (1991).

ASHCROFT, BILL, GRIFFITHS, GARETH, and TIFFIN, HELEN, *The Empire Writes Back: Theory and Practice in Post-colonial Literatures* (London: Routledge, 1989).

—— —— —— *Key Concepts in Post-colonial Studies* (London: Routledge, 1998).

ATKINSON, DAVID W., *Gandhi and Tagore: Visionaries of Modern India* (Hong Kong: Asian Research Services, 1989).

ATMAPRANA, PRAVRAJIKA, *Sister Nivedita of Ramakrishna-Vivekananda* (Calcutta: Sister Nivedita Girls' School, 1977).

AUROBINDO, (Sri) (Aurobindo Ghose), *Bankim-Tilak-Dayananda* (1918; Pondicherry: Sri Aurobindo Ashram, 1955).

—— *Birth Centenary Library*, 30 vols. (Pondicherry: Sri Aurobindo Ashram, 1972–6).

—— *The Brain of India* (1921; Calcutta: Arya Publishing House, 1948).

—— *Collected Poems and Plays*, 2 vols. (Pondicherry: Nolini Kanta Gupta, 1942).

—— *The Doctrine of Passive Resistance* (Calcutta: Arya Publishing House, 1948).

—— *The Human Cycle* (Pondicherry: Sri Aurobindo Ashram, 1949).

—— *The Ideal of the Karmayogin* (Pondicherry: Sri Aurobindo Ashram, 1950).

—— *The Life Divine* (New York: Sri Aurobindo Library, 1949).

—— *Letters* (Bombay: Sri Aurobindo Circle, 1949).

—— *Letters on Savitri* (Pondicherry: Sri Aurobindo Ashram, 1951).

—— *Love and Death* (Madras: M. Chattopadhyay, 1921).

AUROBINDO (*cont.*), *Poems Past and Present* (Pondicherry: Sri Aurobindo Ashram, 1946).

—— *The Renaissance in India*, trans. Rameshwar De (Chandernagore: Prabartak Publishing, 1923).

—— *Speeches* (Calcutta: Arya Publishing House, 1948).

—— *Views and Reviews* (Madras: Sri Aurobindo Library, 1946).

BAGCHEE, MONI, *Sister Nivedita: A Study of the Life and Works* (Calcutta: Presidency Library, 1956).

BAKHTIN, MIKHAIL, *The Dialogic Imagination*, trans. Caryl Emerson and Michael Holquist (Austin: University of Texas Press, 1981).

BANERJEE, SURENDRANATH, *A Nation in the Making: Being Reminiscences of Fifty Years of Public Life* (Oxford: Oxford UP, 1963).

BAUDRILLARD, JEAN, *Fatal Strategies*, trans. Philip Beitchman and W. G. J. Niesluchkowski (London: Pluto, 1999).

BEER, GILLIAN, *Open Fields: Science in Cultural Encounter* (Oxford: Clarendon Press, 1996).

BELL, MICHAEL, *Literature, Modernism and Myth: Belief and Responsibility in the Twentieth Century* (Cambridge: Cambridge UP, 1997).

BENJAMIN, WALTER, *Illuminations: Essays and Reflections*, ed. Hannah Arendt, trans. Harry Zohn (New York: Schocken, 1969).

BESANT, ANNIE, *India and the Empire: A Lecture and Various Papers* (London: Theosophical Publishing Society, 1914).

BHABHA, HOMI K., *The Location of Culture* (London: Routledge, 1995).

—— (ed.), *Nation and Narration* (London: Routledge, 1990).

BHANA, SURENDRA, *Gandhi's Legacy: The Natal Indian Congress 1894–1994* (Pietermaritzburg: Natal UP, 1997).

BIRCH, DINAH (ed.), *Ruskin and the Dawn of the Modern* (Oxford: Clarendon Press, 1999).

BLAUT, JAMES M., *The National Question: Decolonizing the Theory of Nationalism* (London: Zed, 1987).

BLAVATSKY, H. P., *Raja-Yoga or Occultism* (Bombay: Theosophy Co., 1931).

BLUNT, W. S., *India under Ripon: A Private Diary* (London: Fischer Unwin, 1909).

—— *My Ideas about India* (London: Kegan Paul, Trench and Co., 1885).

—— *Poems* (London: Macmillan, 1923).

—— *The Secret History of the English Occupation of Egypt, Being a Personal Narrative of Events* (London: T. Fisher Unwin, 1907).

BOEHMER, ELLEKE, *Colonial and Postcolonial Literature: Migrant Metaphors* (Oxford: Oxford UP, 1995).

—— (ed.), *Empire Writing: An Anthology of Colonial Literature 1870–1918* (Oxford: Oxford UP, 1998).

—— (ed.), *South African War? 1899–1902*, *Kunapipi*, 21.3 (1999).

—— 'Without the West: Southern African and Indian Women Writers in the 1990s', *African Studies*, 58.2 (2000).

BOOTH, HOWARD, and RIGBY, NIGEL (eds.), *Modernism and Empire* (Manchester: Manchester UP, 2000).

BRANTLINGER, PATRICK, *Rule of Darkness: British Literature and Imperialism, 1830–1914* (Ithaca, NY: Cornell UP, 1988).

—— 'A Postindustrial Prelude to Postcolonialism: John Ruskin, Morris and Gandhism', *Critical Inquiry*, 22 (1996).

BRASTED, HOWARD, 'Indian Nationalist Development and the Influence of Irish Home Rule, 1870–1886', *Modern Asian Studies*, 14.1 (1980).

—— 'Irish Home Rule Politics and India 1873–1886', unpublished Ph.D. thesis (Edinburgh: University of Edinburgh, 1974).

BREEN, DAN, *My Fight for Irish Freedom* (Dublin: Talbot Press, 1924).

BRENNAN, TIMOTHY, *At Home in the World: Cosmopolitanism Now* (Cambridge, Mass.: Harvard UP, 1997).

BROWN, JUDITH, *Gandhi: Prisoner of Hope* (New Haven: Yale UP, 1989).

—— and PROZESKY, MARTIN (eds.), *Gandhi and South Africa: Principles and Politics* (Pietermaritzburg: University of Natal Press, 1996).

BROWN, TONY (ed.), *Edward Carpenter and Late Victorian Radicalism* (Ilford: Frank Cass, 1990).

BURTON, ANTOINETTE, *At the Heart of the Empire: Indians and the Colonial Encounter* (Berkeley and Los Angeles: University of California Press, 1998).

BUTLER, JUDITH, *Gender Trouble and the Subversion of Identity* (London: Routledge, 1990).

CAIRNS, DAVID, and RICHARDS, SHAUN, *Writing Ireland* (Manchester: Manchester UP, 1988).

CANNADINE, DAVID, *Orientalism: How the British Saw their Empire* (London: Allen Lane, 2001).

CARPENTER, EDWARD, *From Adam's Peak to Elephanta* (London: Swan Sonnenschein, 1892).

—— *Towards Democracy* (London: Swan Sonnenschein, 1905).

CASELY HAYFORD, J. E., *Ethiopia Unbound* (London: C. M. Phillips, 1911).

CÉSAIRE, AIMÉ, *Discourse on Colonialism*, trans. Joan Pinkham (New York: Monthly Review Press, 1972).

CHAMBERS, IAIN, and CURTI, LIDIA (eds.), *The Post-colonial Question: Common Skies, Divided Horizons* (London: Routledge, 1996).

CHATTERJEE, PARTHA, *The Nation and its Fragments: Colonial and Postcolonial Histories* (Princeton: Princeton UP, 1994).

—— *Nationalist Thought and the Colonial World: A Derivative Discourse?* (London: Zed, 1986).

CHAUDHURI, HARIDAS, and SPIEGELBERG, FREDERIC (eds.), *The Integral Philosophy of Sri Aurobindo: A Commemorative Symposium* (London: George Allen and Unwin, 1960).

CHAUDHURI, NIRAD C., *Scholar Extraordinary: The Life of Friedrich Max Müller* (London: Chatto and Windus, 1974).

—— *Thy Hand, Great Anarch! India 1921–1952* (London: Hogarth, 1990).

CHENG, VINCENT, *Joyce, Race and Empire* (Cambridge: Cambridge UP, 1995).

CHENNELLS, ANTHONY, 'Plotting South African History: Narrative in Sol Plaatje's *Mhudi*', *English in Africa*, 24.1 (1997).

CHEW, SHIRLEY, 'Leonard Woolf's Exemplary Tale "Pearls and Swine"', *Journal of Commonwealth Literature*, 13.1 (Aug. 1978).

CHIROL, VALENTINE, *Indian Unrest* (London: Macmillan, 1910).

CHOW, REY, *Writing Diaspora: Tactics of Intervention in Contemporary Cultural Studies* (Bloomington: Indiana UP, 1993).

CHRISMAN, LAURA, 'Fathering the Black Nation of South Africa: Gender and Generation in Sol Plaatje's *Native Life in South Africa* and *Mhudi*', *Social Dynamics*, 23.2 (Summer 1997).

—— *Rereading the Imperial Romance: British Imperialism and South African Resistance in Haggard, Schreiner, and Plaatje* (Oxford: Oxford UP, 2000).

COLLINI, STEFAN, *Public Moralists: Political Thought and Intellectual Life in Britain 1850–1930* (Oxford: Clarendon Press, 1991).

CONRAD, JOSEPH, *Heart of Darkness* (1900; Harmondsworth: Penguin, 1973).

COOK, S. B., *Imperial Affinities: Nineteenth-Century Analogies and Exchanges between India and Ireland* (New Delhi: Sage Publications, 1993).

COUZENS, TIM, 'The Dark Side of the World', *English Studies in Africa*, 14.2 (1971).

—— 'Editor's View', in Sol Plaatje, *Mhudi* (Cape Town: Francolin Press, 1996).

—— *The New African: A Study of the Life and Work of H. I. E. Dhlomo* (Johannesburg: Ravan Press, 1985).

—— 'Sol T. Plaatje and the First South African Epic', *English in Africa*, 14.2 (1987).

—— 'Sol Plaatje's *Mhudi*', *Journal of Commonwealth Literature*, 8.1 (1973).

COWASJEE, SAROS (ed.), *Stories from the Raj: From Kipling to Independence* (London: Bodley Head, 1982).

COXHEAD, ELIZABETH, *Daughters of Erin: Five Women of the Irish Renaissance* (Gerrards Cross: Colin Smythe, 1979).

CRAWFORD, ROBERT, *The Savage and the City in the Work of T. S. Eliot* (Oxford: Clarendon Press, 1987).

CROZIER, F. P., *Ireland for Ever* (London: Cape, 1932).

—— *A Word to Gandhi: The Lesson of Ireland* (London: William Norgate Ltd., 1931).

CULLINGFORD, ELIZABETH, *Yeats, Ireland and Fascism* (Basingstoke: Macmillan, 1981).

DASGUPTA, R. K. (ed.), *Swami Vivekananda: A Hundred Years since Childhood* (Belur: Ramakrishna Math, 1994).

DAVIS, MARY, *Sylvia Pankhurst: A Life in Radical Politics* (London: Pluto, 1999).

DAVIS, R. P., 'Griffith and Gandhi: A Study in Non-violent Resistance', *Threshold*, 3.2 (1959).

DAVITT, MICHAEL, *The Boer Fight for Freedom* (New York: Funk and Wagnalls Co., 1902).

DE LAURETIS, TERESA, *Technologies of Gender: Essays on Theory, Film, and Fiction* (London: Macmillan, 1987).

DELEUZE, GILLES, and GUATTARI, FÉLIX, *On the Line*, trans. John Johnson (New York: Semiotext(e), 1983).

DERRIDA, JACQUES, and TLILI, MUSTAPHA (eds.), *For Nelson Mandela* (New York: Holt, 1986).

DEWEY, CLIVE, 'Celtic Agrarian Legislation and the Celtic Revival: Historicist Implications of Gladstone's Irish and Scottish Land Acts 1870–1886', *Past and Present*, 64 (1974).

DHAR, S. N., *A Comprehensive Biography of Swami Vivekananda* (Calcutta: Vivekananda Prakashan Kendra, 1975).

DIJK, A. M. G. VAN, 'Europese Invloeden op het Denken van Sri Aurobindo', unpublished Ph.D. thesis (Utrecht: Rijksuniversiteit te Utrecht, 1977).

DU BOIS, W. E. B., *The Souls of Black Folk* (London: Archibald Constable, 1905).

DUTTA, KRISHNA, and ROBINSON, ANDREW, *Rabindranath Tagore: The Myriad-Minded Man* (London: Bloomsbury, 1995).

ELLMAN, MAUD, *The Hunger Artists: Starving, Writing and Imprisonment* (Cambridge, Mass.: Harvard UP, 1993).

ELLMAN, RICHARD, *Yeats: The Man and the Masks* (Harmondsworth: Penguin, 1979).

FANON, FRANTZ, *Black Skin, White Masks*, trans. Charles L. Markmann, introd. Homi Bhabha (London: Pluto, 1986).

—— *The Wretched of the Earth*, trans. Constance Farrington (Harmondsworth: Penguin, 1986).

FOSTER, R. F., *Modern Ireland 1600–1972* (Harmondsworth: Penguin, 1988).

—— *W. B. Yeats: A Life*, i: *The Apprentice Mage 1865–1914* (Oxford: Oxford UP, 1997).

FOXE, BARBARA, *Long Journey Home: A Biography of Margaret Noble (Nivedita)* (London: Rider and Co., 1975).

GANDHI, LEELA, *Postcolonial Theory: A Critical Introduction* (Edinburgh: Edinburgh UP, 1998).

GANDHI, M. K., *An Autobiography; or The Story of my Experiments with Truth*, trans. Mahadev Desai (1927; Ahmedabad: Navajivan Publishing House, 1958).

—— *Hind Swaraj and Other Writings*, ed. Anthony J. Parel (Cambridge: Cambridge UP, 1997).

—— *Satyagraha in South Africa* (Ahmedabad: Navajivan Press, 1928).

GANGULI, B. N., *Dadabhai Naoroji and the Drain Theory* (London: Asia Publishing House, 1965).

GELLNER, ERNEST, *Nations and Nationalism* (Oxford: Blackwell, 1983).

GEORGE, ROSEMARY M., *The Politics of Home: Postcolonial Relocations and Twentieth-Century Fiction* (Cambridge: Cambridge UP, 1996).

GIBBONS, LUKE, *Transformations in Irish Culture* (Cork: Cork UP and Field Day, 1996).

GIKANDI, SIMON, *Maps of Englishness: Writing Identity in the Culture of Colonialism* (New York: Columbia UP, 1996).

GILROY, PAUL, *The Black Atlantic: Modernity and Double Consciousness* (London: Verso, 1993).

GONNE, MAUD, *A Servant of the Queen* (London: Victor Gollancz, 1938).

GOONERATNE, YASMINE, 'Leonard Woolf's Waste Land: *The Village in the Jungle*', *Journal of Commonwealth Literature*, 7.1 (1972).

—— 'A Novelist at Work: The Manuscript of Leonard Woolf's *The Village in the Jungle*', *Journal of Commonwealth Literature*, 18.1 (1983).

GORDON, LEONARD A., *Bengal: The Nationalist Movement 1876–1940* (New York: Columbia UP, 1974).

GOULD, FREDERICK J., *Hyndman: Prophet of Socialism* (London: George Allen and Unwin, 1928).

GRAY, STEPHEN, 'Plaatje's Shakespeare', *English in Africa*, 4.1 (1977).

GREGORY, Lady AUGUSTA, *Poets and Dreamers: Studies and Translations from the Irish* (Gerrards Cross: Colin Smythe, 1974).

GREWAL, INDERPAL, *Home and Harem: Nation, Gender, Empire and the Cultures of Travel* (London: Leicester UP, 1996).

GUPTA, MAHENDRANATH, *The Gospel of Sri Ramakrishna*, trans. Swami Nikhilananda (New York: Ramakrishna-Vedanta Center, 1942).

GUPTA, PARTHA SARATHI, *Imperialism and the British Labour Movement, 1914–1964* (New York: Holmes and Meier Publishers, 1975).

HALL, WAYNE E., *Shadowy Heroes: Irish Literature of the 1890s* (Syracuse, NY: Syracuse UP, 1980).

HAND, SEÁN (ed.), *The Levinas Reader* (Oxford: Blackwell, 1999).

HANSON, VIRGINIA (ed.), *H. P. Blavatsky and the Secret Doctrine: Commentaries* (Wheaton, Ill.: Theosophical Publishing House, 1971).

HARDING, ELIZABETH U., *Kali: The Black Goddess of Dakshineswar* (York Beach, Me.: Nicolas-Hays, 1993).

HATTENSTONE, SIMON, 'The Man with No Past: An Interview with Gerry Adams', *Guardian* (30 Apr. 2001).

HEEHS, PETER, *The Bomb in Bengal: The Rise of Revolutionary Terrorism in India 1900–1910* (New Delhi: Oxford UP, 1993).

HOBSBAWM, ERIC, *Nations and Nationalism since 1780: Programme, Myth, Reality* (Cambridge: Cambridge UP, 1990).

—— *Primitive Rebels: Studies in Archaic Forms of Social Movement* (Manchester: Manchester UP, 1963).

HOBSON, J. A., *Imperialism: A Study* (London: James Nisbet and Co., 1902).

HOGAN, PATRICK COLM, *Colonialism and Cultural Identity* (Albany: State University of New York Press, 2000).

—— and PANDIT, LALITA (eds.), *Literary India: Contemporary Studies in Aesthetics, Colonialism, and Culture* (Albany: State University of New York Press, 1995).

HOLMES, MICHAEL, and HOLMES, DENIS (eds.), *Ireland and India: Connections, Comparisons, Contrasts* (Dublin: Folens, 1997).

HOOPER, MYRTLE, 'Rewriting History: the "Feminism" of *Mhudi*', *English Studies in Africa*, 35.1 (1992).

HOWE, STEPHEN, *Ireland and Empire: Colonial Legacies in Irish History and Culture* (Oxford: Oxford UP, 2000).

HOWES, MARJORIE, *Yeats's Nations: Gender, Class and Irishness* (Cambridge: Cambridge UP, 1996).

HUGHES, EMRYS, *Keir Hardie* (London: National Labour Press, 1940).

HULME, T. E., *Speculations: Essays on Humanism and the Philosophy of Art*, introd. Herbert Read (London: Kegan Paul, Trench, Trubner and Co., 1924).

HUNT, J. D., 'Gandhi and the Black People in South Africa', *Gandhi Marg* (Apr.–June 1989).

HYNDMAN, H. M., *The Awakening of Asia* (London: Cassell, 1919).

—— *The Bankruptcy of India: An Enquiry into the Administration of India under the Crown* (London: Swan Sonnenschein, Lowrey and Co., 1886).

—— *England for All* (1881; Brighton: Harvester, 1973).

INNES, C. L., *The Devil's Own Mirror: The Irishman and the African in Modern Literature* (New York: Three Continents Press, 1990).

—— *Woman and Nation in Irish Literature and Society 1880–1935* (Hemel Hempstead: Harvester Wheatsheaf, 1993).

ISHERWOOD, CHRISTOPHER, *Ramakrishna and his Disciples* (London: Methuen, 1965).

JACKSON, HOLBROOK, *The Eighteen Nineties* (1913; London: Harvester, 1976).

JAMESON, FREDRIC, 'Modernism and Imperialism', Field Day Pamphlet 14 (Derry: Field Day Theatre Co., 1988).

JAMESON, FREDRIC (*cont.*), *The Political Unconscious: Narrative as a Socially Symbolic Act* (London: Methuen, 1981).

—— 'Third World Literature in the Era of Multinational Capital', *Social Text*, 15 (Fall 1986).

JAYAWARDENA, KUMARI, *The White Woman's Other Burden: White Women and South Asia during the British Colonial Period* (London: Routledge, 1995).

JEFFARES, A. NORMAN (ed.), *In Excited Reverie: A Centenary Tribute to W. B. Yeats 1865–1939* (New York: St Martin's Press, 1965).

JEFFERY, KEITH (ed.), *'An Irish Empire': Aspects of Ireland and the British Empire* (Manchester: Manchester UP, 1996).

JOHNSON, DAVID, 'Literature for the Rainbow Nation: The Case of Sol Plaatje's *Mhudi*', *Journal of Literary Studies*, 10.3/4 (1994).

—— *Shakespeare and South Africa* (Oxford: Clarendon Press, 1996).

JOSHI, SVATI (ed.), *Rethinking English: Essays in Literature, Language, History* (New Delhi: Trianka, 1991).

KAPLAN, CAROLA M., and SIMPSON, ANNE B. (eds.), *Seeing Double: Revisioning Edwardian and Modernist Literature* (Basingstoke: Macmillan, 1996).

KAPUR, NARINDER, *The Irish Raj* (Antrim: Greystone Press, 1997).

KAVIRAJ, SUDIPTA, *The Imaginary Institution of India* (New Delhi: Teen Murti Publications, 1991).

KEE, ROBERT, *The Green Flag*, ii: *The Bold Fenian Men* (Harmondsworth: Penguin, 1989).

KENNEDY, LIAM, *Colonialism, Religion and Nationalism in Ireland* (Belfast: Queen's University Institute of Irish Studies, 1996).

KER, DAVID I., *The African Novel and the Modernist Tradition* (New York: Peter Lang, 1998).

KERN, STEPHEN, *Modernism, Orientalism and the American Poem* (Cambridge: Cambridge UP, 1998).

KERR, DOUGLAS, 'Colonial Habitats: Orwell and Woolf in the Jungle', *English Studies*, 78.2 (1997).

KHILNANI, SUNIL, *The Idea of India* (London: Hamish Hamilton, 1997).

KIBERD, DECLAN, *Inventing Ireland* (London: Cape, 1995).

KIERNAN, V. G., *The Lords of Human Kind* (London: Century Hutchinson, 1988).

KING, RICHARD, *Orientalism and Religion: Postcolonial theory, India and 'the Mystic East'* (London: Routledge, 1999).

KOSS, STEPHEN (ed.), *The Pro-Boers: The Anatomy of an Antiwar Movement* (Chicago: University of Chicago Press, 1973).

KRIPAL, JEFFREY, *Kali's Child: The Mystical and the Erotic in the Life and Teachings of Ramakrishna* (Chicago: Chicago UP, 1995).

KRIPALANI, KRISHNA, *Rabindranath Tagore: A Biography* (London: Oxford UP, 1962).

KRISTEVA, JULIA, *Power of Horror: An Essay on Abjection*, trans. Léon S. Roudiez (New York: Columbia UP, 1982).

KUMAR, RADHA, *The History of Doing: An Illustrated Account of Movements for Women's Rights and Feminism in India* (London: Verso, 1993).

LAGO, MARY (ed.), *Imperfect Encounter: Letters of William Rothenstein and Rabindranath Tagore 1911–1941* (Cambridge, Mass.: Harvard UP, 1972).

—— *Rabindranath Tagore* (Boston: Twayne Publishers, 1976).

LAWRENCE, KAREN R. (ed.), *Decolonizing Tradition: New Views of Twentieth-Century 'British' Literary Canons* (Urbana: University of Illinois Press, 1992).

—— (ed.), *Transcultural Joyce* (Cambridge: Cambridge UP, 1998).

LAZARUS, NEIL, *Nationalism and Cultural Practice in the Postcolonial World* (Cambridge: Cambridge UP, 1999).

LEE, HERMIONE, *Virginia Woolf* (London: Chatto and Windus, 1996).

LENNON, JOSEPH, *Irish Orientalism* (Syracuse NY: Syracuse UP, 2004).

LEVENSON, SAMUEL, *Maud Gonne* (London: Cassell, 1976).

LEVINAS, EMMANUEL, *Alterity and Transcendence*, trans. Michael B. Smith (London: Athlone Press, 1999).

—— *Ethics and Infinity*, trans. R. A. Cohen (Pittsburgh: Duquesne UP, 1985).

—— *Otherwise than Being or Beyond Essence*, trans. Alphonse Lingis (The Hague: Martinus Nijhoff, 1981).

LLOYD, DAVID, *Anomalous States: Irish Writing and the Post-colonial Moment* (Dublin: The Lilliput Press, 1993).

—— *Nationalism and Minor Literature: James Clarence Mangan and the Emergence of Irish Nationalism* (Berkeley and Los Angeles: University of California Press, 1987).

LONGENBACH, JAMES, *Stone Cottage: Pound, Yeats and Modernism* (Oxford: Oxford UP, 1988).

LONGFORD, ELIZABETH, *A Pilgrimage of Passion: The Life of Wilfrid Scawen Blunt* (London: Weidenfeld and Nicolson, 1979).

LOOMBA, ANIA, *Colonialism/Postcolonialism* (London: Routledge, 1998).

—— 'Overworlding the "Third World"', in Robert Young (ed.), *Neocolonialism, Oxford Literary Review*, 3 (1991).

LOWRY, DONAL (ed.), *The South African War Reappraised* (Manchester: Manchester UP, 2000).

LUEDEKING, LEILA, and EDMOND, MICHAEL, *Leonard Woolf: A Bibliography* (Winchester: St Paul's Bibliographies, 1992).

LYONS, F. S. L., *Ireland since the Famine* (London: Weidenfeld and Nicolson, 1971).

LYONS, G. A., *Some Recollections of Griffith and his Times* (Dublin: Talbot Press, 1923).

MACBRIDE WHITE, ANNA, and JEFFARES, A. NORMAN (eds.), *The Gonne-Yeats Letters 1893–1918* (London: Pimlico, 1993).

MCCLINTOCK, ANNE, *Imperial Leather: Race, Gender and Sexuality in the Colonial Context* (London: Routledge, 1995).

MCCRACKEN, DONAL P., *The Irish Pro-Boers 1877–1902* (Johannesburg: Perskor, 1989).

MCCRACKEN, SCOTT, and LEDGER, SALLY (eds.), *Cultural Politics at the Fin de Siècle* (Cambridge: Cambridge UP, 1995).

MCKAY, CLAUDE, *A Long Way from Home* (New York: Arno Press, 1969).

MCKINLEY, DALE, *The ANC and the Liberation Struggle: A Critical Biography* (London: Pluto Press, 1997).

MCLACHLAN, NOEL, 'The Path Not Taken: Michael Davitt and Passive Resistance', *Times Literary Supplement* (12 Feb. 1999).

MCMINN, JOSEPH M. (ed.), *The Internationalism of Irish Literature and Drama* (Gerrards Cross: Colin Smythe, 1992).

MAJEED, JAVED, *Ungoverned Imaginings: James Mill's The History of British India and Orientalism* (Oxford: Clarendon Press, 1992).

MANSERGH, NICOLAS, *The Irish Question 1840–1921* (London: Unwin, 1968).

—— *Nationalism and Independence* (Cork: Cork UP, 1997).

MANSFIELD, KATHERINE, *The Aloe*, ed. Vincent O'Sullivan (London: Virago, 1982).

—— *The Collected Short Stories* (Harmondsworth: Penguin, 1982).

MARCUS, JANE (ed.), *Virginia Woolf and Bloomsbury: A Centenary Celebration* (London: Macmillan, 1987).

MARKS, SHULA, *The Ambiguities of Dependence in South Africa* (Baltimore: Johns Hopkins UP, 1986).

—— and ATMORE, ANTHONY (eds.), *Economy and Society in Pre-industrial South Africa* (London: Longman, 1980).

—— and RATHBONE, RICHARD (eds.), *Industrialization and Social Change in South Africa* (London: Longman, 1982).

MASANI, R. P., *Dadabhai Naoroji: The Grand Old Man of India* (Mysore: Kavyalaya Publications, 1957).

MASON, ELLSWORTH, and ELLMAN, RICHARD (eds.), *The Critical Writings of James Joyce* (New York: The Viking Press, 1959).

MATTHEWS, STEVEN, *Irish Poetry: Politics, History, Negotiation* (Basingstoke: Macmillan, 1997).

MAX MÜLLER, FRIEDRICH, *Ramakrishna: His Life and Sayings* (New York: Charles Scribner and Sons, 1899).

MAZUMDAR, A. K. (ed.), *Nivedita Commemoration Volume* (Calcutta: Vivekananda Janmotsava Samiti, 1968).

MELI, FRANCIS, *South Africa Belongs to Us: A History of the ANC* (Harare: Zimbabwe Publishing House, 1988).

MENDIS, BASIL, 'The Official Diaries of Leonard Woolf', *Ceylon Daily News* (21 June 1950).

MERCER, KOBENA, *Welcome to the Jungle: New Positions in Black Cultural Studies* (London: Routledge, 1994).

METCALF, THOMAS R., *Ideologies of the Raj, The New Cambridge History of India*, vol. iii.4 (Cambridge: Cambridge UP, 1994).

MEYEROWITZ, SELMA, *Leonard Woolf* (Boston: Twayne, 1982).

MILLER, CHRISTOPHER, *Nationalists and Nomads: Essays on Francophone African Literature and Culture* (Chicago: University of Chicago Press, 1999).

MITRA, SISIRKUMAR, *The Liberator: Sri Aurobindo, India and the World* (New Delhi: Jaico, 1954).

MITTER, PARTHA, *Art and Nationalism in Colonial India 1850–1922*: Occidental Orientations (Cambridge: Cambridge UP, 1994).

MOODY, T. W., *Davitt and the Irish Revolution, 1846–1882* (Oxford: Oxford UP, 1981).

MOOKERJEE, AJIT, *Kali: The Feminine Force* (London: Thames and Hudson, 1988).

MORGAN, KENNETH O., *Keir Hardie: Radical and Socialist* (London: Phoenix, 1975).

MPE, PHAWANE, '"Naturally these stories lost nothing by their retelling": Plaatje's Mediation of Oral History in *Mhudi*', *Current Writing*, 8.1 (1996).

MUKHERJEE, HARIDAS, and MUKHERJEE, UMA, *Bipin Chandra Pal and India's Struggle for Swaraj* (Calcutta: Firma K. L. Mukhopadhyay, 1958).

—— —— *India's Fight for Freedom or the Swadeshi Movement (1905–6)* (Calcutta: Firma K. L. Mukhopadhyay, 1958).

—— —— (eds.), *Sri Aurobindo and the New Thought in Indian Politics* (Calcutta: Firma K. L. Mukhopadhyay, 1958).

NAIRN, TOM, *The Break-up of Britain: Crisis and Neo-nationalism* (London: New Left Books, 1977).

—— 'What Nations are for', *London Review of Books* (8 Sept. 1994).

NANDY, ASHIS, *The Illegitimacy of Nationalism: Rabindranath Tagore and the Politics of Self* (New Delhi: Oxford UP, 1994).

—— *The Intimate Enemy: Loss and Recovery of Self under Colonialism* (New Delhi: Oxford UP, 1983).

NAOROJI, DADABHAI, *Poverty and Un-British Rule in India* (London: Swan Sonnenschein and Co., 1901).

—— *The Poverty of India* (London: Vincent Brooks, Day and Son, 1878).

NASTA, SUSHEILA (ed.), *Motherlands: Black Women's Writing* (London: Women's Press, 1991).

NATH, RAKHAL CHANDRA, *The New Hindu Movement 1886–1911* (Calcutta: Minerva, 1982).

NEUFELDT, R. W., *Friedrich Max Müller and the Rg Veda* (New Delhi: Oxford UP, 1980).

NEWMAN, JUDIE, *The Ballistic Bard: Postcolonial Fictions* (London: Arnold, 1995).

NGUGI WA THIONG'O, *A Grain of Wheat* (London: HEB, 1967).

NIVEDITA (Margaret Noble), *Aggressive Hinduism* (Madras: G. A. Natesan, 1905).

—— *Complete Works*, 2nd edn., 6 vols., ed. Pravrajika Atmaprana (Calcutta: Advaita Ashrama, 1982).

—— *Kali, the Mother* (1900; Calcutta: Advaita Ashrama, 1989).

—— *The Master as I Saw Him* (London: Longmans, Green, and Co., 1910).

—— *The Web of Indian Life* (London: William Heinemann, 1904).

NIXON, ROB, *Homelands, Harlem and Hollywood* (London: Routledge, 1994).

NOCHLIN, LINDA, *The Body in Pieces: The Fragment as a Metaphor of Modernity* (London: Thames and Hudson, 1992).

NORTH, MICHAEL, *The Dialect of Modernism: Race, Language and Twentieth Century Literature* (Oxford: Oxford UP, 1994).

O'GORMAN, FRANCIS, *Late Ruskin, New Contexts* (Aldershot: Ashgate, 2000).

O'HARA, BERNARD, *Michael Davitt Remembered* (Straide: Michael Davitt Memorial Association, 1984).

OLIPHANT, ANDRIES W., 'The Interpreter', in Elleke Boehmer (ed.), *South African War? 1899–1902, Kunapipi*, 21.3 (1999).

OLSON, CARL, *The Mysterious Play of Kali: An Interpretative Study of Ramakrishna* (Atlanta, Ga.: Scholars Press, 1990).

ORWELL, GEORGE, *Collected Essays* (London: Secker and Warburg, 1975).

OWEN, ALEX, *The Darkened Room: Women, Power and Spiritualism in Late Victorian England* (London: Virago, 1989).

PAL, BIPIN CHANDRA, *Swadeshi and Swaraj*, introd. T. Chakravarti (Calcutta: Yugayatri Prakashak Ltd., 1954).

PANDEY, B. N., *The Indian Nationalist Movement, 1885–1947: Select Documents* (London: Macmillan, 1979).

PANKHURST, SYLVIA, *The Home Front: A Mirror to Life in England during the World War* (London: Hutchinson and Co., 1932).

—— *The Suffrage Movement* (London: Virago, 1977).

PAREKH, BHIKHU, *Gandhi's Political Philosophy* (Basingstoke: Macmillan, 1989).

PARKER, ANDREW, et al. (eds.), *Nationalisms and Sexualities* (London: Routledge, 1992).

PARRY, BENITA, 'The Circulation of Empire in Metropolitan Writing', unpublished University of Leeds seminar paper (3 Nov. 1999).
—— *Delusions and Discoveries: Studies on India in the British Imagination* (London: Verso, 1998).
—— 'Signs of our Times: Discussion of Homi Bhabha's *The Location of Culture*', *Third Text*, 28–9 (Autumn–Winter 1994).
—— 'Some Problems in Current Theories of Colonial Discourse', *Oxford Literary Review*, 9 (1987).
PETHICA, JAMES (ed.), *Lady Gregory's Diaries, 1892–1902* (Gerrards Cross: Colin Smythe, 1996).
PHELPS, J. M., 'Sol Plaatje's *Mhudi* and Democratic Government', *English Studies in Africa*, 36.1 (1993).
PHILIPS, C. H. (ed.), *The Evolution of India and Pakistan 1858 to 1947: Select Documents* (London: Oxford UP, 1962).
PHILLIPS, KATHY J., *Virginia Woolf against the Empire* (Knoxville: University of Tennessee Press, 1994).
PICK, DANIEL, *Faces of Degeneration* (Cambridge: Cambridge UP, 1989).
PITT, MAIR, *The Maha-Yogi and the Mask: A Study of Rabindranath Tagore and W. B. Yeats* (Salzburg: University of Salzburg Studies in English Literature, 1997).
PLAATJE, SOLOMON T., *Mafeking Diary: A Black Man's View of a White Man's War*, ed. John Comaroff, Brian Willan, and Andrew Reed (1973; London: James Currey, 1990).
—— *Mhudi*, ed. Stephen Gray, introd. Tim Couzens (1930; London: William Heinemann, 1989).
—— *Native Life in South Africa before and since the European War and the Boer Rebellion*, 2nd edn. introd. Brian Willan, foreword Bessie Head (1916; Johannesburg: Ravan Press, 1995).
—— *Sol Plaatje: Selected Writings*, ed. Brian Willan (Johannesburg: Witwatersrand UP, 1996).
PORTER, BERNARD, *Critics of Empire: British Radical Attitudes to Colonialism in Africa, 1895–1914* (London: Macmillan, 1968).
POUND, EZRA, 'Rabindranath Tagore', *Fortnightly Review*, 99 (1913).
—— *Selected Letters of Ezra Pound 1907–1941*, ed. D. D. Paige (London: Faber and Faber, 1950).
—— 'Tagore's Poems', *Poetry*, 1.3 (Dec. 1912).
PRAKASH, GYAN (ed.), *After Colonialism: Imperial Histories and Postcolonial Displacements* (Princeton: Princeton UP, 1995).
PRATT, MARY LOUISE, *Imperial Eyes: Travel Writing and Transculturation* (London: Routledge, 1992).
PURANI, A. B., *The Life of Sri Aurobindo* (1958; Pondicherry: Sri Aurobindo Ashram, 1964).

QUAYSON, ATO, *Strategic Transformations in Nigerian Writing* (Oxford: James Currey, 1997).

RAO, AMRUTA, *Sister Nivedita and Dr Annie Besant* (New Delhi: APC Publications, 1996).

RASKIN, JONAH, *The Mythology of Imperialism* (New York: Random House, 1971).

RAY, RAJAT KANTA (ed.), *Mind, Body and Society: Life and Mentality in Colonial Bengal* (Calcutta: Oxford UP, 1995).

—— *Social Conflict and Political Unrest in Bengal 1875–1927* (New Delhi: Oxford UP, 1984).

RAYCHAUDHURI, TAPAN, *Europe Reconsidered: Perceptions of the West in Nineteenth Century Bengal* (New Delhi: Oxford UP, 1988).

REID, FRED, *Keir Hardie: The Making of a Socialist* (London: Croom Helm, 1978).

RETAMAR, ROBERTO, *Caliban and Other Essays*, foreword Fredric Jameson (Minneapolis: Minneapolis UP, 1989).

REYMOND, LIZELLE, *The Dedicated: A Biography of Nivedita* (New York: The John Day Company, 1953).

RICHARDS, DAVID, *Masks of Difference: Cultural Representations in Literature, Anthropology and Art* (Cambridge: Cambridge UP, 1995).

RICHARDS, THOMAS, *The Imperial Archive: Knowledge and the Fantasy of Empire* (London: Verso, 1993).

RISHABCHAND, *The Integral Yoga of Sri Aurobindo* (1953; Pondicherry: Sri Aurobindo Ashram, 1959).

ROBBINS, KEITH, *John Bright* (London: RKP, 1979).

ROLLAND, ROMAIN, *The Life of Vivekananda*, trans. E. F. Malcolm-Smith (Mayavati: Advaita Ashrama, 1947).

ROTHENSTEIN, WILLIAM, *Men and Memories: Recollections 1872–1938*, introd. Mary Lago (London: Chatto and Windus, 1978).

ROY, PARAMA, *Indian Traffic: Identities in Question in Colonial and Postcolonial India* (Berkeley and Los Angeles: University of California Press, 1998).

RUSKIN, JOHN, *Unto This Last and Other Writings* (Harmondsworth: Penguin, 1985).

SAID, EDWARD W., *Culture and Imperialism* (London: Cape, 1993).

—— *The World, the Text, and the Critic* (London: Faber, 1984).

—— 'Yeats and Decolonization', Field Day Pamphlet 15 (Derry: Field Day Theatre Co., 1988).

SANGARI, KUMKUM, and VAID, SUDESH (eds.), *Recasting Women: Essays in Indian Colonial History* (New Brunswick, NJ: Rutgers UP, 1990).

SARKAR, SUMIT, *Modern India, 1885–1947* (New Delhi: Macmillan, 1989).

—— *The Swadeshi Movement in Bengal 1903–1908* (New Delhi: People's Publishing House, 1973).

SCHALKWYK, DAVID, 'Portrait and Proxy: Representing Plaatje and Plaatje Represented', *Scrutiny2*, 4.2 (1999).

SCHIFFMAN, RICHARD, *Sri Ramakrishna: A Prophet for a New Age* (Calcutta: Ramakrishna Mission Institute, 1994).

SCHNEER, JONATHAN, *London 1900: The Imperial Metropolis* (New Haven: Yale UP, 1999).

SCHREINER, OLIVE, *Thoughts on South Africa* (London: T. Fisher Unwin, 1923).

—— *Trooper Peter of Mashonaland* (London: T. Fisher Unwin, 1897).

—— *Woman and Labour* (London: T. Fisher Unwin, 1911).

SEAL, ANIL, *The Emergence of Indian Nationalism: Competition and Collaboration in the Later Nineteenth Century* (Cambridge: Cambridge UP, 1968).

SEN, AMIYA, *Swami Vivekananda* (New Delhi: Oxford UP, 2000).

SHARPE, ERIC J., *The Universal Gita* (London: Duckworth, 1985).

SHARPE, JENNY, *Allegories of Empire: The Figure of the Woman in the Colonial Text* (Minneapolis: University of Minnesota Press, 1993).

SHEEHY-SKEFFINGTON, FRANCIS, *Michael Davitt* (London: T. Fisher Unwin, 1967).

SINGH, KARAN, *Prophet of Indian Nationalism: A Study of the Political Thought of Sri Aurobindo Ghosh, 1893–1910* (London: George Allen and Unwin, 1963).

SINGH, K. N. (ed.), *Indian Writing in English* (New Delhi: Heritage, 1979).

SINGH, SIMON, *Fermat's Last Theorem* (London: Fourth Estate, 1998).

SINHA, MRINALINI, *Colonial Masculinity: The 'Manly Englishman' and the 'Effeminate Bengali' in the Late Nineteenth Century* (Manchester: Manchester UP, 1995).

SMITH, ANGELA, *Katherine Mansfield and Virginia Woolf: A Public of Two* (Oxford: Clarendon Press, 1999).

SMITH, ANTHONY D., *National Identity* (London: Penguin, 1991).

—— *Theories of Nationalism* (London: Duckworth, 1971).

SMITH, MICHAEL PETER, and GUARNIZO, LUIS EDUARDO (eds.), *Transnationalism from Below* (Somerset, NJ: Transaction, 1998).

SPATER, GEORGE, and PARSONS, IAN, *A Marriage of True Minds: An Intimate Portrait of Leonard and Virginia Woolf* (London: Jonathan Cape and the Hogarth Press, 1977).

SPIVAK, GAYATRI, *A Critique of Postcolonial Reason: Toward a History of the Vanishing Present* (Cambridge, Mass.: Harvard UP, 1999).

—— *In Other Worlds: Essays in Cultural Politics* (London: Routledge, 1987).

SRINIVASA IYENGAR, K. R., *Sri Aurobindo: A Biography and a History* (Calcutta: Arya Publishing House, 1945).

SRIVASTAVA, GITA, *Mazzini and his Impact on the Indian National Movement* (New Delhi: Chugh Publications, 1982).

SUNDER RAJAN, RAJESWARI (ed.), *The Lie of the Land* (New Delhi: Oxford UP, 1992).

SUNDER RAJAN, RAJESWARI *(cont.)* (ed.), *Real and Imagined Women: Gender, Culture and Postcolonialism* (London: Routledge, 1993).

SWAN, MAUREEN, *Gandhi: The South African Experience* (Johannesburg: Ravan Press, 1985).

SWITZER, LES, 'Gandhi in South Africa: The Ambiguities of Satyagraha', *Journal of Ethnic Studies*, 14.1 (1986).

TAGORE, RABINDRANATH, *Collected Poems and Plays* (London: Macmillan, 1938).

—— *Gitanjali (Song Offerings)* (London: Macmillan, 1913).

—— *Gora*, trans. Surendranath Tagore (1910; London: Macmillan, 1924).

—— *The Home and the World (Ghare Baire)*, trans. Surendranath Tagore, rev. R. Tagore (1916/1919; Madras: Macmillan India, 1992).

—— *I Won't Let You Go: Selected Poems*, trans. Ketaki Kushari Dyson (Newcastle: Bloodaxe, 1991).

—— *My Reminiscences* (London: Macmillan, 1917).

—— *Nationalism* (London: Macmillan, 1917).

—— *Selected Short Stories*, trans. William Radice (Harmondsworth: Penguin, 1991).

TAYLOR, ANNE, *Annie Besant: A Biography* (Oxford: Oxford UP, 1992).

TERDIMAN, RICHARD, *Discourse/Counter Discourse* (Princeton: Princeton UP, 1985).

THOMPSON, E. P., *Alien Homage: Edward Thompson and Rabindranath Tagore* (New Delhi: Oxford UP, 1993).

—— *William Morris* (London: Merlin Press, 1977).

TORGOVNIK, MARIANNA, *Gone Primitive: Savage Intellects, Modern Lives* (Chicago: University of Chicago Press, 1990).

TRIVEDI, HARISH, *Colonial Transactions: English Literature and India* (Manchester: Manchester UP, 1995).

TROTTER, DAVID, 'Modernism and Empire: Reading *The Waste Land*', *Critical Quarterly*, 28.1/2 (1986).

TSUZUKI, CHUSHICHI, *Edward Carpenter: Prophet of Human Fellowship* (Cambridge: Cambridge UP, 1980).

VARMA, VISHWANATH PRASAD, *The Political Philosophy of Sri Aurobindo* (London: Asia Publishing House, 1960).

VERTOVEC, STEVEN, 'Conceiving and Researching Transnationalism', *Ethnic and Racial Studies*, 22.2 (1999).

VISRAM, ROZINA, *Ayahs, Lascars and Princes: The Story of Indians in Britain 1700–1947* (London: Pluto, 1986).

VISWANATHAN, GAURI, *Masks of Conquest: Literary Study and British Rule in India* (New York: Columbia UP, 1989).

—— *Outside the Fold: Conversion, Modernity and Belief* (Princeton: Princeton UP, 1998).

VOIGT, JOHANNES H., *F. Max Müller: The Man and his Ideas* (Calcutta: Firma K. L. Mukhopadhyay, 1967).

WALCOTT, DEREK, *Collected Poems* (London: Faber, 1992).

WALSHE, PETER, *The Rise of African Nationalism in South Africa: The African National Congress 1912–1952* (Berkeley and Los Angeles: University of California Press, 1971).

WARD, MARGARET, *Maud Gonne: Ireland's Joan of Arc* (London: Pandora, 1990).

WARE, VRON, *Beyond the Pale: White Women, Racism and History* (London: Verso, 1992).

WASHINGTON, PETER, *Madame Blavatsky's Baboon: Theosophy and the Emergence of the Western Guru* (London: Secker and Warburg, 1993).

WILLAN, BRIAN, *Sol Plaatje: South African Nationalist 1876–1932* (London: Heinemann, 1984).

WILLIAMS, RAYMOND, *The Country and the City* (Oxford: Oxford UP, 1973).

—— *The Politics of Modernism: Against the New Conformists*, ed. Tony Pinkney (London: Verso, 1989).

WILLIS, J. H., *Leonard and Virginia Woolf as Publishers: The Hogarth Press, 1917–1941* (Charlottesville: University Press of Virginia, 1992).

WILSON, DUNCAN, *Leonard Woolf: A Political Biography* (London: Hogarth Press, 1978).

WOLLAEGER, MARK, 'Woolf, Postcards, and the Elision of Race: Colonizing Women in *The Voyage Out*', *Modernism/Modernity*, 8.1 (Jan. 2001).

WOOLF, LEONARD, *Beginning Again: An Autobiography of the Years 1911–1918* (London: Hogarth Press, 1964).

—— *Diaries in Ceylon 1908–1911: Records of a Colonial Administrator, and Stories from the East, Ceylon Historical Journal*, ed. S. Saparamadu, 9. 1–4 (July 1959–Apr. 1960).

—— *Diaries in Ceylon 1908–1911* (London: Hogarth Press, 1961).

—— *Downhill All the Way: An Autobiography of the Years 1919–1939* (London: Hogarth Press, 1967).

—— *Economic Imperialism* (London: Swarthmore Press, 1920).

—— *Empire and Commerce in Africa: A Study in Economic Imperialism*, introd. Peter Cain (London: Routledge/Thoemmes Press, 1998).

—— *Growing: An Autobiography of the Years 1904–1911* (London: Hogarth Press, 1961).

—— *Imperialism and Civilization* (London: Hogarth Press, 1928).

—— *Letters of Leonard Woolf*, ed. Frederic Spotts (London: Bloomsbury, 1990).

—— *Stories from the East* (London: Hogarth Press, 1921).

WOOLF, LEONARD (*cont.*), *The Village in the Jungle* (1913; London: Hogarth Press, 1961).
—— *The Wise Virgins* (London: Edward Arnold, 1914).
WOOLF, VIRGINIA, *Mrs Dalloway* (1922; Harmondsworth: Penguin, 1982).
—— *Three Guineas* (1938; London: Hogarth Press, 1986).
—— *The Voyage Out* (1915; Oxford: Oxford UP, 1992).
YEATS, W. B., *The Collected Letters of W. B. Yeats, 1865–1895*, vol. i, ed. John S. Kelly and Eric Domville (Oxford: Oxford UP, 1986).
—— *The Collected Letters of W. B. Yeats, 1896–1900*, vol. ii, ed. John S. Kelly, Warwick Gould, and Deirdre Toomey (Oxford: Oxford UP, 1997).
—— *The Collected Poems*, ed. Richard Finneran (London: Macmillan, 1993).
—— *Essays and Introductions* (Basingstoke: Macmillan, 1989).
—— *The Letters of W. B. Yeats*, ed. Allen Wade (London: Rupert Hart-Davis, 1954).
—— *Uncollected Prose*, vol. i, ed. John Frayne (London: Macmillan, 1970).
YOUNG, ROBERT J. C., *Colonial Desire: Hybridity in Theory, Race and Culture* (London: Routledge, 1995).
—— (ed.), *Neocolonialism, Oxford Literary Review*, 3 (1991).
—— *Postcolonialism: An Historical Introduction* (Oxford: Blackwell, 2001).
ZIMMERMAN, GEORGES-DENIS, *Songs of Irish Rebellion: Political Street Ballads and Rebel Songs 1780–1900* (Dublin: Allen Figgis, 1967).

MANUSCRIPT SOURCES

Leonard Woolf Papers (University of Sussex Library Manuscripts Collection).
MSS 29817–19, Fred Allan Papers (National Library of Ireland, Dublin).
Sinn Féin, 1906–7, microfiche (National Library of Ireland, Dublin).
United Irishman, 1899–1906, microfiche (National Library of Ireland, Dublin).

Index